Beginning Oracle SQL for Oracle Database 18c

From Novice to Professional

Ben Brumm

Apress®

Beginning Oracle SQL for Oracle Database 18c: From Novice to Professional

Ben Brumm
Melbourne, VIC, Australia

ISBN-13 (pbk): 978-1-4842-4429-6   ISBN-13 (electronic): 978-1-4842-4430-2
https://doi.org/10.1007/978-1-4842-4430-2

Managing Director, Apress Media LLC: Welmoed Spahr
Acquisitions Editor: Jonathan Gennick
Development Editor: Laura Berendson
Coordinating Editor: Jill Balzano

Cover designed by eStudioCalamar

Cover image designed by Freepik (www.freepik.com)

Distributed to the book trade worldwide by Springer Science+Business Media New York, 233 Spring Street, 6th Floor, New York, NY 10013. Phone 1-800-SPRINGER, fax (201) 348-4505, e-mail orders-ny@springer-sbm.com, or visit www.springeronline.com. Apress Media, LLC is a California LLC and the sole member (owner) is Springer Science + Business Media Finance Inc (SSBM Finance Inc). SSBM Finance Inc is a **Delaware** corporation.

For information on translations, please e-mail rights@apress.com, or visit www.apress.com/rights-permissions.

Apress titles may be purchased in bulk for academic, corporate, or promotional use. eBook versions and licenses are also available for most titles. For more information, reference our Print and eBook Bulk Sales web page at www.apress.com/bulk-sales.

Any source code or other supplementary material referenced by the author in this book is available to readers on GitHub via the book's product page, located at www.apress.com/9781484244296. For more detailed information, please visit www.apress.com/source-code.

Printed on acid-free paper

Table of Contents

About the Author

Ben Brumm is a software developer and business analyst with over 11 years of experience. Based in Melbourne, Australia, he has been working with databases and SQL both during his full-time job and as the founder of the DatabaseStar dot com site where he teaches Oracle database topics. His passion for software and databases began when he started computer classes in high school in the late 1990s and it has only grown since then.

About the Technical Reviewer

Michelle Hardwick (Kolbe) is the Director of Data Science & Analytics at Salt Lake Community College (SLCC). SLCC serves over 60,000 students annually and has ten campuses in Salt Lake County. Her team at SLCC provides the data strategy, analytics, research, and is the backbone behind all data initiatives at the college. Michelle's team is driven by the goal of helping improve outcomes for every student at SLCC.

With over 11 years of experience in Business Intelligence, Michelle has overseen multiple implementations of data warehouses, BI, and analytics. Prior to SLCC, Michelle was a Consultant at Red Pill Analytics working on various analytics projects in multiple industries. In her past role as the Manager of Data & Insights at Backcountry.com, she guided all business intelligence projects at Backcountry. The focus was on eliminating manual work and enabling data-driven decisions throughout the company. She also mentored her team to ensure team growth and learning, consistency, and ensuring that projects will be maintainable for years, not months.

Michelle is also an Adjunct Professor at the Utah State University, teaching database and analytics courses at the undergraduate and master's level.

Michelle has a BS in Computer Science from Winona State University and an MBA from Utah State University. She served as President for the Utah Oracle Users Group for years and is currently the Executive Vice President of the Independent Oracle Users Group. She previously held a Board Position on the Healthcare Data Warehousing Association. Michelle also serves on the Advisory Council of the MIS Department at Utah State University and is a Contributing Editor on the Select Journal published by the Independent Oracle Users Group.

Michelle is recognized as an Oracle ACE Director and is a frequent speaker at conferences including Oracle OpenWorld, Collaborate, UTOUG, Kscope, and the Oracle OTN Latin America Tour.

Acknowledgments

I'd like to thank Jonathan Gennick at Apress who originally contacted me with the idea for this book and for everything he has helped me with while writing this book. I'd also like to thank Jill Balzano for assisting with getting the book organized and completed, and Michelle Kolbe who ensured the high quality and accuracy of the material in her role as Technical Reviewer. Finally, I'd like to thank my wife Fiona for her support while creating this book.

Introduction

Welcome to "Beginning SQL for Oracle Database 18C"! Thanks for picking up this book. It's safe to say you're interested in learning about Oracle database, as that's what this book is about. Why Oracle database, and why this book?

Oracle Database is one of the most popular database management systems in the world. The website `db-engines.com`, which ranks the popularity of databases based on several factors, has Oracle at #1 as of late 2018. It's used in many large organizations, and the main competitor is Microsoft's SQL Server. Learning Oracle SQL will put you in a good position when looking for a job with any company using an Oracle database.

Why this book? This book will help you get started with learning SQL on the latest version of Oracle's database: 18c. Version 18c was announced in late 2017 by Oracle and released in mid-late 2018 for the developer community. Learning how to use the latest version of Oracle will be very helpful for your career, because when organizations upgrade their version of Oracle to version 18c, you'll know how to work with it.

This book is also targeted toward beginners. You'll start by learning what a database is, how to install the tools you need, and all of the commands of SQL (Structured Query Language) to get you up and running with Oracle database. No experience with databases is needed at all. If you have worked with other databases such as SQL Server or MySQL, you might pick up the concepts easier because there are some common areas.

What You'll Learn

This book is broken up into several different parts, and many different chapters. Here's a summary of what you'll learn.

Part I: Setting Up

Chapter 1: What is a Database? This chapter explains what a database is. It explains some of the common terms such as table, row, and what SQL is. It also mentions who the different vendors are, such as Oracle.

Chapter 2: Setting Up. In this chapter you'll learn how to set up your very own Oracle database. You'll learn how to download the required software from the Oracle website, which includes Oracle's free version of their database called Oracle Express, and a development tool called Oracle SQL Developer. There are step-by-step instructions along with screenshots.

Part II: Viewing Data

Chapter 3: Retrieving Data. This chapter introduces the SELECT statement, which you can use to retrieve data from the database and view it.

Chapter 4: Selecting Specific Columns. This chapter expands on the previous chapter and shows you how to view individual columns using the SELECT statement.

Chapter 5: Restricting the Results. You'll learn how to use the WHERE clause to see only some of the records in a table, because there are times you don't want to see every record.

Chapter 6: Comparing Data. Sometimes you may want to filter on a partial match, and you'll learn how to do that in this chapter.

Chapter 7: Applying Multiple Filters. SQL allows you to filter the records on multiple criteria. In this chapter, you'll learn how to do that.

Chapter 8: Working with Nulls. Databases have a concept called NULL, which represents an unknown value. You'll learn more about what this means and how to handle it in your queries.

Chapter 9: Removing Duplicate Results. You'll occasionally get duplicate results when writing queries. This chapter will explain how to remove the duplicates and just see the unique results.

Chapter 10: Applying Filters on Lists and Ranges of Values. This chapter will explain how to filter your results using multiple values more efficiently by using lists of values.

Chapter 11: Ordering Your Data. If you ever need to show your data in a specific order, you'll know how to do that after reading this chapter.

Chapter 12: Applying Table and Column Aliases. You'll learn what table aliases and column aliases are, and their advantages, in this chapter.

Part III: Adding, Updating, Deleting Data

Chapter 13: Understanding the Data Types. Oracle supports many different types of data, each of which have their own purpose. In this chapter, you'll learn about a few of the main data types.

Chapter 14: **Creating a Table**. Data is stored in tables in a database, and this chapter will show you how you can create a table.

Chapter 15: **Adding Data to a Table**. To view data in a table, it first needs to be added to a table. This chapter explains how to do that in SQL.

Chapter 16: **Updating and Removing Data**. Occasionally you'll need to make changes to data that already exists in the database. You can do that in Oracle SQL and this chapter will show you how.

Chapter 17: **Updating or Deleting a Table**. This chapter explains how to make changes to the structure of a table or delete it if it's no longer needed.

Part IV: Joining Tables

Chapter 18: Inner Join. In this chapter, you'll learn what a join is, and how to display data from two tables using an "inner join."

Chapter 19: **Outer Join**. This chapter explains the concept of an "outer join," and how to use it in SQL.

Chapter 20: **Other Join Types**. Other than an inner join and outer join, there are a few other types of joins. These are explained in this chapter.

Chapter 21: **Joining Many Tables**. You'll often need to join more than two tables together in your queries. This chapter explains how to do that.

Part V: Functions

Chapter 22: Using Functions in SQL. SQL includes functions that perform calculations and transformations on your data. You'll learn what they are and how to use them in this chapter.

Chapter 23: **Writing Conditional Logic**. In this chapter, you'll learn how to implement conditional logic, which displays one value if a condition is true and another if it is false.

Chapter 24: Understanding Aggregate Functions. Some functions in SQL are called aggregate functions, which combine multiple rows of data together. This chapter explains what they are and how to use them.

Chapter 25: Grouping Your Results. When using aggregate functions, you may want to group your results. This chapter explains what that means and how to do it.

Chapter 26: What are Indexes? In this chapter, you'll learn what an index is, how to create one, and some tips for doing so.

Part VI: Command Line

Chapter 27: Using the Command Line. This chapter will explain what SQL*Plus is and how to use it to connect to your database. It also explains what SQLcl is, and how to download and use it.

Part VII: Appendixes

Appendix: How to Find and Navigate the Oracle SQL Reference. Oracle's website contains a lot of information about SQL. This appendix will explain how to find this website and how to navigate it.

About the Author

I've been working with Oracle databases ever since I went to university in 2004. My first role after university was supporting a series of applications that were built on an Oracle database and have had a range of roles in the software development industry since then. In that time, I obtained the "Oracle SQL Expert" certification, and studying for that helped me improve my knowledge of the Oracle database. I also run the website databasestar.com, which offers practical advice for database developers, with a focus on Oracle SQL.

Now you know a bit about me, and what you'll learn in this book, it's time to get started with learning SQL with Oracle Database 18c.

PART I

Setting Up

CHAPTER 1

What is a Database?

One of the main features of software is that it lets you interact with data in a certain way. This could be a grocery list app that lets you add items to a shopping list on your phone, a website that lets you write and publish articles, or a customer relationship management program where you store information about customers.

All of these programs let you view information in a certain way, edit this information, and then store it somewhere. Without the ability to store this information, the software wouldn't work that well. Imagine having a grocery list app, but when you entered the items you needed to buy, the app wouldn't save and the list disappeared when you closed the application. Such an application wouldn't be very useful!

Software needs a place to store data. The most common way to store this is in a database. A database is a defined structure of files and information that lets users and software store, retrieve, and update data in an efficient way.

Databases are used by grocery list apps, websites for publishing articles, customer relationship management systems, and many more types of software. The data that is stored in a database is used by the software in many ways, and allows the users to view, save, and edit information in the software.

For example, a grocery list app may store the following information in a database:

- The names of each item on your grocery list (the items you need to buy from the shop)

- A list of categories of items (e.g., vegetables, dairy, spices)

- The quantities or amounts of each item you want to buy (e.g., 3 apples, 2 cups of flour)

So why is a database used, other than to store information?

First, it's efficient. The way that the data is stored in the database makes it easy for users and software to read the data, add new data, update or delete existing data.

3

© Ben Brumm 2019
B. Brumm, *Beginning Oracle SQL for Oracle Database 18c,*
https://doi.org/10.1007/978-1-4842-4430-2_1

Databases also let you make updates to a small area of data without impacting all of the other data, if required. For example, you can add a new item to your grocery list without having to make changes to every other item in the database.

One consideration of using databases to store data is that they need a "database management system." This is a type of software that lets users or applications interact with the file. It allows you to easily enter commands, and the database management system takes care of changes to the data and all of the complexity involved. Another advantage would be handling multiple users viewing or editing the data.

Alternatives to Databases

A database isn't the only way to store data. Data can also be stored directly in files. An example of this would be a text file. If you open Notepad and create a new document, enter some text, and save it, a file is saved onto your computer. There is no database created in this example. The file is just saved to your computer.

Storing your data in a text file is simpler than working with a database, and it's OK if you're the only one working on the file.

However, there are problems that may occur with storing data in files when the software starts to get used by multiple people or gets larger over time, such as ensuring different users' changes are not overwritten, ensuring data can be saved and retrieved quickly, and only updating parts of a file. These problems are all addressed if a database is used.

There are a few different database-related terms I want to explain, to help you understand what a database is and how to interact with it.

Tables

A table is a logical structure for storing related data in a database. Most of the data in a database is stored within tables. Databases usually have multiple tables, and we'll be referring to tables a lot throughout this book.

If you've used a spreadsheet program before, such as Microsoft Excel, a table can be thought of like a worksheet. Information is stored in a table in a similar way that it is stored on a worksheet. You have rows of data that are divided into columns.

Rows

A row represents a single record of information in a table. For example, a row may represent a customer in a customer relationship management system, or a product in a grocery list app. A row in a database is similar to a row in a spreadsheet file. Purists won't appreciate my putting things that way, but the analogy is useful.

Columns

A column is a way to represent a particular piece of information for the records or rows within a table. It's an attribute or a value of each row.

For example, a customer's first name may be a column, and a value may then be recorded for the rows. A customer's last name could be a different column, and can be recorded separately and would likely be different to each customer's first name.

It may help to form a mental picture of columns in a spreadsheet file. For example:

```
First Name    Last Name
Jacinda       Ardern
Malcolm       Turnbull
Theresa       May
```

Each row in this example represents a prime minister. Thus, the table would be a table of prime ministers. Each row in the table represents one prime minister specifically. Then each column describes an attribute—such as first and last—that one would expect a prime minister to have.

Query

You've learned that data is stored in a database, and it can be added, updated, or retrieved. Software interacts with this database using a database management system in a few different ways:

- Retrieving the data from the database

- Changing values in the database

- Adding some new data to the database

- Removing some existing data from the database

These types of commands are called queries, which are specific commands using a certain type of code that let the software interact with the database, using the database management system. These queries are easily readable, and we'll learn how to read and write them in this book.

SQL

SQL stands for Structured Query Language. It is the language or type of code that is used to write queries on the database. This is the language that we'll be learning in this book.

This can be pronounced as an abbreviation, "ess cue ell." However, it can also be pronounced as "see kwel," as though the word is "sequel." In either way, SQL is the language we'll use.

Indexes

Earlier we explained what tables were. Tables are a type of object on the database. Tables are used to store data. Indexes are another type of object on the database, and are used to make it easier to find data stored in tables.

An index is an object that improves the efficiency of a query. It's kind of like an index at the back of a book. If you were looking for information on a particular topic, you wouldn't skim through every page until you found it. You would look up the topic in the index and it would tell you what page to go to.

Vendors

The SQL language and related database features follow a standard: the ISO SQL standard. This standard specifies how the language works.

With many programming languages, such as Java, there is only one vendor. However, with SQL, there are many vendors. These vendors have created their own versions of a database management system that uses SQL.

Some of these vendor implementations are:

- Oracle Database

- Microsoft SQL Server

- Oracle MySQL

- PostgreSQL

All of these vendor implementations are similar in that they all implement the SQL standard. The same code that is defined in the standard will work in the same way in each vendor's database. At least, that's the hope.

However, each vendor has added on extra functionality and features that don't work the same across the different platforms. For example, Oracle implements extensions to SQL that work on their database platform but are not found in, say, PostgreSQL. All vendors do the same thing, so in practice it can be difficult to write SQL that is perfectly compatible across vendor implementations.

Sometimes the vendor-specific changes are small, such as the names of particular functions, or the names of data types. Sometimes they are larger changes, such as new types of objects or ways to structure a database.

What does this mean for you? If you learn the SQL that applies to one vendor's database, most of that knowledge is transferrable to other vendors. You should be able to use most of what you learn about one database vendor on another database vendor.

In this book, you'll learn about Oracle SQL. This means you'll learn all of the basic commands on Oracle's database management system that uses the SQL language. If you were to go and try to work with a Microsoft SQL Server database, you should be able to pick up Microsoft's implementation pretty quickly after learning about the differences.

Summary

A database is a method of storing data used by applications. Data in a database is stored in tables, which have rows for each record and columns for each type of data that needs to be stored.

A query is a command that is run on the database to retrieve, add, or update data. These queries are written in a language called SQL, which stands for Structured Query Language.

Several vendors offer their own version of database management systems that use SQL. Some of these vendors are Oracle, Microsoft SQL Server, MySQL, and PostgreSQL. We'll be learning about Oracle in this book.

CHAPTER 2

Setting Up

This chapter introduces you to the different tools we'll use in this book, and shows you how to download and set them up. You'll create a table and set up some sample data as well.

What Tools Do We Need?

We'll use two different tools to teach Oracle SQL in this book: Oracle Express, and Oracle SQL Developer. Oracle Express is a smaller version of Oracle's enterprise-level database. The Express Edition, or Oracle Express, is free and easy to set up. It's popular with people learning Oracle SQL and for creating their own projects at home.

Oracle SQL Developer is a program developed by Oracle that lets you connect to the database and run SQL on the database. It's also free and easy to set up.

Last, there's another tool provided by Oracle called LiveSQL. It's a website with sample datasets that lets you connect to a database, upload your own data, and run SQL queries on it. You don't need to install Oracle Express or Oracle SQL Developer to use LiveSQL.

While LiveSQL is a handy tool for learning and working with Oracle SQL, the focus of this book will be on Oracle SQL Developer and Oracle Express. This is because the book will teach you not only how to work with SQL the language, but how to use Oracle SQL Developer—one of the most widely used tools for working with Oracle Database. This focus on SQL Developer makes you more prepared for real-world application of SQL, as companies would use Oracle SQL Developer (or a similar tool) to work with databases rather than LiveSQL.

© Ben Brumm 2019
B. Brumm, *Beginning Oracle SQL for Oracle Database 18c*,
https://doi.org/10.1007/978-1-4842-4430-2_2

Versions

Examples in the book are built around the following versions of Express Edition and SQL Developer. However, SQL is a mature and stable language. The beginning content in this book should work just fine with any reasonably recent version of the database.

- Oracle Express Edition 18c. This version was released in early 2018, with the Express Edition released in late 2018.

- Oracle SQL Developer 18.2. This version was released in July 2018.

The history of Oracle version numbers started at 2 and went up to version 12c in 2017. Every 2 or 3 years a new major version was released, and the "c" in "12c" stands for "cloud," which was the focus of that version (previous versions used other letters such as "g" for grid computing and "i" for Internet). Even though the c stands for cloud, 12c is available for on-premise installs and on the cloud.

Oracle Corporation announced in 2017 that their versioning would change to an annual release and therefore the numbering would change to reflect the year of release. This explains the version 18c. There is no Oracle version number 13 to 17. They were skipped in favor of moving to 18c.

The same concept was used for Oracle SQL Developer. The latest version is 18, and the version before that was version 4.

Now we've explained what tools we're going to use, let's look at how to set them up.

Download Oracle Express

Oracle Express (or Oracle Database XE) is the database management system we'll be using. It has all of the database features we need. The limitations it has are related to database size and its use in commercial products, but it's great for learning with.

To download Oracle Express:

1. Visit Oracle's website at www.oracle.com.

2. Navigate to Menu ➤ Products ➤ Databases ➤ Application Development. This can be done by hovering your mouse over each section and clicking Oracle Express, as shown in Figure 2-1.

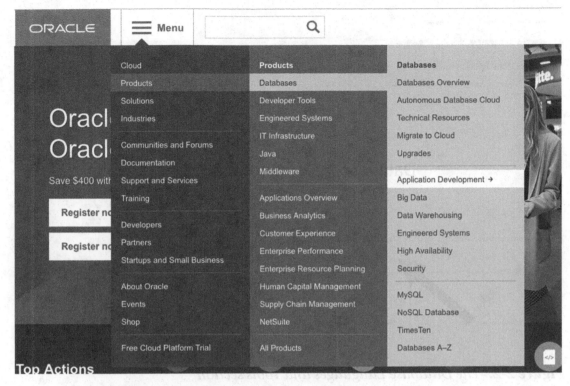

Figure 2-1. *The menu options for selecting Application Development*

3. Scroll down the page and click Database Express Edition (as shown in Figure 2-2).

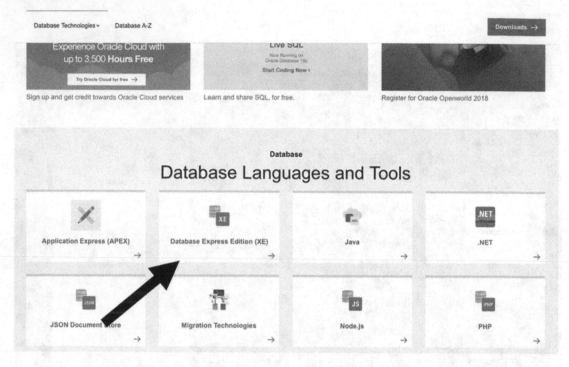

Figure 2-2. *The Database Languages and Tools section*

4. Scroll down and click Download Oracle Database XE under the
    Resources section (Figure 2-3).

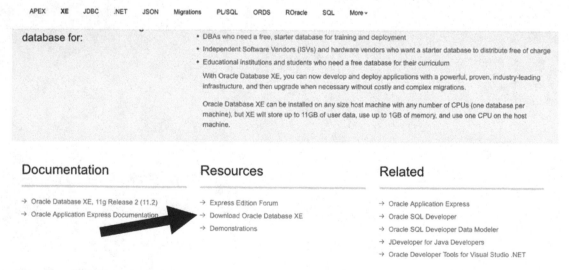

Figure 2-3. *The bottom of the Oracle Database XE page*

The page that loads will show information about Oracle Express (Figure 2-4).

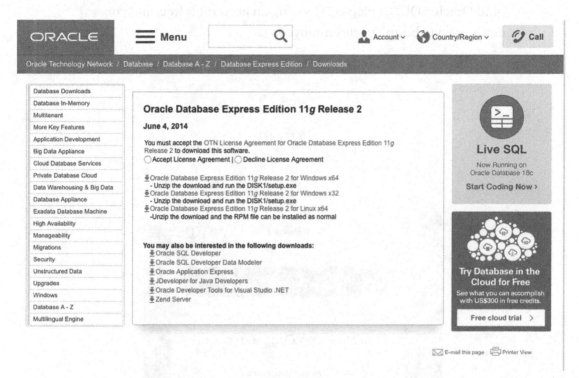

Figure 2-4. *The Oracle Express download page*

Note   The screenshots in this section show Oracle Express 11g. At the time of writing, this is the latest version released for Windows. By the time you're reading this, the 18c version should be available. The installation process is the same.

---

5. Read and click the Accept License Agreement. The download links will then appear.

6. Choose the version that corresponds to your operating system and click the link. If on Windows, go with 32- or 64-bit to match the version of Windows you are running. If in doubt about that, then choose the 32-bit version for a smoother experience.

You'll then be asked to log in or create an Oracle account
(Figure 2-5). This is required so you can download Oracle Express
(and Oracle SQL Developer). Creating an account is free, and you
don't need to be an Oracle employee.

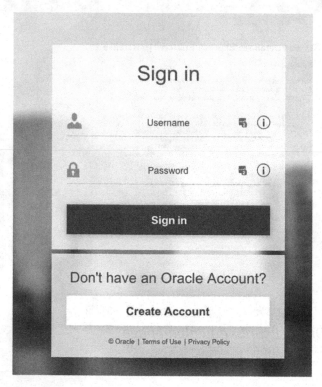

Figure 2-5. *Sign in or create account*

7. Click Create Account. The Create Your Oracle Account screen will then be displayed, as shown in Figure 2-6.

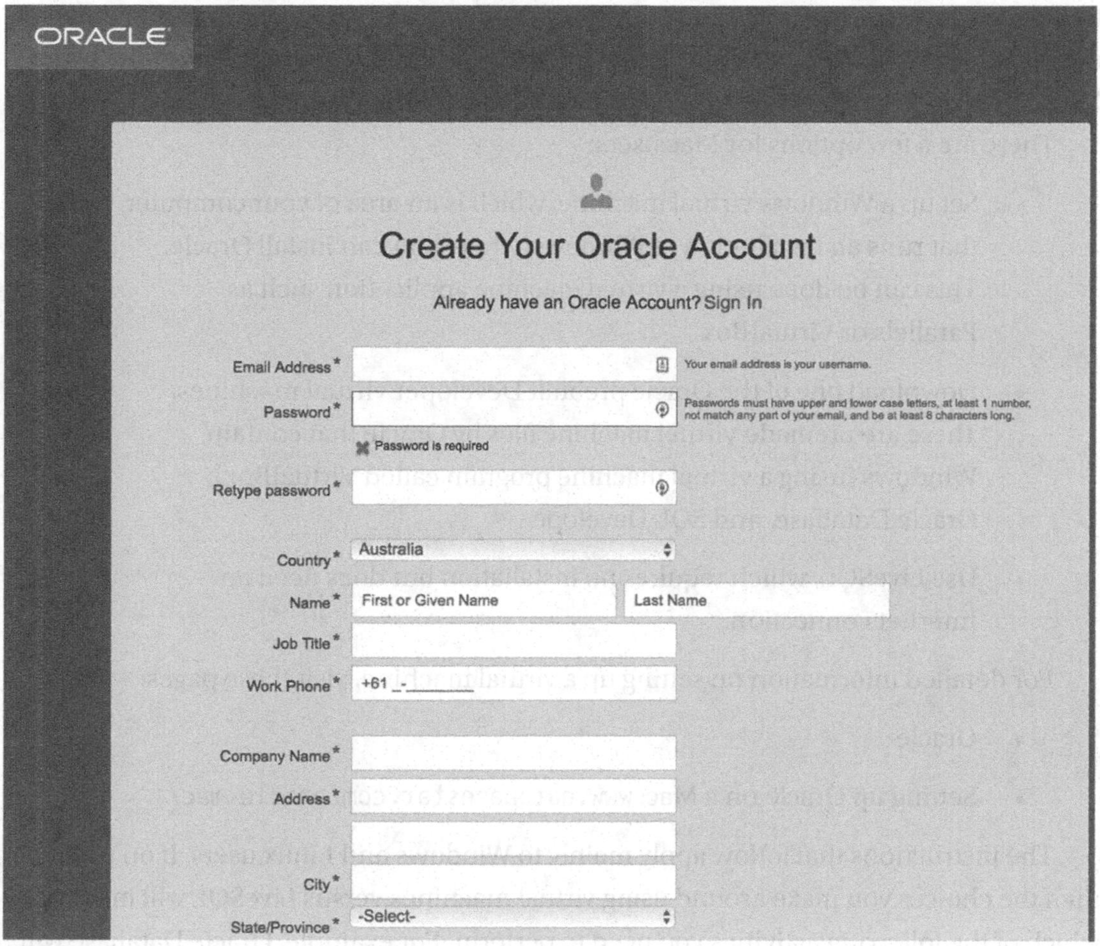

Figure 2-6. *The Create Your Oracle Account screen*

8. Enter your details and click Create Account. Your account should now be created.

9. Login using your newly created account. Oracle Express should then start downloading to your computer.

Depending on your browser settings, the download will either start automatically (in a default Downloads folder), or you'll be asked to specify the location.

Windows, Linux, and What About Mac?

You've probably noticed there is a Windows and a Linux version of Oracle Express, but there's no Mac version. Oracle currently doesn't offer a Mac version of Oracle Express for download. However, it is possible to use Oracle Express and learn Oracle if you're using a Mac. I use a Mac and am able to run an Oracle database on it.

There are a few options for Mac users:

- Set up a Windows virtual machine, which is an area of your computer that runs an installation of Windows, where you can install Oracle. This can be done using a virtual machine application such as Parallels or VirtualBox.

- Download one of the Oracle prebuilt Developer virtual machines. These are premade virtual machine files by Oracle that contain Windows (using a virtual machine program called VirtualBox), Oracle Database, and SQL Developer.

- Use LiveSQL, which requires no installation but does need an Internet connection.

For detailed information on setting up a virtual machine, visit these pages:

- Oracle

- Setting up Oracle on a Mac: www.databasestar.com/oracle-mac/

The instructions that follow apply mainly to Windows and Linux users. If on a Mac, then the choices you make around using virtual machines versus LiveSQL will influence which of the following activities you need to perform. For example, Oracle Database will be preinstalled on a prebuilt virtual machine from Oracle, whereas you'll need to install the database yourself on a virtual machine that you create from scratch.

Install Oracle Express

Now that we have downloaded Oracle Express, it's time to install it. The steps that follow are for the Windows installation, but the Linux installation should be similar.

1. Browse to the location where you downloaded the file. This will either be in a default Downloads folder or where you specified it. If you've still got your browser open, you should be able to click the file and select Show in Folder (or a similar option) to open the location where the file is saved.

2. As the file is a ZIP file, it needs to be extracted. Open the file and extract it, or right click the file and select Extract.

   The file is extracted into a folder called DISK1.

3. Open the DISK1 folder and run the setup file (Figure 2-7).

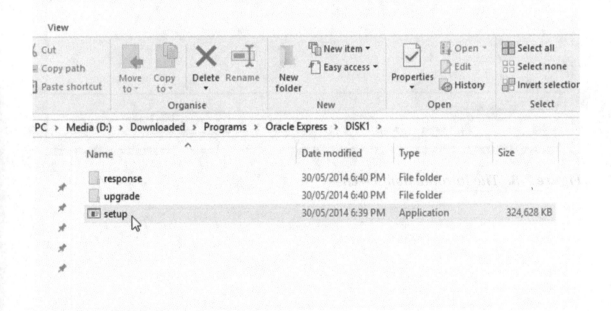

Figure 2-7. *The DISK1 folder*

4. The file will load and an introduction screen will be displayed (Figure 2-8). Click Next.

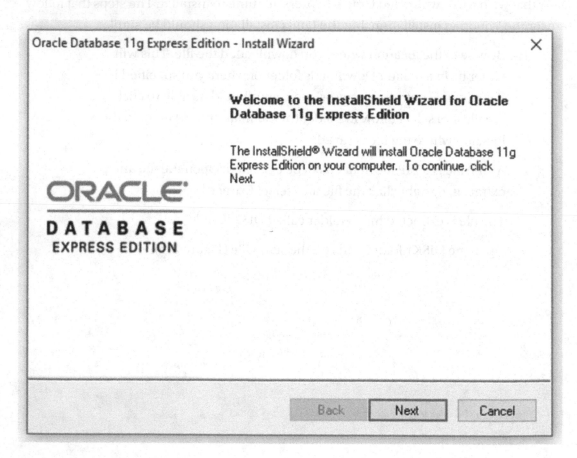

Figure 2-8. *The Introduction screen*

5. Read the terms and click "I accept"; then click Next (Figure 2-9).

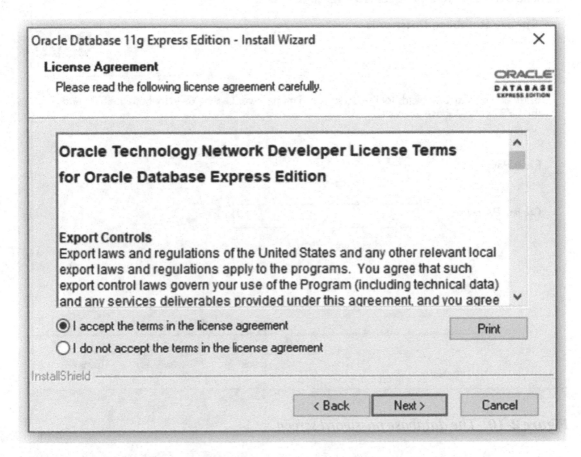

Figure 2-9. *The License Agreement*

6. On the "Choose a destination location" screen, click Next. You can change the location you want to install into, but the default location (C:\oraclexe) is OK.

7. The "Specify Database Passwords" screen is displayed as shown in Figure 2-10. Enter a password you would like to use for the system administrator accounts (called SYS and SYSTEM) and click Next.

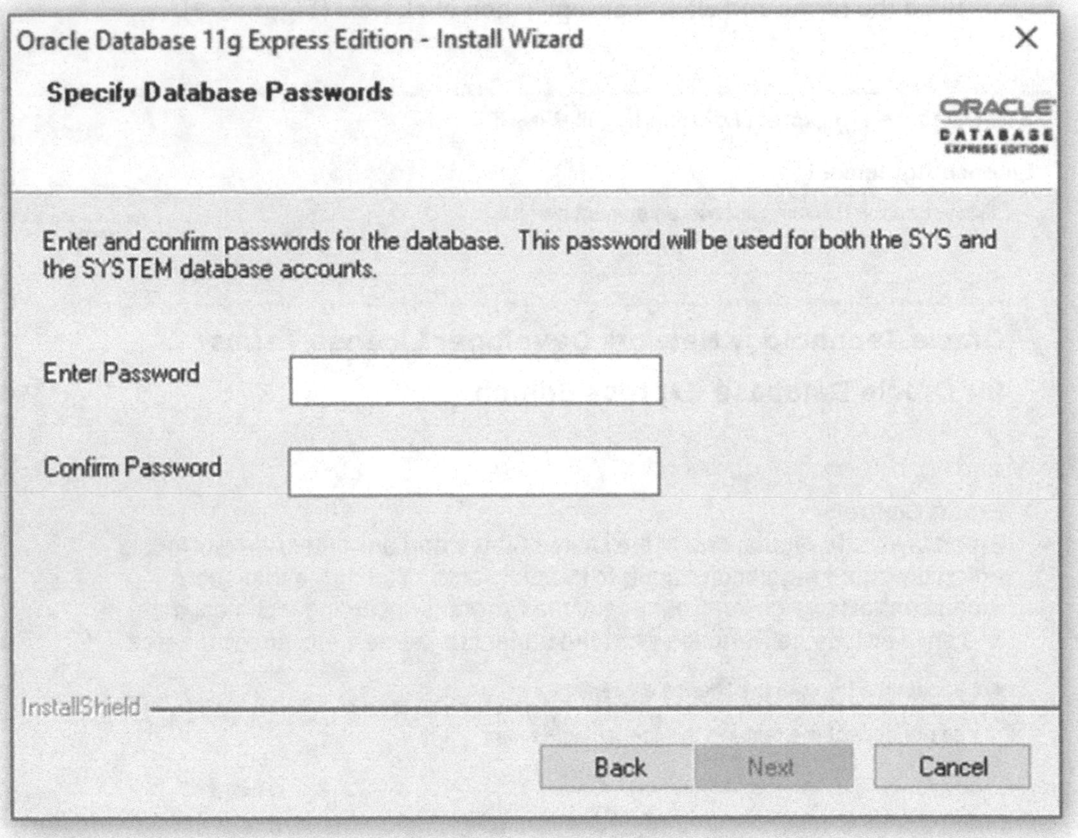

Figure 2-10. *The database password screen*

Note   You need to remember this password, as you'll use it to log in to the database later, and in case you ever need to reset another password. If you forget the password, you may need to reinstall Oracle Express.

---

8. On the Summary screen, click Install.

Oracle Express will then be installed. This installation usually takes a few minutes. A message is displayed once the installation is complete.

Now you have installed Oracle Express, it's time to download and set up Oracle SQL Developer so you can use this database.

Download Oracle SQL Developer

Oracle SQL Developer is Oracle's free application for accessing and working with Oracle databases. This application is called an integrated development environment (IDE). It's a type of application that lets developers work with code.

To download SQL Developer:

1. Visit Oracle's website at `www.oracle.com`.

2. Under the menu, navigate to Products ➤ Databases ➤ Application Development.

3. Scroll down and select SQL Developer.

4. Click the Download button, as shown in Figure 2-11.

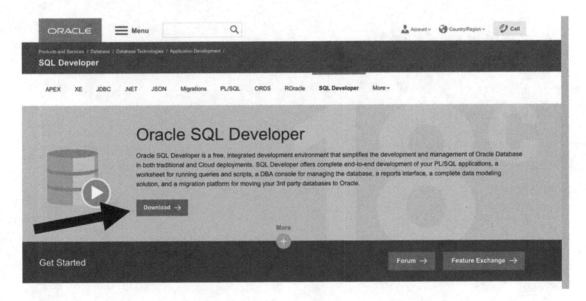

Figure 2-11. *Oracle SQL Developer download*

The page shows many different options for downloading SQL
Developer (Figure 2-12):

- Windows 64-bit with JDK included

- Windows 32-bit or 64-bit

- Mac OSX

- Linux

- Other

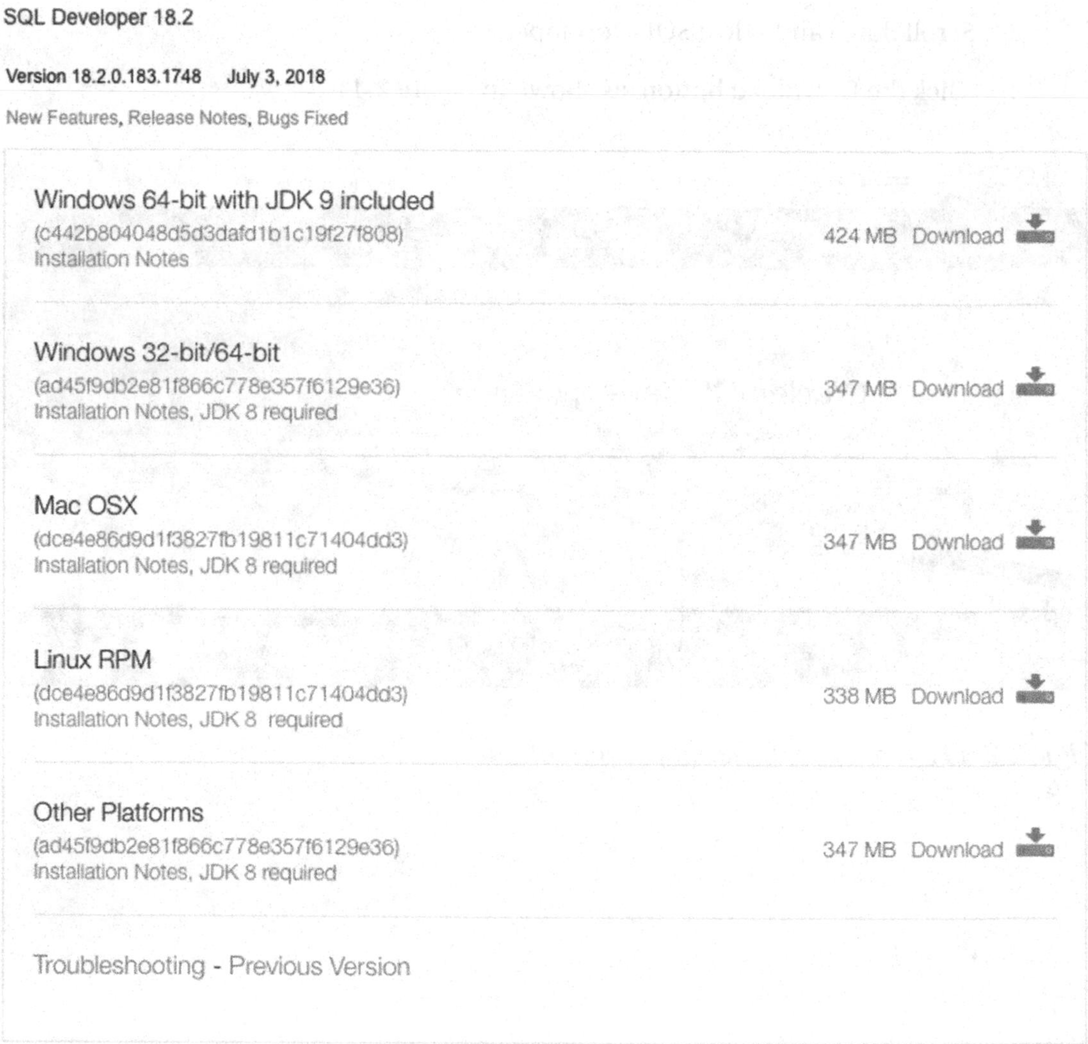

SQL Developer 18.2

Version 18.2.0.183.1748   July 3, 2018

New Features, Release Notes, Bugs Fixed

Windows 64-bit with JDK 9 included
(c442b804048d5d3dafd1b1c19f27f808)   424 MB Download
Installation Notes

Windows 32-bit/64-bit
(ad45f9db2e81f866c778e357f6129e36)   347 MB Download
Installation Notes, JDK 8 required

Mac OSX
(dce4e86d9d1f3827fb19811c71404dd3)   347 MB Download
Installation Notes, JDK 8 required

Linux RPM
(dce4e86d9d1f3827fb19811c71404dd3)   338 MB Download
Installation Notes, JDK 8 required

Other Platforms
(ad45f9db2e81f866c778e357f6129e36)   347 MB Download
Installation Notes, JDK 8 required

Troubleshooting - Previous Version

Figure 2-12. *Oracle SQL Developer download versions*

You should choose the version of Oracle SQL Developer that matches your operating system and the version of Oracle Express you chose earlier (either 32-bit or 64-bit). The easiest way to get started is to use the "Windows 64-bit with JDK included." That's if you are running a 64-bit version of Windows. Oracle SQL Developer runs on a Java platform, and this is the only version that includes the JDK (Java Development Kit) with it. So, it's simpler to install because it's only the one process.

However, if you aren't running Windows 64-bit, you'll need to choose one of the other versions. The other versions don't come with the JDK included, so you'll need to install that separately. We'll explain how to do that later in this chapter.

5. Click the Download link for the version you wish to download. As with Oracle Express, depending on your browser settings the file will be downloaded to the default location or you'll get to specify the location.

Once the file is downloaded, it's ready to set up.

Run Oracle SQL Developer

The good thing about Oracle SQL Developer is that it doesn't need to be installed. The file that you have downloaded is a ZIP file. To get SQL Developer up and running:

1. Browse to the location where you downloaded SQL Developer.

2. Extract the ZIP file by double-clicking the file, or right clicking and select Extract.

3. Once the file is extracted, you can create a shortcut to the file to make it easier to run. Right click "sqldeveloper.exe" and select Send to Desktop as Shortcut. This will place a shortcut to the file on the desktop.

4. Run the "sqldeveloper.exe" file. SQL Developer will now open.

5. If you downloaded a version that did not come with JDK included, you may get asked to specify the path to your Java files. Click Browse and locate the java.exe file. This will usually be in "C:\ Program Files\Java\jdk1.8.0_144\bin\".

The landing page or splash screen should then be shown.

Download the JDK

If you have downloaded one of the SQL Developer versions that did not come with the JDK included, you may need to download it. If you've already got it on your computer, perhaps from other development work you've done, then you won't need to download it again. However, if you do need to download it, here's how:

1. Visit www.oracle.com.

2. Under the menu, select Products ➤ Developer Tools ➤ Java SE SDK.

3. Click the Downloads tab at the top of the page, as shown in Figure 2-13.

Figure 2-13. Java downloads

4. Click the Download button next to JDK, as shown in Figure 2-14.

Figure 2-14. *Java download page*

5. Click "Accept License Agreement," then click the link that represents the file for your operating system, as shown in Figure 2-15.

| Overview | **Downloads** | Documentation | Community | Technologies | Training |

Java SE Development Kit 10 Downloads

Thank you for downloading this release of the Java™ Platform, Standard Edition Development Kit (JDK™). The JDK is a development environment for building applications, and components using the Java programming language.

The JDK includes tools useful for developing and testing programs written in the Java programming language and running on the Java platform.

See also:

- Java Developer Newsletter: From your Oracle account, select **Subscriptions**, expand **Technology**, and subscribe to **Java**.

- Java Developer Day hands-on workshops (free) and other events

- Java Magazine

JDK 10.0.2 checksum

Java SE Development Kit 10.0.2

You must accept the Oracle Binary Code License Agreement for Java SE to download this software.
Thank you for accepting the Oracle Binary Code License Agreement for Java SE; you may now download this software.

Product / File Description	File Size	Download
Linux	306 MB	jdk-10.0.2_linux-x64_bin.rpm
Linux	338.43 MB	jdk-10.0.2_linux-x64_bin.tar.gz
macOS	395.46 MB	jdk-10.0.2_osx-x64_bin.dmg
Solaris SPARC	207.07 MB	jdk-10.0.2_solaris-sparcv9_bin.tar.gz
Windows	390.25 MB	jdk-10.0.2_windows-x64_bin.exe

Figure 2-15. Java download links

Once the file is downloaded, you can install it.

1. Click the file in your browser to run the installation file. Alternatively, you can browse to the location where you downloaded it to, and run the file.

2. Follow the steps in the process by clicking Next at each stage. There's no need to change any of the default options.

The JDK should take a few minutes to be installed. You can now run SQL Developer.

Create a Connection

Once you have opened SQL Developer, you're ready to connect to the Oracle database you just installed. This will allow you to interact with the database by running queries. We're going to do a few things:

1. Create a new connection using the administrator account

2. Create a new user

3. Create a new connection using the new user

Why do we need to create a new user? Can't we just use the system account that we created in the install? We could indeed use the system account, but using the system account for creating tables and working with data in this way is not a good thing to do. That's because system administrator accounts have a lot of privileges and are used by database administrators for a variety of tasks. In a working environment, you won't have access to a system administrator account, so it's better to use your own account.

To create a new connection:

1. In SQL Developer, click the green + button in the Connections tab on the left of the screen, as shown in Figure 2-16.

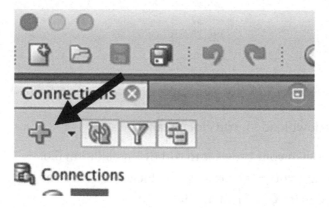

Figure 2-16. *The new connection button*

If you don't see the Connections tab, click the View menu and click Connections.

The New Connection window is then displayed, as shown in Figure 2-17. The existing connections are shown on the left, and fields for creating a new connection are on the right. Your list of connections on the left will be empty.

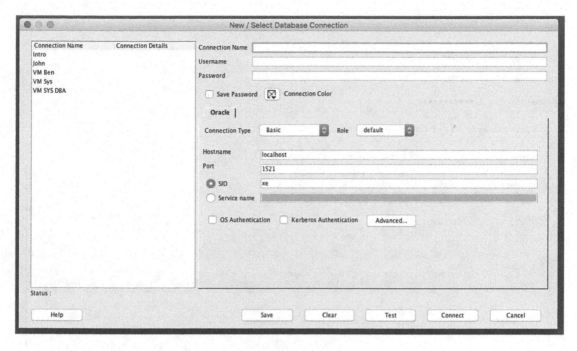

Figure 2-17. *The new connection window*

2.   Enter in a Connection Name. This can be anything you like, and is used so you can identify the connection in the list of all other connections. I would suggest the word "System" because this is the connection for the SYSTEM account. In the future if you are connecting to multiple databases, it's good to put the name of the database along with the username in this Connection Name field.

3.   Enter the word "SYSTEM" as the Username.

4.   In the password field, enter the password that you entered when you installed Oracle Express. This was the password you needed to remember.

5.   Check the Save Password box so you don't need to enter the password each time. The screen should look like Figure 2-18.

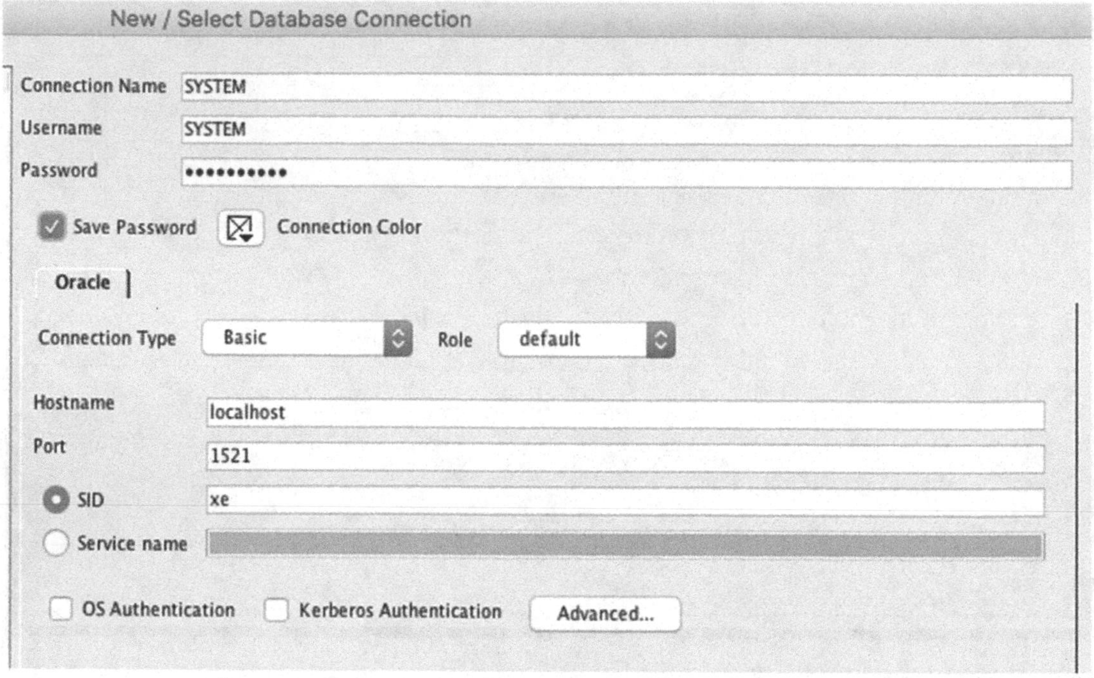

Figure 2-18. *Data in the new connection window*

6. For the Connection information, if you are at a company, your DBA would typically give you this information on how to connect. For connecting to our Oracle Express database, leave the Hostname, Port, and SID fields as their default values. The Hostname should be "localhost," the Port should be 1521, and the SID should be "xe".

7. Click the Test button. This will test your connection to the database and see if you have entered the correct information.

   If the test is successful, it should say "Status: Success" in the lower left hand corner, as shown in Figure 2-19.

Figure 2-19. *The success message from testing a connection*

Click Save. The new connection is saved into the list on the left, as shown in Figure 2-20.

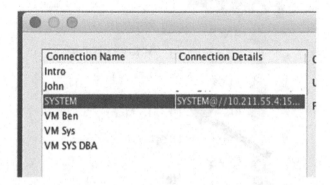

Figure 2-20. *The new connection in the list*

8. Click Connect. SQL Developer will use this connection and connect to the database. Once it is connected, a new tab is shown in the SQL Developer window with the name of your connection.

Create a New User

We could proceed with creating a table as the SYSTEM account, but working as SYSTEM is a practice we want to avoid. We'll create a new user that will then create our table. On the left side of the SQL Developer window, you should see the word Connections, and then the connection you just created under that. Find your new connection. Then perform the following steps:

1. Click the arrow to the left of the connection name to expand the items under the connection. This will show all the different categories of objects.

2. Scroll to the bottom of this list, right click Other Users, and select Create User, as shown in Figure 2-21.

Figure 2-21. *Create User menu option*

3. In the window that appears, enter the name for the new user,
    as shown in Figure 2-22. This is case insensitive and should not
    contain special characters or reserved words like "system." If
    you're not sure what to use, use your own name or "intro_user" as
    a username.

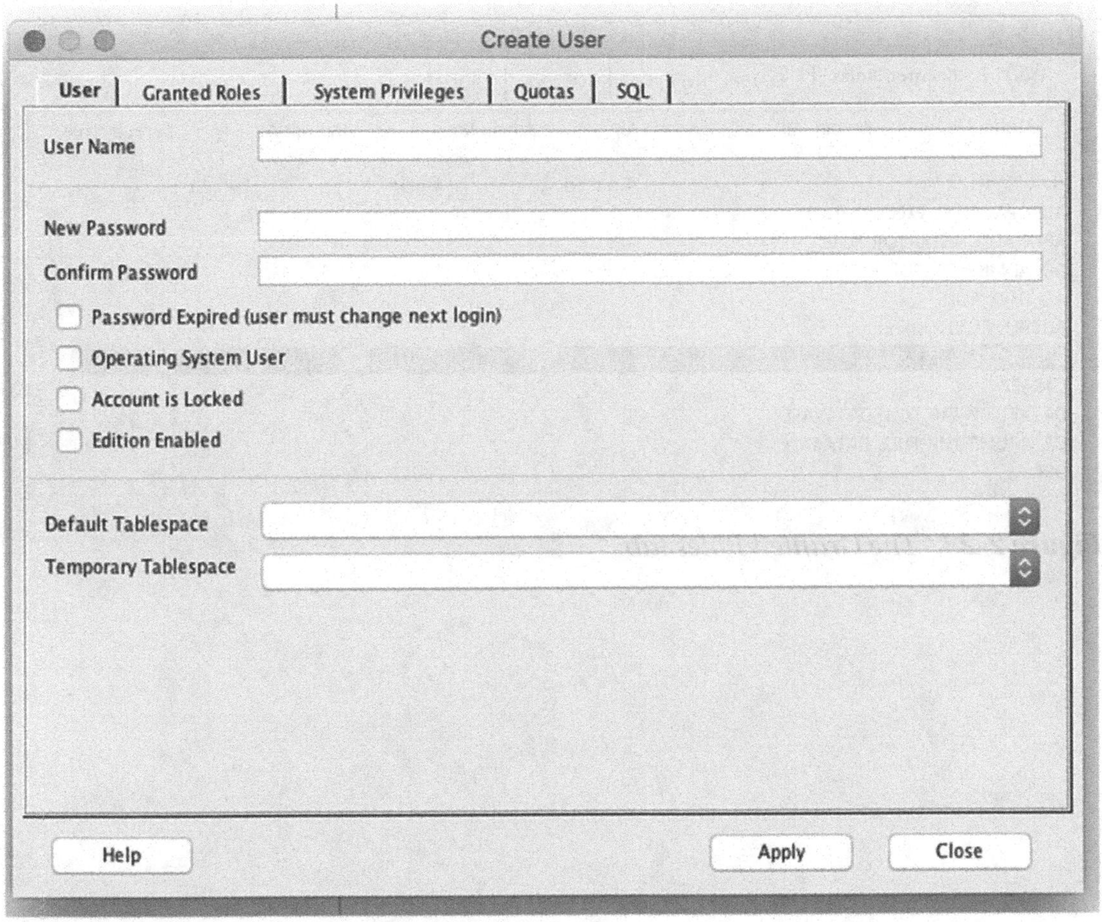

Figure 2-22. *The Create User window*

4. Enter a password in the New Password and Confirm Password boxes.

5. Leave all of the other options blank: the checkboxes and the tablespace fields.

6. Click the Granted Roles tab. A list of available roles will appear.

7. Click the Granted checkbox next to the CONNECT role, as shown in Figure 2-23. This "CONNECT" role allows the user to make a connection to the database.

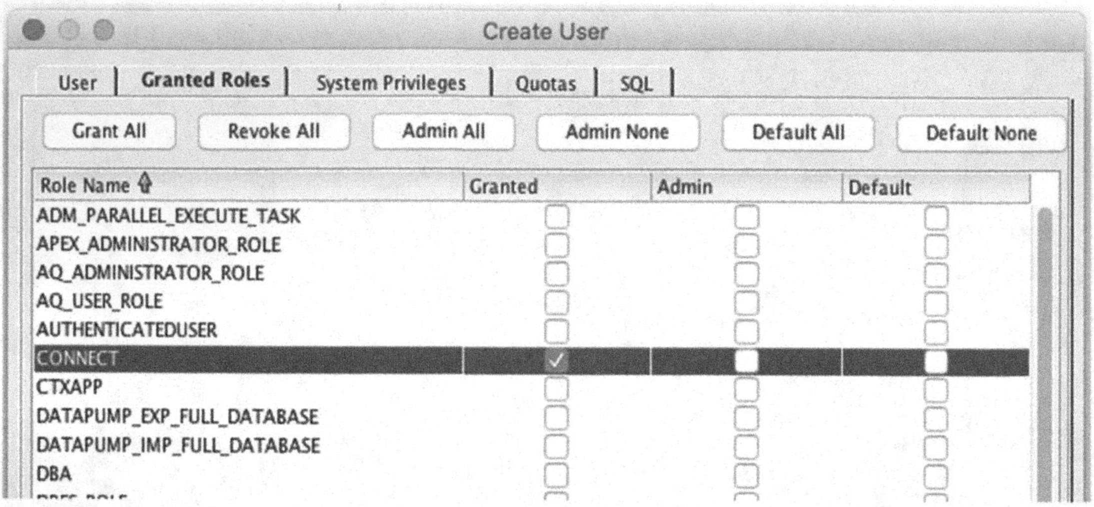

Figure 2-23. *The Granted Roles tab*

8. Click the System Privileges tab. A list of available privileges will
    appear, as shown in Figure 2-24.

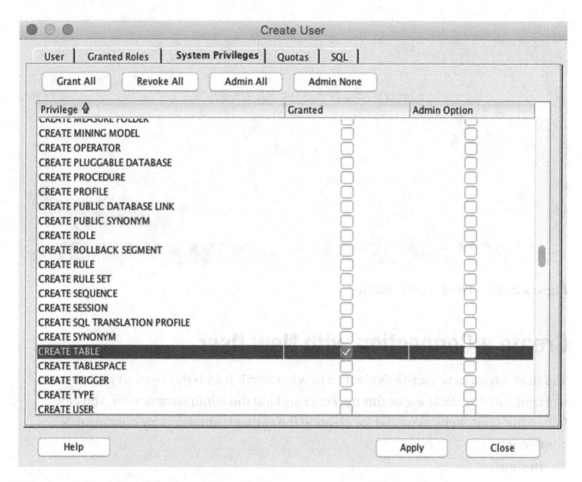

Figure 2-24. *The System Privileges tab*

9. Click the Granted checkbox next to the CREATE TABLE privileges.
    This will allow you to create a table.

10. Click the Apply button. The new user will be created and a message is displayed, as shown in Figure 2-25.

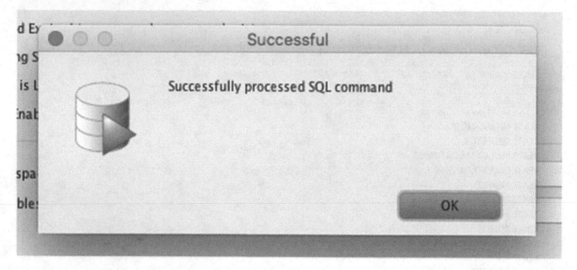

Figure 2-25. *The success message*

Create a Connection with New User

You now have a new user. Let's create a new connection with this user, so you can start working with the database as this new user and not the administrator user. You can follow the same steps as we did for creating the earlier connection for creating this connection.

In short:

1. Click the green plus sign on the left of SQL Developer to show the Create New Connection window.

2. Enter a new name for the connection, and enter the username and password you used when you created the user.

3. Leave the rest of the connection info as the defaults.

4. Click Save to save the connection.

5. Finally, click Connect to connect as this user.

Well done! You've now installed an Oracle database, opened SQL Developer, and created a new user and a connection with that user.

Create a Table

The last things we need to do before we can start learning some basic SQL is to create some sample data. This will involve two steps: creating a table, and then adding data to that table.

Each of these steps can be done in two ways. We can use the menu and dialog boxes inside SQL Developer, or we can run some SQL code to do this. By the end of the book you'll learn how to do both in SQL code, but for now, we'll create a table using the menus. Once you are connected to the Oracle database as your new user, you're ready to create a table.

To do this:

1. Expand the name of the connection on the left side of the window to see all of the available objects.

2. Right click the option that says "Tables (Filtered)," and select New Table. This should appear at the top of the list, as shown in Figure 2-26.

Figure 2-26. *The New Table menu option*

The Create Table window should appear.

3. Enter in a name for the table. For this table, we'll store data about employees, so we'll enter the word "employee" into the Name field, as shown in Figure 2-27. Upper case, lower case, the case does not matter. Oracle stores table names all in the one case.

Figure 2-27. *The name of the new table*

4. A table needs to have columns in it. In the Columns section, select
   the first value in the Name column (currently called "COLUMN1")
   by double-clicking it, as shown in Figure 2-28.

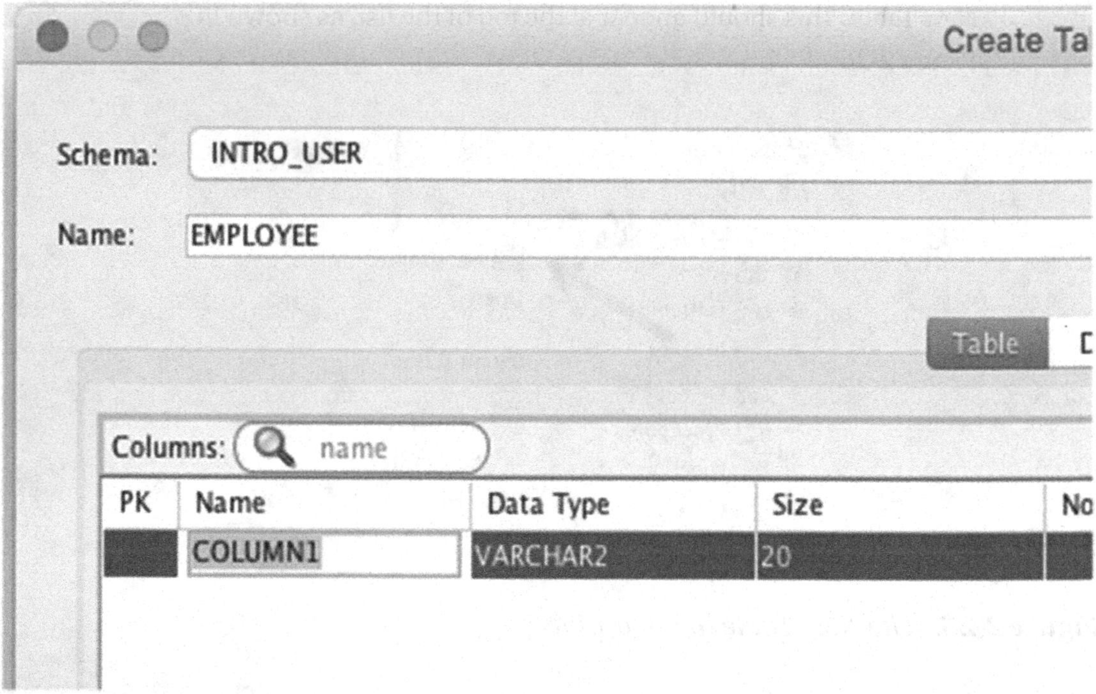

Figure 2-28. *Editing the name of a new column*

5. Enter a new name for the column. We'll call ours ID.

6. Select a Data Type value of NUMBER, as shown in Figure 2-29.

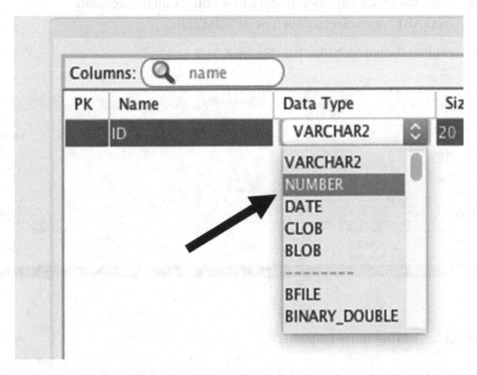

Figure 2-29. *The data type of the new column*

7. Click the green + symbol on the right to add a new entry, as shown in Figure 2-30.

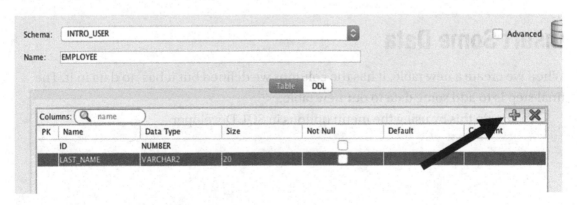

Figure 2-30. *Adding a new column*

8. Repeat the same steps to name this column "LAST_NAME." Leave the data type as VARCHAR2.

9. Click the green + symbol to add a new entry. Call this column "SALARY" and select a data type of NUMBER.

Your window should look like this (Figure 2-31).

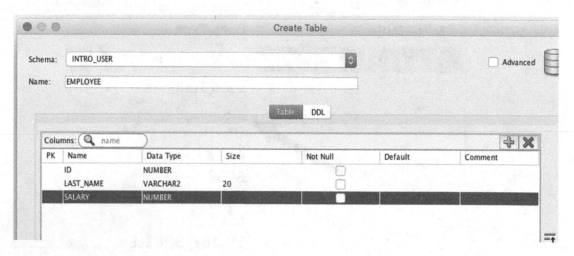

Figure 2-31. *Adding more columns*

10. Click the OK button. Your table will now be created. It will also appear under the "Tables (Filtered)" item on the right of the screen.

Congratulations! You have now created your very first table.

Insert Some Data

When we create a new table, it has the columns we defined but it has no data in it. The final step is to add some data to our new table.

We can do this by using the menu options in SQL Developer.

To do this:

1. Expand the name of your connection on the left window, and then expand the Tables (Filtered) entry, as shown in Figure 2-32.

Figure 2-32. *The table listed under the connection*

2. Click the EMPLOYEE table once. A new tab opens on the left that shows information about the table, such as the three columns you added when you created the table, as shown in Figure 2-33.

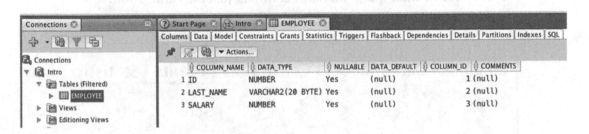

Figure 2-33. *The Employee columns*

3. On the second row of tabs, click the Data tab. This should be on the left next to Columns, as shown in Figure 2-34.

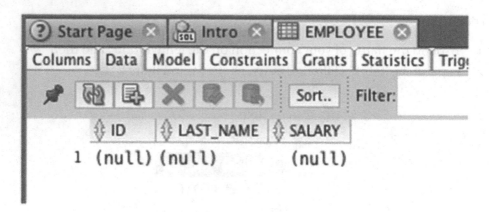

Figure 2-34. *The data in the Employee table*

4. Click the Insert Row button. This is the third button from the left, which has a white square and a green + symbol on it. A new row will be added.

5. Enter a value of 1 in the ID column, a value of JONES in the LAST_NAME column, and a value of 20000 in the SALARY column. You don't need to enter quote marks or commas, just the values. Your screen should look like Figure 2-35.

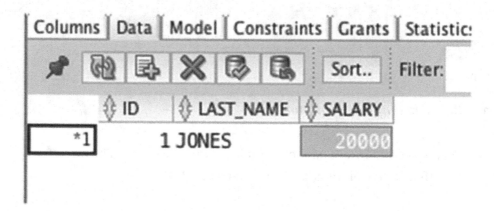

Figure 2-35. *The first row of data*

6. Click the Insert Row button and enter the following values into the row that appears. Repeat until all of these values are in the table and it looks like Figure 2-36.

ID	LAST_NAME	SALARY
2	SMITH	35000
3	KING	40000
4	SIMPSON	52000
5	ANDERSON	31000

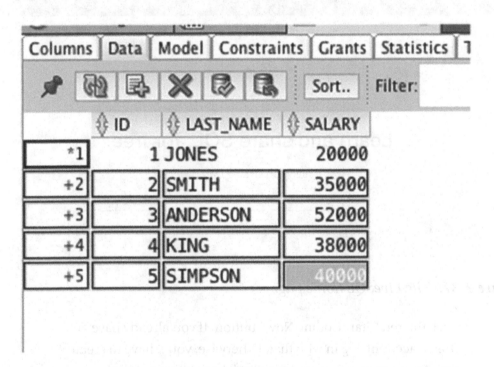

Figure 2-36. *More rows added to the table*

7. Click the Commit Changes button. This is a grey box with a cylinder and a green tick icon two buttons to the right of the Insert New Row icon.

This will save this data to the database. After a moment, the changes will be saved. Some messages will appear in the log at the bottom of the screen.

Now we have our data in our table.

LiveSQL

Oracle has an online database called LiveSQL, which lets you create your own data and run your own queries. It's great for testing out SQL or for when you don't have access to a computer with Oracle installed on it.

All of the example code in this book can be run on LiveSQL. However, you'll need to know how to use LiveSQL first. To access LiveSQL:

1. Visit `https://livesql.oracle.com` in your web browser, which should display as shown in Figure 2-37.

Figure 2-37. *The LiveSQL home page*

2. Click the red "Start Coding Now" button. If you already have an Oracle account, log in with that. Otherwise, you'll have to create one. An account is free, and you don't have to be an Oracle employee.

3. Once you are logged in and have accepted the Application Disclaimer, you'll have several areas available for you to visit, as shown in Figure 2-38. You can look at scripts or code other people have made available, or you can start with a new window. For this book, we'll start at a new window.

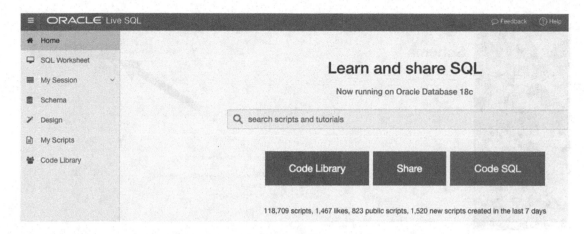

Figure 2-38. *The LiveSQL page after logging in*

4. Click the red Code SQL button or the SQL Worksheet link on the left to open a new LiveSQL session.

   You'll be presented with a new query window, as shown in Figure 2-39.

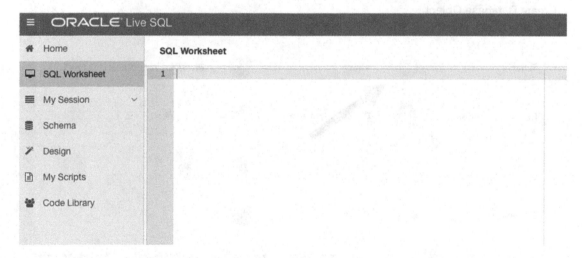

Figure 2-39. *The SQL worksheet*

5. Enter (or copy and paste) any code we have mentioned in this book into this query window, and click the Run button. The code should run and the results will be displayed.

6. To create a new table using a wizard similar to the SQL Developer instructions, click Schema and choose Create Database Object.

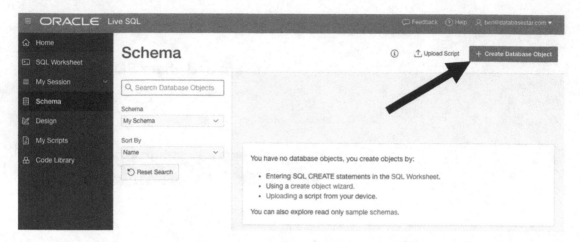

Figure 2-40. *The LiveSQL Schema window*

7. In the popup that appears, choose Table.

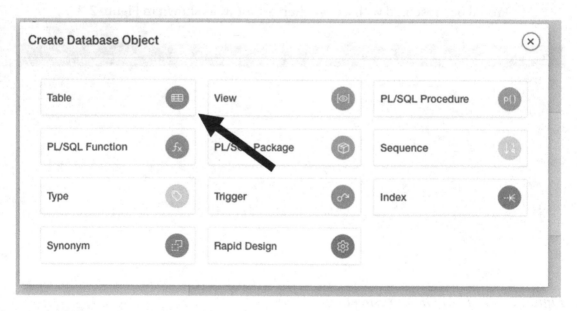

Figure 2-41. *The Create Database Object window*

The Create Table window is shown in Figure 2-42.

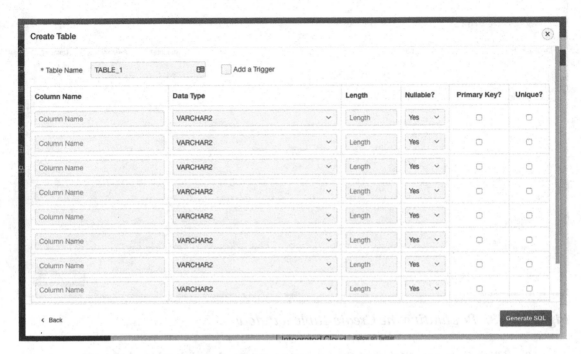

Figure 2-42. The Create Table window

8. Enter a Table Name for your table.

9. Enter the column names and select data types, in the same way as you did in Oracle SQL Developer.

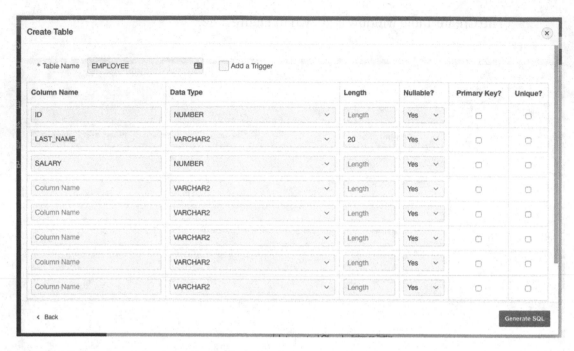

Figure 2-43. *Populating the Create Table window*

10. Click Generate SQL. The SQL is then generated and displayed in
    a query window. LiveSQL will generate the SQL code rather than
    create the table automatically. You'll learn how to create a table
    using SQL code later in this book.

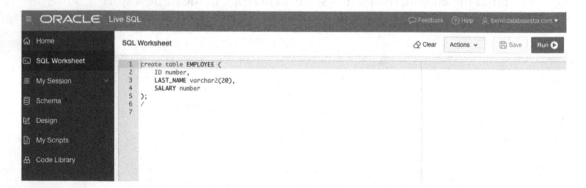

Figure 2-44. *The CREATE TABLE query in LiveSQL*

11. Click Run in the top right corner of the window to run the query.
     The EMPLOYEE table will then be created.

You're now able to run queries and see results on an Oracle database.

Summary

To run Oracle on our own computer, we can run Oracle Express Edition and Oracle SQL Developer, which are both free tools offered by Oracle.

Setting these up involved installing Oracle Express, setting up a new connection, and creating a new user in Oracle SQL Developer.

We then created a table, and added some data to this table, using the menu and screens within SQL Developer.

In the next chapter, we'll look at running some basic SQL queries to see this data.

PART II

Viewing Data

PART II

Viewing Data

CHAPTER 3

Retrieving Data

In this chapter, you'll learn how to see the data that's in your database. You'll look at your first SQL statement, the SELECT statement, and see some examples of this on the table you just created.

How Can You See the Data?

In the last chapter, you achieved a lot:

- You downloaded and installed Oracle Express.

- You downloaded and ran SQL Developer.

- You created two new connections and a new user.

- You created a new table and populated it with sample data.

When you created the table and added the sample data, you used the user interface of SQL Developer—the menu and the fields that appeared on the screen. However, SQL is a text-based language. You'll be learning how to write SQL code to work with this data, because this code can be used in other applications, to develop reports, or in other scripts.

There is a statement or command in the SQL language that allows you to view data in the database. It's called the SELECT statement.

What Is the SELECT Statement?

The SELECT statement is a type of statement in SQL that lets you read data from the database. A SELECT statement must be written in a certain pattern. This pattern is called *syntax,* and each of the statements you'll learn about has a different pattern or syntax. The word syntax is commonly used in SQL and programming to describe how code needs to be written.

© Ben Brumm 2019
B. Brumm, *Beginning Oracle SQL for Oracle Database 18c,*
https://doi.org/10.1007/978-1-4842-4430-2_3

To write a SELECT statement in Oracle SQL, it needs to follow this syntax:

```
SELECT your_columns
FROM your_table;
```

Let's look at each part of this statement. First, you start with the SELECT keyword. I've called it a *keyword* as it's a special word in SQL that does something (in this case, retrieves some data). A SELECT statement starts with the SELECT keyword.

You then have a space, and then the placeholder word "your_columns." This placeholder is where you list the columns you want to show in your results. When you write a SELECT statement (which you will do shortly), you replace the "your_columns" part with something else, generally a list of column names.

Next, you have the FROM keyword. The FROM keyword is part of the SELECT statement. It specifies the table that the data is being retrieved from. The FROM keyword is not a statement, because an SQL statement cannot start with the FROM keyword. FROM is actually a keyword that is part of other statements (such as SELECT).

You then have a space, then the word "your_table." This is also a placeholder, and you can replace this with the name of the table.

Finally, you have a semicolon ";". This specifies the end of the statement. Writing the semicolon is optional, but it's a good habit to get into. When you start to have multiple statements in an SQL window or start writing more SQL code, the semicolon will be important. Adding a semicolon to the end of your SQL statements is a good habit to start early.

A Few Things to Note

There are a few things in the SELECT statement syntax you might be wondering about, such as the capitalization and the separate lines. I've written part of that syntax in capital letters and part in lower case:

```
SELECT your_columns
FROM your_table;
```

Why is that? Basically, it's about formatting. When you write SQL, it's helpful to stick to a consistent format, to make it easier to read for others and easier to maintain.

I prefer to write SQL keywords, such as SELECT and FROM, in capital letters. This makes them stand out wherever you read them, whether it's in SQL Developer, another IDE, application code, or a script.

Other people prefer to write their SQL keywords in lower case, such as "select" and "from." The choice comes down to personal preference and there's no shortage of articles online that specify how and why SQL should be written in either upper case or lower case.

Fortunately, SQL is not a case-sensitive language. It doesn't matter to the Oracle database whether you write SELECT or select. The code will still run.

Which way should you write your SQL? I recommend upper case for keywords. However, I also think that it's more important to be consistent with your formatting with the rest of your team or the application. If your team prefers lower case, then use lower case. If you have the choice, if you're learning for yourself and not in a team, then I suggest using upper case.

What about the spacing? Why did I put the word FROM on a new line? SQL doesn't need keywords to be on a new line.

However, putting the FROM keyword (and many other keywords) on a new line will help to make the query easier to read and easier to maintain. So, I recommend writing your queries like this.

Our First SELECT Statement

Now that you've looked at the syntax of a SELECT statement and explained some of the formatting, let's write your very first SELECT statement.

First, you start with the SELECT keyword:

```
SELECT
```

Then, you add in the columns you want to see. In this example, we will show all of the columns available in this table. To do that in SQL, you use the asterisk character "*". Add this to the end of the SELECT keyword, after a space.

```
SELECT *
```

This variation of the SELECT statement is often called a "select all" or a "select star," as you are selecting all of the columns.

Next, you start a new line and add the word FROM.

```
SELECT *
FROM
```

Now you need to specify which table the data comes from. You can use the table you created in the last chapter, which was employee.

```
SELECT *
FROM employee
```

Finally, add a semicolon.

```
SELECT *
FROM employee;
```

This is your very first SELECT statement!

What about the rows? You have specified you want to see all columns, but what about the rows?

The database will use this statement and find all rows that match the criteria you provide. By default, all rows are returned, unless you specify criteria that you should check. You'll learn about displaying rows that meet certain criteria later in this book, but for now you aren't adding any, so the database will show you all rows.

What do you do with it? You run it on your database using an SQL worksheet or editor.

Running a Statement in SQL Developer

To run your SELECT statement, you can use SQL Developer. You can do this by following these steps:

1. Open SQL Developer. It should be in the location that you extracted it in the previous chapter. A loading screen will appear and within 5 to 10 seconds the application will load.

2. In the Connections menu on the left of the screen (Figure 3-1), there should be two connections (one for SYSTEM and one for Intro User or the user you created).

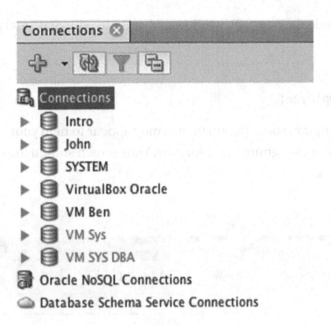

Figure 3-1. *The Connections panel*

3. Double-click your Intro User connection (or the connection that is not for the SYSTEM user).

    A new SQL worksheet will open on the main screen. Notice that on the top right corner, the drop-down box contains the name of your connection, as shown in Figure 3-2.

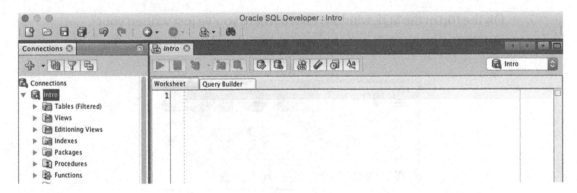

Figure 3-2. *The new SQL worksheet*

4. Click inside the new SQL window and enter in your SQL query as follows:

```
SELECT *
FROM employee;
```

As you enter it, some popup menus may appear to help your typing. You can ignore those for now. Your screen should look like Figure 3-3.

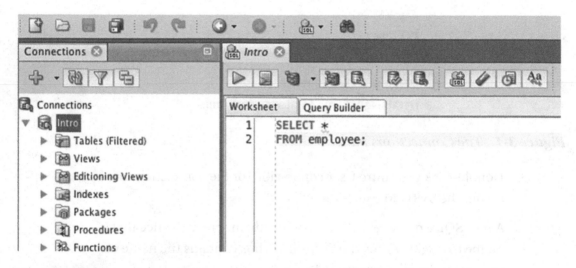

Figure 3-3. *Entering an SQL query*

On the top of the SQL window, above where you've just written your SELECT statement, there is a row of buttons, as shown in Figure 3-4.

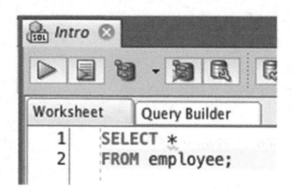

Figure 3-4. *The Run buttons*

The first button, the big green arrow, is Run Statement, and the second is Run Script. I'll show you what happens when you use those buttons. You can ignore the other buttons for now.

5. Click the Run Statement button, which is the first button on the toolbar.

The SQL statement is run, and after a moment, a set of data is shown at the bottom of the screen (Figure 3-5).

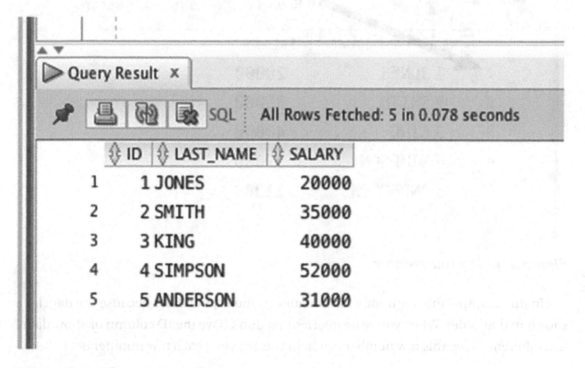

Figure 3-5. *The query results*

You'll notice that the data is shown in rows, and there are five rows. On the left of each row, there is a number, as shown in the screenshot in Figure 3-6. This number represents the row number of your result.

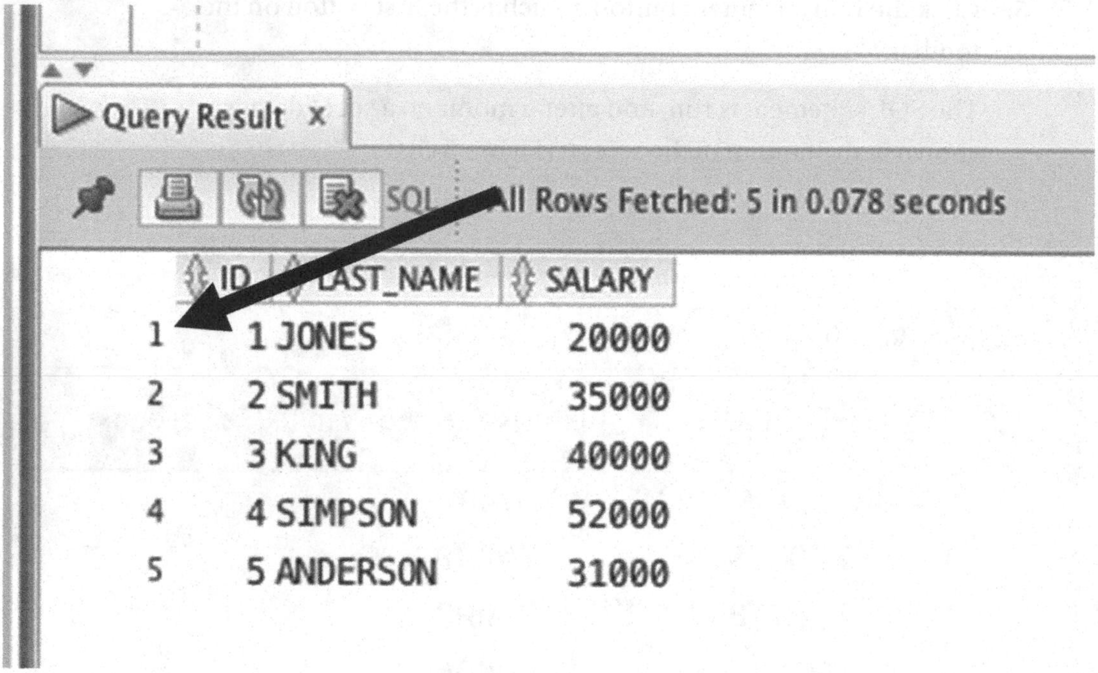

Figure 3-6. *The row number*

In this example the row number is the same as the ID, but that's because the data is shown in that order. When you write queries that don't have the ID column or show data in a different order, this row number can help you see what each row number is.

Results

When a SELECT statement is run on a database, the results of the statement are shown to you. This is called the results, or your *result set*, as it's a set of data that results from a query.

In your previous example, you wanted to see all columns in the employee table. When you run this statement, a table or grid appears at the bottom of the screen. This grid is your result set, and it is all of the columns and rows in the employee table.

This is the same data that you entered in the previous chapter. It shows the ID column, the last_name column, and the salary column. It shows all of the rows you entered.

Run Script

Another way you can run your query is to use the Run Script button in SQL Developer. This button will run all of the commands in your SQL window, which may include more than one. It will also display it in a text-based output, and not a table.

Once you have your SELECT query written in the SQL window, click the Run Script button. Figure 3-7 shows what your output would look like.

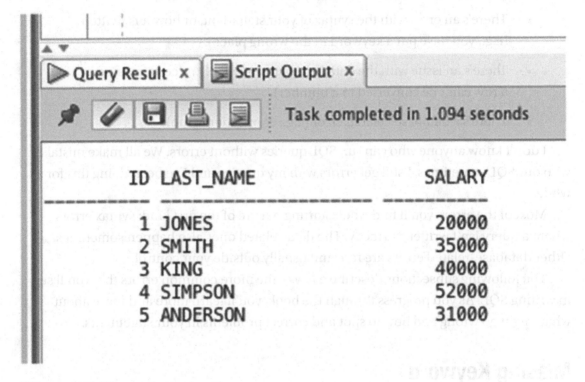

Figure 3-7. *The script output*

This shows the same output as the Run Statement button. However, it's shown in a text-based format. This makes it easy to copy and paste into a text file, or to run several statements at once. If you execute multiple queries, the results will be displayed one after each other in this text output, with the first query's results at the top.

It's good to know how to use the Run Script feature, and what it does. However, in this book, you'll be using the Run Statement button most of the time.

Errors in SQL

Running those queries seemed pretty simple right? You run a statement, and data is displayed. However, not all SQL statements are that simple, and not all of them give you the result you want.

Occasionally you'll run a query and instead of getting the result set from the database, you'll get an error message.

Error messages are shown for many reasons, such as:

- There's an error with the syntax of your statement, or how it is written (e.g., you have put a keyword in the wrong place).

- There's an issue with the data being processed (e.g., a certain value in a row can't be converted to a number).

- There's a database-related error (e.g., connection issue).

I don't know anyone who can run SQL queries without errors. We all make mistakes with our SQL sometimes. I still get errors with my queries and I've been doing this for a while.

Most of the errors you'll find when starting out are of the first kind: syntax errors where a query isn't written correctly. The data-related ones also happen sometimes. Other database-related errors are rare and usually outside your control.

The following subsections describe a few of the more common errors that you'll see in writing SQL. As you progress through the book, you'll learn more and more about what might go wrong and how to spot and correct problems in your statements.

Missing Keyword

Our example query earlier looked like this:

```
SELECT *
FROM employee;
```

Let's say that you forget to add the FROM keyword to your query, and your query looks like this:

```
SELECT * employee;
```

If you run that statement, you'll get this error:

```
ORA-00923: FROM keyword not found where expected
00923. 00000 -  "FROM keyword not found where expected"
*Cause:
*Action:
Error at Line: 1 Column: 10
```

All Oracle error messages start with a three letter code, followed by a dash and then five numbers. This is the error code. Most errors have an ORA error code, but some will have a PLS code.

The preceding error in the example has a code of ORA-00923, and the message says "FROM keyword not found where expected."

An error description is shown on the second line, but it is the same as the error message. Often, a cause and action is shown. But for this error, there is no cause or action displayed. The final line says the line and column that the error occurred on: in this case at Line 1, Column 10.

The error in this case is self-explanatory: "the FROM keyword is not found." If you look at your SQL statement, you'll see that there is no FROM keyword, so the statement does not run.

Table Does Not Exist

Sometimes you'll have a query like the following, and get an error:

```
SELECT *
FROM emplyoee;

ORA-00942: table or view does not exist
00942. 00000 -  "table or view does not exist"
*Cause:
*Action:
Error at Line: 2 Column: 6
```

The error says ORA-00942: table or view does not exist.

You're probably thinking, "That can't be right, the table does exist, I just created it!" I've made this same mistake many times. The issue with this query is that the table you have specified does not actually exist, but that's because it's misspelt. The query mentions "emplyoee" and not "employee."

You'll get this error if you misspell a table. However, this error can also appear for a few other reasons related to roles and security.

Summary

In this chapter, you've looked at the SELECT statement, which allows you to see the data that exists in a table. You used SELECT * to show all of the columns and rows in a table and learned what kind of errors can appear as you're writing your queries.

In the next chapter, you'll learn about specifying which columns in a table you want to display.

CHAPTER 4

Selecting Specific Columns

In this chapter, you'll learn how to show specific columns from your table. It is not always necessary or desirable to return all columns as we did in Chapter 3. As you'll recall, we executed the following query in that chapter:

```
SELECT *
FROM employee;
```

Figure 4-1 shows the results, which are all the columns from the employee table. Fortunately, in this instance there are few columns, so the results are not overwhelming.

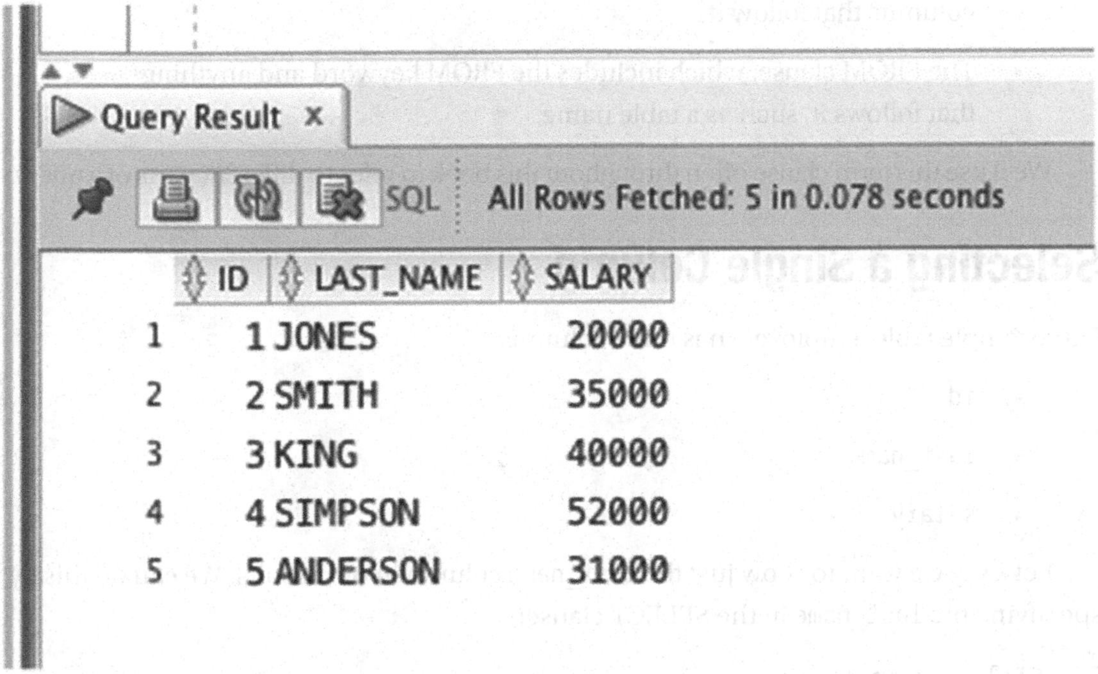

> Query Result ×
>
> SQL   All Rows Fetched: 5 in 0.078 seconds
>
> | | ID | LAST_NAME | SALARY |
> |---|---|---|---|
> | 1 | 1 | JONES | 20000 |
> | 2 | 2 | SMITH | 35000 |
> | 3 | 3 | KING | 40000 |
> | 4 | 4 | SIMPSON | 52000 |
> | 5 | 5 | ANDERSON | 31000 |

Figure 4-1. *The results of a query on the employee table*

© Ben Brumm 2019
B. Brumm, *Beginning Oracle SQL for Oracle Database 18c*,
https://doi.org/10.1007/978-1-4842-4430-2_4

Consider the case when a table has dozens or even maybe a hundred columns! Sometimes we don't want to see all columns in our query results. This could be because we're using a query in a certain part of the application where we only want to display some of the data and not all of the data in the table.

How can we do this in SQL? We specify each of the columns in the SELECT clause. The syntax for this kind of query looks as follows:

```
SELECT column_name, column_name...
FROM table_name;
```

This syntax looks very similar to that from Chapter 3. However, instead of specifying the * character (which indicates all columns), we specify each individual column we want to show. We separate each column name with a comma. The three dots "…" at the end of the syntax there just indicate that the column name syntax can be repeated.

One more thing: I used a term that we haven't covered yet, which is *clause*. A clause is a line of SQL code that starts with a keyword and includes everything related to that keyword.

We've seen two clauses so far:

- The SELECT clause, which includes the SELECT keyword and columns that follow it

- The FROM clause, which includes the FROM keyword and anything that follows it, such as a table name.

We'll use this term clause often throughout this book to refer to different parts of a query.

Selecting a Single Column

Our example table, employee, has three columns:

- id

- last_name

- salary

Let's say we want to show just the last_name column in our results. We can do this by specifying the last_name in the SELECT clause:

```
SELECT last_name
FROM employee;
```

This means the query will only show the last_name column in our results, and not the ID or the salary columns. A query like this would be used in an area of an application that needed to display the last names of employees. Let's run this query on our database.

First, open SQL Developer, if you haven't done so already. Then, connect to your database by double-clicking the new user's connection you created in an earlier chapter. This was not the system user: it was the other user you created. In Figure 4-2, this is called Intro.

Figure 4-2. *The connection in SQL Developer*

Double-clicking the connection in the list will cause SQL Developer to connect to the database. A new SQL worksheet window is also displayed on the screen.

What if no SQL worksheet is displayed? Or you closed it? You can open a new one pretty easily.

To do this:

1. Click the New SQL Worksheet button in the middle of the icons on the toolbar.

Figure 4-3. *The new SQL Worksheet icon*

2. The Select Connection window will pop up as shown in Figure 4-4.

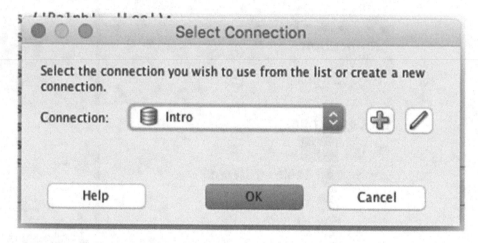

Figure 4-4. *The Select Connection window*

3. Select the connection you want to use, such as "Intro," and click OK.

    A new SQL worksheet is created, and it is displayed as a new tab within SQL Developer, as shown in Figure 4-5.

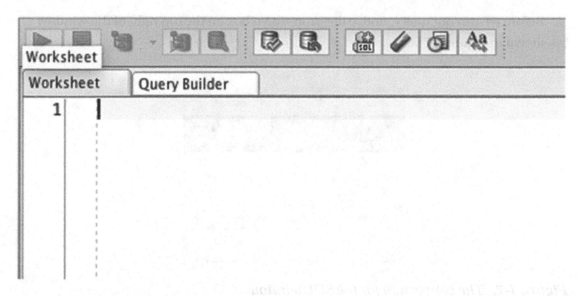

Figure 4-5. *The new worksheet*

Once the new file is displayed as a new tab on the screen, you can enter your query. Let's enter the query we used in the earlier example into our new window, as shown in Figure 4-6.

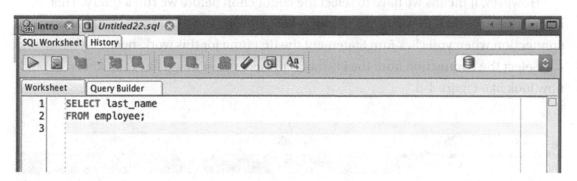

Figure 4-6. *Our query written in SQL Developer*

Before we run our query, notice the drop-down box on the top right of the window (as shown in Figure 4-7).

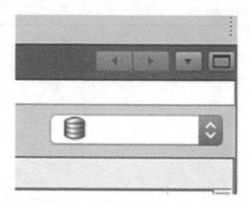

Figure 4-7. *The connection for the SQL window*

This is the connection that is used for this file. Each tab, or file, in SQL developer needs to have a connection to the database to be able to run code. The good thing is that you can have a separate connection for each tab, if you're working on multiple users or databases.

However, it means we have to select the connection before we run a query. This box is where we do it. If you forget this step, SQL Developer will prompt you to choose a connection when you click Run Statement the first time for this worksheet.

Select the connection from the list that represents your new user. Your screen should now look like Figure 4-8.

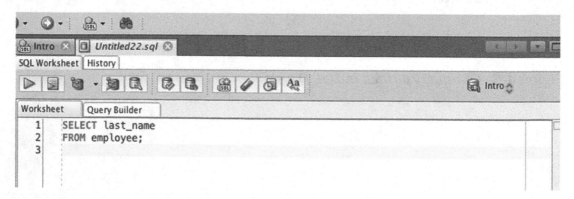

Figure 4-8. *An SQL query after selecting a connection*

Now we can run the query. Click Run Query to run it on the database and see the results (Figure 4-9).

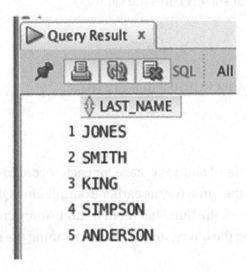

Figure 4-9. *Results of our query*

The results here show only the last_name from the employee table. It does not show the ID or the salary columns, because we did not specify them in the SELECT clause in the query.

Selecting Multiple Columns

In SQL, you can specify more than one column in your SELECT clause. You do this by specifying multiple column names separated by commas, as we saw in the beginning of this chapter:

```
SELECT column1, column2, column_n...
FROM your_table;
```

If we want to show both the ID and the last_name columns, we would write our query like this:

```
SELECT id, last_name
FROM employee;
```

71

You might notice a space between the comma and the next column name. This space is not required. The statement will still run if it's missing the space. For example, the following is less legible, but still executes the same:

```
SELECT id,last_name
FROM employee;
```

However, I think it's easier to read if there's a space:

```
SELECT id, last_name
FROM employee;
```

This query will show the id and last_name for each record in the employee table. You can run this query in the same way as earlier examples in SQL Developer. Enter it into SQL Developer and click the Run Statement button. Your screen should look like Figure 4-10 before running the query, and 4-11 after running the query.

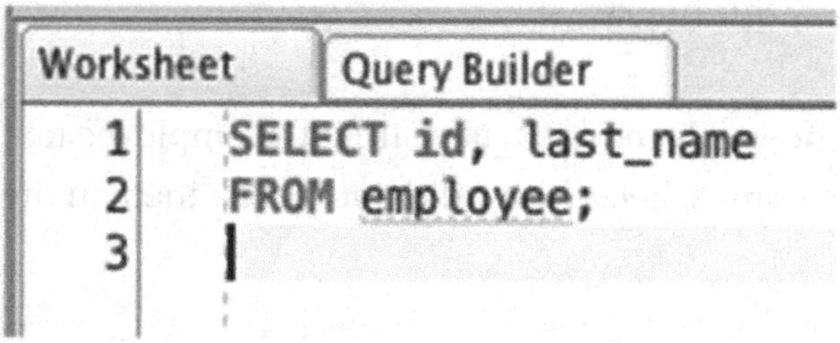

Figure 4-10. Before running the query

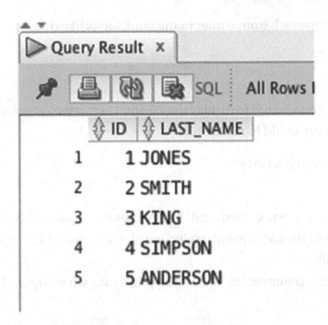

Figure 4-11. *After running the query*

The results can also be represented like this:

ID	LAST_NAME
1	JONES
2	SMITH
3	KING
4	SIMPSON
5	ANDERSON

The results at the bottom of the screen will show all records with both the ID and the last_name columns.

Selecting All Columns

You can use the same method for displaying all columns in a table. You can choose to write SELECT *, or you can choose to enumerate all the column names.

The SELECT * approach from earlier in the book looks like this:

```
SELECT *
FROM employee;
```

For example, if you wanted to display the ID, the last name, and the salary of all employees, your query could look like this:

```
SELECT id, last_name, salary
FROM employee;
```

The three columns are specified, and their names are separated by commas. Both approaches will show the same results: selecting all columns using * or selecting all columns individually.

You can enter this statement in SQL Developer, as shown in Figure 4-12.

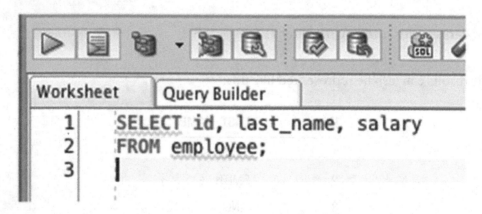

Figure 4-12. *Selecting all columns*

When you run the query, you'll see the id, last_name, and salary for all employee records, as shown in Figure 4-13.

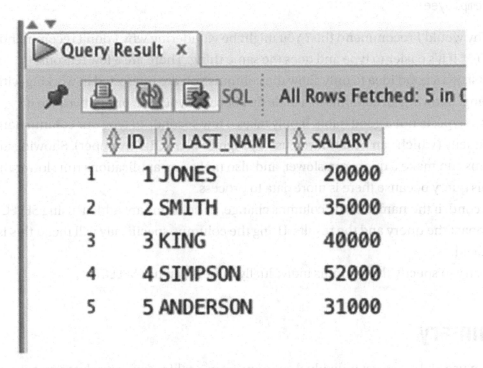

Figure 4-13.   *The results of all columns*

SELECT Columns or SELECT *?

If you want to show all columns in a table, you can do this in two ways:

- Use SELECT *
- Use SELECT and then specify each column individually

Which method is better? Which one should you use? I recommend specifying each of the columns individually. This means your query should look like this:

```
SELECT id, last_name, salary
FROM employee;
```

Rather than look like this:

```
SELECT *
FROM employee;
```

Why would I recommend this? You might be wondering why I don't recommend SELECT * if it's easier to type and does the same thing. There are a few reasons.

First, it's a good idea to only show the columns you are interested in working with or seeing. Showing all columns in a table just because you can, or just because it's easier to type, is not a good habit. It only takes a few seconds to type our column names individually (which can be fast if you use a program like SQL Developer). Showing all columns can make a query run slower, and also make any applications run slower that use this query because there is more data to process.

Second, if the names of the columns change, or columns are added, using SELECT * can impact the query and the results. Using the columns specifically will mean this issue is reduced.

So, try to specify the columns individually rather than use SELECT *.

Summary

You can use SQL to select individual columns from a table. You can select one column, multiple columns, or every column in the table. Specifying the individual columns is recommended rather than using SELECT * because it's easier to maintain and reduces the load by the application and database.

CHAPTER 5

Restricting the Results

We have just learned how to display certain columns from a table. In this chapter, we'll look at how to display certain rows from a table.

Why Restrict Data?

In our earlier examples, we looked at all columns in a table and one or two columns from a table. One of the queries looked like this:

```
SELECT id, last_name, salary
FROM employee;
```

This query will show the `id`, `last_name`, and `salary` columns for all employees in the table. What if you didn't want to see all employees in the table? In our example table, there are five records. But what if the table had one hundred, or one thousand records? In real databases that you might encounter in the workplace, a table with over a million records is not uncommon.

So why would you want to only show some records? Essentially, if you have a requirement to only show records that meet certain criteria, then you only need to find those records in the database.

Some examples could be:

- Find all information for a particular employee.

- Find all orders places for a customer.

- Find all student enrollments during a particular year.

You might be thinking, "Can't we just get all records in the table and let the application find what it needs?" We could do that, but it would be very slow. Finding all of the data in a table, sending it from the database to the application, for the application to discard the records it does not need would take a lot of time and memory. It also has

© Ben Brumm 2019
B. Brumm, *Beginning Oracle SQL for Oracle Database 18c*,
https://doi.org/10.1007/978-1-4842-4430-2_5

an impact on network traffic, because sending all data to the application typically results in a lot of network traffic and is a lot slower than the database examining the rows before sending them back.

It's a much better use of the database and time to only find the data that we want. Luckily, we can do that easily in SQL with the *WHERE* clause.

What is the WHERE Clause?

The WHERE clause is a clause that lets you filter the data from your query to only show you what meets the criteria you specify. A clause, as we mentioned in an earlier chapter, is a combination of an SQL keyword and everything related that comes after it.

The WHERE clause looks like this:

```
WHERE criteria
```

The clause seems simple, but it's quite powerful. You put the WHERE clause into a SELECT query immediately after the FROM clause. For example:

```
SELECT columns
FROM table
WHERE criteria;
```

The semicolon is moved to the very end of the statement, after the WHERE clause.

Example with a Text Value

Let's take a look at some examples. We'll begin with some text values. Here is the query we ran last chapter, which shows all of the records in the employee table.

```
SELECT id, last_name, salary
FROM employee;
```

Our results look like these:

ID	LAST_NAME	SALARY
1	JONES	20000
2	SMITH	35000
3	KING	40000
4	SIMPSON	52000
5	ANDERSON	31000

Let's say you wanted to find all of the columns, or fields, for employees with a `last_name` of SMITH.

You can write your query like this:

```
SELECT id, last_name, salary
FROM employee
WHERE last_name = 'SMITH';
```

There are a few new components to this query:

- First, you add in the `WHERE` keyword.
- Then, you specify the `last_name` column. This is because you want to check the value of the `last_name` column against another value.
- You then add an equals sign "=".
- Finally, you add the term 'SMITH'. This is because you want to see all records with a `last_name` of SMITH.

SMITH is inside single quotes because this is a specific value you want to look for. The value of SMITH is called a "string," which is the word in software development for a text value. The value of SMITH is inside single quotes because you want the database to know you want that treated as a text value and not as a column name. If you did not have the single quotes, your query would look like this:

```
SELECT id, last_name, salary
FROM employee
WHERE last_name = SMITH;
```

Then, the Oracle database would be looking for a column called SMITH, and an error would be shown because the column does not exist. So, any time you're looking for a text value, ensure it is inside single quotes:

```
SELECT id, last_name, salary
FROM employee
WHERE last_name = 'SMITH';
```

How does this query work? The Oracle database will run this query, and for each row in the employee table, it will check if the `last_name` of that row is equal to `'SMITH'`. If it is, then the row is included in the results displayed to you. If not, then it is not displayed. If you run this query, your output would be:

```
ID LAST_NAME SALARY
2  SMITH 35000
```

Only one record is shown, because only one record has a `last_name` value of SMITH. When you use the WHERE clause with text values, the **values are case sensitive**. Earlier in this book we mentioned that SQL is not a case-sensitive language, which means SELECT and select both perform the same thing.

However, when working with text values, such as 'SMITH', this check is case sensitive. This means that looking for 'Smith' will not show the same results as looking for 'SMITH'.

```
SELECT id, last_name, salary
FROM employee
WHERE last_name = 'Smith';
```

```
No results found.
```

This is because the value in the table is equal to `'SMITH'`, which is different to `'Smith'`.

Note   Text values (those inside single quotes) are case sensitive in SQL. So, 'SMITH' is not equal to 'Smith'.

Notice the spaces surrounding the equals sign. They are not required, but without them the query is more difficult to read. For example:

```
SELECT id, last_name, salary
FROM employee
WHERE last_name='Smith';
```

This query will execute, but I recommend the spaces around operators like the equal sign for reasons of readability. Good use of white space makes the query easier to read for the next programmer who needs to maintain it.

Example with a Number Value

You don't always need to filter on text values. You can also filter on number values. Let's say you wanted to find any employees who had a salary of 52,000. Your query would look like this:

```
SELECT id, last_name, salary
FROM employee
WHERE salary = 52000;
```

There are a few differences between this query and the earlier query:

- We want to see records with a specific salary, so we have specified
  WHERE salary.

- We don't care what the last_name value is, so we have removed any
  condition for that column from the WHERE clause.

- We have also used the equals sign, and then specified a number:
  52000. Doing so will show us all records with a salary of 52000.

You might be wondering, "What about a dollar sign? Can I add a comma as a thousand separator?" You might be trying to run a query like this:

```
SELECT id, last_name, salary
FROM employee
WHERE salary = $52000;
```

Or like this:

```
SELECT id, last_name, salary
FROM employee
WHERE salary = 52,000;
```

The good news is that you don't have to type commas and dollar signs. One of the factors of good database design is that each column has an appropriate data type. While the last_name column is stored as a text value, the salary is stored as a number.

You can't store the currency symbol (a $ symbol or a € symbol) in the salary column, because that would mean the field is no longer a number. However, you can store the salary as a number without the currency symbol, and any application that uses this salary value can determine how to display the value (for example, adding a currency symbol).

You also don't need to store any commas or other characters as thousand separators. These should be used only for displaying data in a report or an application, so the place that the salary is displayed will determine if any thousand separators are needed. In the database, we simply store the number value. You can also add this when you SELECT the column from the database.

Unlike text values in SQL, you shouldn't enclose number values within single quotes. Specifying salary = 52000 will work.

To recap, our query looks like this:

```
SELECT id, last_name, salary
FROM employee
WHERE salary = 52000;
```

If you run your query, your results will look like these:

```
ID   LAST_NAME   SALARY
4    SIMPSON     52000
```

This result shows a single record that meets your criteria: the salary is equal to 52000. None of the other records have that same salary value.

Finding Rows Not Equal to a Value

So far, you have looked at records that match certain criteria exactly. What if you want to find all records that don't match certain criteria?

You can find records that don't match certain criteria in SQL with a slightly different symbol that represents "not equal to." The "not equal to" operation is represented by <>. This symbol is two angled brackets next to each other.

Let's see an example of finding records that don't match certain criteria, where you want to see all employees where the last_name is not SMITH.

Your query would look like this:

```
SELECT id, last_name, salary
FROM employee
WHERE last_name <> 'SMITH';
```

This query looks exactly the same as the one earlier to find all employees named SMITH, except we use <> instead of =. Thus, our new version of the query will show us all records where the last_name does not equal SMITH.

ID	LAST_NAME	SALARY
1	JONES	20000
3	KING	40000
4	SIMPSON	52000
5	ANDERSON	31000

Finally, there is another symbol that can be used for not equals: "!=". The exclamation point and equals sign also specify "not equal to." This means your query could also be written like this:

```
SELECT id, last_name, salary
FROM employee
WHERE last_name != 'SMITH';
```

The results would be the same:

ID	LAST_NAME	SALARY
1	JONES	20000
3	KING	40000
4	SIMPSON	52000
5	ANDERSON	31000

If there are two symbols that do the same thing, which one do you use? I would recommend using the two angled brackets "<>", because they are part of the SQL standard whereas "!=" is not. This makes it easier for others to understand and also makes it easier in the future for code changes.

Greater Than

We've looked at equal to, and not equal to. You can also find records using a "greater than" check, which means you can find all records where a column is greater than a specific value. The greater than symbol is ">", a single angled bracket that points to the right.

Let's say you wanted to find all employee records where the salary was greater than 35000. Your query would look like this:

```
SELECT id, last_name, salary
FROM employee
WHERE salary > 35000;
```

Just like with finding values equal to a number, you shouldn't enclose the number inside single quotes. This applies to all the work you do with numbers.

This query will look at each record, determine if the salary is greater than 35000, and if it is, the record will be shown in these results. If not, the record won't be shown. The greater than symbol does not include values that match what you have specified. So, a value of 35000 would not be returned, but a value of 35001 would be.

Our results would look like this:

```
ID   LAST_NAME   SALARY
3    KING        40000
4    SIMPSON     52000
```

The results show the two records where the salary is greater than 35000. It does not include employee 'SMITH', as they have a salary of 35000 exactly, which is not greater than 35000.

Greater Than or Equal To

What if you wanted to include that 'SMITH' record? You could change your query to be > 34999. Another way to do it would be to use "greater than or equal to." Including the 'SMITH' record can be checked using a ">=" symbol, which is a combination of the greater than symbol and the equals signal.

If you wanted to write a query that shows all employees with a salary greater than or equal to 35000, it would look like this:

```
SELECT id, last_name, salary
FROM employee
WHERE salary >= 35000;
```

This query would show the following results:

```
ID    LAST_NAME    SALARY
2     SMITH        35000
3     KING         40000
4     SIMPSON      52000
```

It shows both 'KING' and 'SIMPSON' because they are over 35000, and 'SMITH' because the 35000 meets the "greater than or equal to 35000" criteria. It doesn't show 'JONES' or 'ANDERSON' because their salary values are less than 35000.

Less Than

Just like with the "greater than" criteria, you can look for records that are less than a specific value using a "less than" symbol. This symbol is "<". It's used in the same way as the greater than symbol. If you wanted to write a query to show all employees with a salary of less than 40000, it would look like this:

```
SELECT id, last_name, salary
FROM employee
WHERE salary < 40000;
```

Your results would be:

```
ID    LAST_NAME    SALARY
1     JONES        20000
2     SMITH        35000
5     ANDERSON     31000
```

Out of the five records in the table, 'KING' (40000) and 'SIMPSON' (52000) are not shown as their salary values are not less than 40000. The salary value for 'KING' is equal to 40000 which is not less than 40000.

Less Than or Equal To

SQL supports a "less than or equal to" check in the same way as the "greater than or equal to" check. It uses a combination of the less than symbol and the equals symbol, which is "<=". To see all employees where the salary is less than or equal to 40000, a query like this would work:

```
SELECT id, last_name, salary
FROM employee
WHERE salary <= 40000;
```

The results of this query would be:

```
ID   LAST_NAME   SALARY
1    JONES       20000
2    SMITH       35000
3    KING        40000
5    ANDERSON    31000
```

The result shows 'JONES', 'SMITH', and 'ANDERSON', as they all have a salary of less than 40000. The result also shows 'KING', as their salary is equal to 40000. In summary, the different symbols that can be used are shown in Table 5-1.

Table 5-1. *Available Comparison Operators*

Meaning	Symbol
Equal to	=
Not equal to	<> or !=
Greater than	>
Greater than or equal to	>=
Less than	<
Less than or equal to	<=

Best Practices

The WHERE clause in SQL is quite flexible, just like the SQL language overall, as you've seen in this chapter. The formatting and structure of your query can be different to the way that other people write a query that would show the same result.

There are a few "best practices" or tips that I can suggest for improving your use of this WHERE clause and your query overall. This will ensure that your query is easy to read and easy to understand by yourself and others in the future.

Specify Columns on the Left

When writing your WHERE clause, you should place your columns on the left, and values or other columns on the right of each comparison statement. This makes the code consistent and easier to read. This means your query would say:

```
WHERE last_name = 'SMITH'
```

Rather than:

```
WHERE 'SMITH' = last_name
```

Both WHERE clauses do the same thing, but the first one follows a more common format that I think is more readable. Most programmers with experience in SQL expect column names on the left and literal values to be on the right.

Select Only What You Need

The columns you mention in the WHERE clause do not have to be listed in the SELECT clause. You can filter on a value without needing to send it back to the application.

For example, let's say you wanted to see all employee IDs where the salary is less than 40000. You could list the salary in both the SELECT and the WHERE clauses:

```
SELECT id, salary
FROM employee
WHERE salary < 40000;
```

However, by listing the salary column in the SELECT clause you are causing all the salary values to be sent over the network to the application when the application doesn't need those values, or possibly exposing data that needs to be secured and kept private.

87

A more efficient version of the query looks like this:

```
SELECT id
FROM employee
WHERE salary < 40000;
```

The database engine can still filter the results on the salary column. However, only the ID values are sent across the network to the application. Network traffic is reduced, and your application users won't be waiting for data to be sent that is not needed or showing salary data to people who shouldn't see it.

Summary

Your results can be filtered using the WHERE clause, which involves the WHERE keyword and some criteria. This means you can show only the records that you are interested in. Filtering your data using the WHERE clause can be done in a range of ways, using symbols such as equals, not equals, greater than, and less than.

CHAPTER 6

Comparing Data

You've just learned how to restrict which rows you want to display, using a range of methods such as the equal to or greater than. Each of these methods checks a column against another value. This other value is checked using an "exact match." The exact value that you specified is used to perform the check.

For example, consider this WHERE clause:

```
WHERE last_name = 'SMITH'
```

This WHERE clause will return all rows where the last_name is equal to 'SMITH'. It does not return records where the last_name is any of the following values:

- Smith

- SMITHERS

- SMITHSONIAN

- Naismith

- SMIT

This is what an exact match does. But what if you want to match on part of a value?

What Is a Partial Match?

In the earlier example, you looked for all employee records that had a last_name of 'SMITH'. What if you wanted to find all employee records that had a last_name starting with the letter S?

You could write a query like this:

```
SELECT id, last_name, salary
FROM employee
WHERE last_name = 'S';
```

© Ben Brumm 2019

B. Brumm, *Beginning Oracle SQL for Oracle Database 18c*,
https://doi.org/10.1007/978-1-4842-4430-2_6

If you run this query, you get the following results:

```
No results found.
```

You don't get any results because there are no `last_name` values that are equal to `'S'`. "Equal to" and "starting with" are different concepts in SQL and programming in general. The ability to find records that "start with" a certain value is called a *partial match*.

A partial match is the ability to match on part of a value. Rather than checking that a value exactly matches another value, with partial match we can check for:

- Starting with a certain value

- Ending with a certain value

- Contains a certain value

- Other combinations of values

You can perform a partial match in SQL by using the *LIKE* keyword.

Syntax of LIKE

The `LIKE` keyword can be used in place of the equals symbol in the `WHERE` clause:

```
WHERE column LIKE compare_string
```

You start with the `WHERE` clause like you've previously seen, and then specify the column you want to look for. You then use the `LIKE` keyword and specify a `compare_string`, which is the value you are looking for.

How do you write this compare string? You use what are called *wildcard characters*. Wildcard characters are characters that are used to represent any other character. This can be better explained with an example.

The Percent Wildcard Character

In our earlier example, you wanted to find all `last_names` that started with "S." To do this, you can use the percent wildcard character, which is "%". This represents "zero or more characters," which means any letter, number, or symbol.

You can have a WHERE clause like this:

```
WHERE last_name LIKE 'S%'
```

This will look for last_name values that have an "S" as the first character, and then zero or more characters after that "S" no matter what those characters are.

This would show values such as:

- SMITHERS
- Smith
- SIMPSON
- Stanley
- Sum
- So

Can you see a pattern here? All of those values start with an "S" and have zero or more characters following it. The actual characters that follow it don't matter. There just needs to be one or more.

You can write a query to show this data:

```
SELECT id, last_name, salary
FROM employee
WHERE last_name LIKE 'S%';
```

Your results would be:

```
ID   LAST_NAME   SALARY
2    SMITH       35000
4    SIMPSON     52000
```

You can see two results here, one for 'SMITH' and one for 'SIMPSON'. Both of those start with "S". There are two other records that have an "S" in them ('ANDERSON' and 'JONES'), but they are not shown because your criteria was "S%", which meant the last_name needed to have a single S at the start, followed by other characters. The values of 'ANDERSON' and 'JONES' don't start with an S.

What if you did want to show those records? What if you wanted to find all records where the last_name had an "S" in it? You can do this by putting a % symbol both before the S and after the S:

```
SELECT id, last_name, salary
FROM employee
WHERE last_name LIKE '%S%';
```

Your results would look like this:

ID	LAST_NAME	SALARY
1	JONES	20000
2	SMITH	35000
4	SIMPSON	52000
5	ANDERSON	31000

These values are shown because they contain an S at any position in the last_name value. It could be at the start, in the middle, or at the end.

You could look for values that end with an S as well, by placing a "%" symbol at the start of your comparison string but not at the end. Your query would look like this:

```
SELECT id, last_name, salary
FROM employee
WHERE last_name LIKE '%S';
```

Our results would look like this:

ID	LAST_NAME	SALARY
1	JONES	20000

The percent wildcard character is helpful for finding a character or set of characters in a string in any position, as you've seen in the preceding examples.

The Underscore Wildcard Character

The other wildcard character available in Oracle SQL is the underscore character "_". The underscore character is used to represent zero or one character of any type. It's similar to the percent character, which represents zero or more characters, except the underscore allows for at most one character in the place that the wildcard is used.

Let's say you had a WHERE clause like this:

```
WHERE last_name LIKE 'SA_'
```

Your results would include:

- SAM
- SAL
- SAr
- SA

However, your results would **not** include:

- SALL
- SANDERS
- SAWS
- Sam

This is because only one character at most is allowed in the place of the underscore, and the second group of examples had two or more characters (or did not start with "SA").

Let's say you wanted to find every last_name that had a single character followed by 'ING'. Your query would look like this:

```
SELECT id, last_name, salary
FROM employee
WHERE last_name LIKE '_ING';
```

The results would be:

```
ID   LAST_NAME   SALARY
3    KING        40000
```

This result shows the value of 'KING' because it contains a single character, followed by the characters 'ING'. If there were records in the table with a last_name value of 'BING' or 'LING', they would also be shown.

You can also mix the percent and underscore characters or include any number of these two characters to find the record you want. Let's say you wanted to find all records that included 'SO' in the last_name but had a single character after it. Your query would be:

```
SELECT id, last_name, salary
FROM employee
WHERE last_name LIKE '%SO_';
```

The WHERE clause compares the last_name to '%SO_', which is any number of characters, then the characters SO, then zero or one character. Your results would be:

ID	LAST_NAME	SALARY
4	SIMPSON	52000
5	ANDERSON	31000

Both 'SIMPSON' and 'ANDERSON' are shown, because they include the characters 'SO' and have a single character following it.

Let's say you wanted to find all records where the last_name included the letter I as the second character and included the letter N at any point after that. Your query would be:

```
SELECT id, last_name, salary
FROM employee
WHERE last_name LIKE '_I%N%';
```

This comparison string, '_I%N%', can be explained as:

- An underscore, which means any single character
- An I, which is in the second position
- A %, which means zero or more of any character
- An N, which needs to be after the I but in any position
- A %, which means zero or more of any character after the N

Your results of this query would be:

ID	LAST_NAME	SALARY
3	KING	40000
4	SIMPSON	52000

Both `'KING'` and `'SIMPSON'` meet the WHERE clause criteria. The N in `'KING'` is immediately after the I, and the N in `'SIMPSON'` is at the end of the value.

Searching for Wildcard Characters

In this chapter you've learned how to use the wildcard characters of % and _ to look for records that partially match a value. These % and _ characters are substituted with other characters when your query is run. However, what if the value in the column actually contained a % character or an _ character?

Let's say that there is a value in your employee table that contained an underscore. The record with this may have been placed there by the application, perhaps during development, and you need to find out more about it. The record would look like this:

```
ID   LAST_NAME          SALARY
11   confirmation_needed (null)
```

The last_name of "confirmation_needed" isn't a valid last_name. You want to write a query to find all employees where a last_name contains an underscore character. You could write this query:

```
SELECT id, last_name, salary
FROM employee
WHERE last_name LIKE '%_%';
```

When you run this query, you'll get this result:

```
ID   LAST_NAME          SALARY
1    JONES              20000
2    SMITH              35000
3    KING               40000
4    SIMPSON            52000
5    ANDERSON           31000
11   confirmation_needed 0
```

This shows all records in the table. The query is searching for '%_%', which means "all characters, followed by one character, followed by all characters." How can you search for all characters with an underscore? You'll need to specify that the underscore should be treated like a value and not a wildcard character. This is done by *escaping* the character.

Escaping a character means you want the character to be treated as part of the value in the column and not as a special symbol (such as a wildcard). Escaping a character is possible in many programming languages, including SQL. To escape a character in SQL, you'll need to do two things:

- Specify a character immediately before the character you want to escape

- Specify in your WHERE clause what this escape character is

A common character to use as an escape character is the backslash character '\', because it's rare this character is used in your data. If it is used, you can choose another character.

To use an escape character in your query, you would write the query like this:

```
SELECT id, last_name, salary
FROM employee
WHERE last_name LIKE '%\_%' ESCAPE '\';
```

This has two changes from the previous query. First, there is a \ character inside the string after the LIKE keyword. This character indicates that the following character (the underscore) is "escaped." There is also a keyword added to the end of the WHERE clause: ESCAPE '\'. This means that the escape character is defined as the '\' character. Without adding this ESCAPE keyword, Oracle won't know what the '\' means inside the LIKE string.

The results of this updated query are:

```
ID   LAST_NAME           SALARY
11   confirmation_needed 0
```

As you can see, the updated query will only show records where the last_name value contains an underscore.

Performance

Another thing to know about the LIKE keyword is that the performance of queries using this keyword is generally not very good.

If you use an exact match, Oracle can usually scan all of the values you're looking at in a column and find those that match. However, using a partial match with the LIKE keyword takes longer, as Oracle needs to look at each value and apply your criteria to it.

We won't go into the performance of Oracle SQL a lot in this book, but I wanted to point out that the LIKE keyword is not known for performing well. You should use it if it's really what you need, and use other methods (such as "equal to") if it can be done that way.

Summary

The = symbol and other symbols are used to perform exact matches or match the specified value exactly. In SQL, the alternative is a partial match, which matches on a part of a value. These parts of values can be specified with the LIKE keyword and using the wildcards of % and _.

CHAPTER 7

Applying Multiple Filters

In the previous chapters, you've learned how to restrict the records you want to see. You looked at using symbols such as "equals to" and "greater than." You also learned how to do partial matches using the LIKE keyword and wildcard characters.

These concepts are useful to know. However, you may have noticed that we only filtered by one criteria in each query. We filtered based on a particular last_name value, or a particular salary value. What if we wanted to filter on two or more criteria?

Why Use Multiple Filters?

Why would you want to use multiple filters in an SQL query? It all depends on the type of query or the results you're looking for. It might be OK to perform a single filter using the WHERE clause for the examples we are using, but when you work with a lot more data or have different results you want to show, then you'll need to learn how to use multiple filters.

Some examples could be:

- Finding all orders in a date range for a specific customer

- Finding all students who are active and in a specific state

- Finding all customers who ordered online and ordered more than a specific amount

Each of these kinds of queries is looking at two or more criteria. You'll learn how to do that with your example data.

99

© Ben Brumm 2019
B. Brumm, *Beginning Oracle SQL for Oracle Database 18c*,
https://doi.org/10.1007/978-1-4842-4430-2_7

The AND Keyword

SQL allows you to use more than one criteria in your WHERE clause to restrict the data to just the records you want to see. There are two ways of doing this. The first way is using the AND keyword.

The AND keyword lets you specify two conditions in your WHERE clause. If a record meets both of the conditions, it is displayed. If a record meets zero or one of the conditions, then it is not displayed. The AND keyword is useful if you want to check for more than one criteria in your query and both of the criteria need to match for a row.

Using the AND keyword looks like this:

```
WHERE condition
AND condition
```

This can be broken down:

- It starts with the WHERE keyword to denote the beginning of the WHERE clause.

- condition: the condition that must be met for a row to be displayed (e.g., last_name = 'SMITH')

- AND: denotes that a second condition must also be met for a row.

- condition: as before, a condition that must be met for a row to be displayed

Let's see some examples of multiple conditions using the AND keyword.

Finding Records That Match a Last Name and a Salary

Let's say you wanted to find records where a last_name contained the letter "S" and the salary was greater than 32000. Your query would look like this:

```
SELECT id, last_name, salary
FROM employee
WHERE last_name LIKE '%S%'
AND salary > 32000;
```

In this query, the AND is written on a new line to make it easier to read. The query will still run if you put the AND on the same line as WHERE (and you might prefer to write it that way). The results of this query would be:

```
ID    LAST_NAME    SALARY
2     SMITH        35000
4     SIMPSON      52000
```

This query shows records for 'SMITH' and 'SIMPSON', as they both have a salary greater than 32000 and an "S" in their last_name. The records for 'JONES' and 'ANDERSON' both have an "S" in their last_name, but their salary is less than 32000. The record for 'KING' has a salary greater than 32000 but does not have an "S" in the last_name. So, only 'SMITH' and 'SIMPSON' are shown.

Finding Records that Match Greater Than and Less Than on Two Columns

Another example of using the AND keyword is using other symbols other than equals to and LIKE. Let's say you wanted to find the records where the ID is greater than or equal to 3 and the salary is less than 40000. Your query would look like this:

```
SELECT id, last_name, salary
FROM employee
WHERE id >= 3
AND salary < 40000;
```

The results would look like this:

```
ID    LAST_NAME    SALARY
5     ANDERSON     31000
```

This is the only record shown, because even though KING and SIMPSON have an ID greater than or equal to 3, their salary is not less than 40000.

The OR Keyword

The second way of using multiple filters on a query is to use the OR keyword. The OR keyword is used in the same way as the AND keyword. However, the difference is that OR means that at least one of the two criteria needs to be met, but it doesn't need to be both like the AND keyword.

Using the OR keyword looks like this:

```
WHERE condition
OR condition
```

The OR keyword works in the same way as the AND keyword. It's used in the WHERE clause and you can use it to specify a second condition to check for. If either one (or both) of the two conditions is true for a row, then it is included in the results. The OR keyword is useful for checking multiple conditions and seeing results where at least one of those conditions is true.

Finding Records that Match a Last Name or a Salary

Let's look at the earlier examples rewritten using OR instead of AND. You want to find records where a last_name contained the letter "S," or the salary was greater than 32000. Your query would look like this:

```
SELECT id, last_name, salary
FROM employee
WHERE last_name LIKE '%S%'
OR salary > 32000;
```

Your results would look like this:

ID	LAST_NAME	SALARY
1	JONES	20000
2	SMITH	35000
3	KING	40000
4	SIMPSON	52000
5	ANDERSON	31000

The results show every record in the table. The records with the last_name of 'JONES', 'SMITH', 'SIMPSON', and 'ANDERSON' are shown, as they all have an "S" in their last_name. The record of 'KING' is shown because they have a salary greater than 32000. Some records only meet one of the two criteria (having an "S" in their last_name or salary greater than 32000), but that's OK; they're still included in the results.

Finding Records that Match Greater Than or Less Than on Two Columns

Let's see another example using OR. You may want to see all records where the ID is greater than or equal to 4, or the salary is less than 40000.

```
SELECT id, last_name, salary
FROM employee
WHERE id >= 4
OR salary < 40000;
```

The results would look like this:

ID	LAST_NAME	SALARY
1	JONES	20000
2	SMITH	35000
4	SIMPSON	52000
5	ANDERSON	31000

We can explain the treatment of each of the records in our table:

- JONES: This is shown because the salary is less than 40000.

- SMITH: This is also shown because the salary is less than 40000.

- KING: This is not shown, as the salary is not less than 40000 and the ID is not greater than or equal to 4.

- SIMPSON: This is shown because the ID is greater than or equal to 4.

- ANDERSON: This is shown because the ID is greater than or equal to 4 and the salary is less than 40000.

More Than Two Conditions

You've seen a few examples of AND and OR with two conditions. What if you wanted to use more than two conditions? What about three conditions, or four conditions? You can do this in SQL using AND and OR. You simply add another AND or OR to the end of the WHERE clause:

```
WHERE condition
[{AND|OR} condition]
[{AND|OR} condition]
```

You'll see syntax like this when you're reading SQL documentation or other code samples online. The square brackets "[" and "]" mean that the part inside is optional. The curly brackets "{" and "}" mean that the part inside is mandatory. Finally, the vertical pipe "|" means that one of the options must be shown.

So, this syntax means that you need to have a WHERE condition, then you could have an AND/OR condition. If you do have an AND/OR condition, you need to write either "AND condition" or "OR condition."

You can add many more AND or OR conditions to your query. You can also use different combinations of AND and OR in your query.

Multiple AND Conditions

Let's see some examples. You may want to see all employees where the last_name contains "S" and the salary is greater than 30000 and less than 40000. Your query would look like this:

```
SELECT id, last_name, salary
FROM employee
WHERE last_name LIKE '%S%'
AND salary > 30000
AND salary < 40000;
```

Your results would look like this:

ID	LAST_NAME	SALARY
2	SMITH	35000
5	ANDERSON	31000

This shows both 'SMITH' and 'ANDERSON' because they meet all three criteria in the query:

- The last_name contains "S."

- The salary is greater than 30000.

- The salary is less than 40000.

Multiple OR Conditions

Let's look at an example using multiple OR keywords. Let's say you want to see all employee records where the salary is less than 25000, or the salary is greater than 50000, or the last_name contains a "G." This is what your query would look like:

```
SELECT id, last_name, salary
FROM employee
WHERE salary < 25000
OR salary > 50000
OR last_name LIKE '%G%';
```

The results of this query would be:

ID	LAST_NAME	SALARY
1	JONES	20000
3	KING	40000
4	SIMPSON	52000

The record for 'JONES' is shown because the salary is less than 25000. The record for 'KING' is shown because the last_name contains a G, and 'SIMPSON' is shown because the salary is greater than 50000. Only one of the conditions needs to be true for the row to be shown.

Combining Multiple AND and OR Conditions

What if you wanted to mix these keywords, by putting both AND/OR into the one query? You can do that. Let's say you had this query:

```
SELECT id, last_name, salary
FROM employee
```

```
WHERE last_name LIKE '%S%'
AND salary > 30000
OR salary < 40000;
```

You have `condition1 AND condition2 OR condition3`. What would these results look like? It would look like this:

```
ID    LAST_NAME   SALARY
1     JONES       20000
2     SMITH       35000
4     SIMPSON     52000
5     ANDERSON    31000
```

How did you get to this result? The `AND` and `OR` keywords are run in a certain order. This is called the *order of operations*. This concept applies to several areas in SQL, and you might remember it from mathematics class in school, where some operations had priority over others.

`AND` and `OR` both have the same priority. They are both used in sequence. So, for this query, the logic says to show records that:

- Have a `last_name` containing S and a `salary` greater than 30000

- Or, have a `salary` less than 40000

These are two separate conditions now. The records for `'SMITH'`, `'SIMPSON'`, and `'ANDERSON'` are shown because they meet the first criteria of having a `last_name` with S and a `salary` greater than 30000. `'JONES'` is shown because they have a `salary` less than 40000. `'KING'` is not shown.

Specifying the Order with Multiple Conditions

What if you want to check your conditions in a specific order? You can do this using brackets: "(" and ")". Adding brackets to your query will force the query to be run in a certain way. The operations inside the brackets are run first, and then they are combined with the operations outside of the brackets. Let's look at this example:

```
SELECT id, last_name, salary
FROM employee
WHERE last_name LIKE '%N%'
```

```
AND salary > 50000
OR last_name LIKE '%T%';
```

This will show records that:

- Have a last_name containing "N" and a salary of greater than 50000

- Or, have a last_name containing "T."

This shows the following results:

```
ID   LAST_NAME   SALARY
2    SMITH       35000
4    SIMPSON     52000
```

If you wanted to show a different set of records, you would write your query like this:

```
SELECT id, last_name, salary
FROM employee
WHERE last_name LIKE '%N%'
AND (salary > 50000
OR last_name LIKE '%T%');
```

Notice that the brackets are around two conditions and the OR keyword. This means those conditions are run first, and then combined with the first condition. This will show records that:

- Have a salary of greater than 50000 or a last_name containing "T"

- And have a last_name containing "N."

The results from this query would be:

```
ID   LAST_NAME   SALARY
4    SIMPSON     52000
```

Each of these records meets the criteria. Without the brackets inside the WHERE clause, the results are different. The reason that the record for 'SMITH' is shown in the first result but not the second is because the first query shows all records where the last_name contains "T" but the second query only shows records where the last_name contains "T" and have a salary of greater than 50000.

Summary

You can use multiple filters in your SQL queries by using a combination of AND and OR keywords. The AND keyword will check that a record meets all of the conditions specified, and the OR keyword will check that a record meets at least one of the conditions specified. Many AND and OR keywords can be added into a query, and they are run in the order they are written. If you want to ensure they are run in a specific order, you can enclose the conditions and keywords in brackets.

CHAPTER 8

Working with Nulls

In this chapter, you'll learn all about a concept in SQL and databases called "null." In the sample table you've been using, every record has a value for every column. However, when working with real databases, this is not always the case. The concept of "null" is used when data is not known.

Missing Data

In a real database, there could be a situation where data is missing. This could be deliberately (we don't know what the value is), or some kind of bug (there should be a value but there isn't). Tables in a database don't require you to store a value in every row and column.

We've been working with a sample table called employee in this book so far. The table looks like this:

```
ID    LAST_NAME    SALARY
1     JONES        20000
2     SMITH        35000
3     KING         40000
4     SIMPSON      52000
5     ANDERSON     31000
```

The table has five rows, and three columns. Every column for every row has a value. However, this is not always the case. It's possibly for values to be missing. What if there was an employee where the salary was not known? Or we had other columns in the table, such as a date of birth, which were not known for some employees?

© Ben Brumm 2019
B. Brumm, *Beginning Oracle SQL for Oracle Database 18c*,
https://doi.org/10.1007/978-1-4842-4430-2_8

This is a valid scenario when working with databases. The question is: how do we store it? Let's say you have a new employee, but you don't currently know what their salary is. It could be represented like this:

ID	LAST_NAME	SALARY
1	JONES	20000
2	SMITH	35000
3	KING	40000
4	SIMPSON	52000
5	ANDERSON	31000
6	COOPER	Unknown

In this example, we've used a text value of "Unknown," to specify that we don't know what the salary value is for the new employee. This isn't a good idea though.

First, the salary column is a number column, which means it only stores numbers and not text values. Using a text value of "Unknown" in this number column will cause an error when trying to add it.

You shouldn't change the type of the salary column to a text value to allow for this "Unknown" value to appear. Well, you could, but then you could do that for every field in the database and it will mean the data types aren't useful at all.

What if you use a value of "n/a"? This also doesn't work, for the same reason. Adding a text value into a number column is not possible. Also, what's to say that the value of "n/a" isn't a legitimate value in this field or other fields? It might not be valid for salary, but what if there was a column called commission which stored an employee's commission amount? The value of "n/a" might mean that commission does not apply to this particular employee.

What if you use 0? You could use 0, but a value of 0 indicates "the salary is zero." You want to capture the fact that the salary is unknown, and unknown is different to 0. If you use 0, you would have to adjust all of our queries that look at the salary column to ignore those with a salary of 0, as it would skew any totals or averages.

What if you use a blank space character " "? That's an option, but it faces the same issues as "Unknown" and "n/a" because it's a text value that is trying to be added to a number field.

How about using an empty string, which means there is nothing inside the quotes: ''? You could try this, but an empty string is treated differently in SQL. It's still a text value, which means it will have issues trying to be used in a number or a date field.

So, you can't use text values like "n/a", or 0, or " ", or empty strings. What can you use? You can use a value of NULL.

What is NULL?

The word NULL is a keyword that means "an unknown value." It's used to represent unknown or missing values in a database table. This keyword is provided because an unknown value is different to an empty string, a blank space, a zero, or another text value that may have a meaning such as "n/a" or "FALSE."

The value of NULL is used quite often in databases, as there is no guarantee that all fields will always have data. What are the advantages of using NULL values in your database (as opposed to zeroes or empty strings)?

- NULL works on any column type: text, number, date. You don't need to change the type of column for it to work.

- NULL has its own set of keywords for performing logic, as it's a special value.

- There are a range of functions that work with NULL.

- It uses no storage, which might not be an issue with small tables but can help with larger tables.

How Should NULL Be Treated?

NULL values require their own treatment, which is probably their only disadvantage. Throughout this book, you'll learn how to work with NULL values, but you'll look at some examples and treatment of NULL values related to what you've learned so far.

You just learned how to check if column values match other values, using symbols such as equals and greater than. This works for text, number, and date values. However, it won't work for NULL values. A value can't be "equal to" NULL, because NULL is an unknown value. To check if a value is NULL, we use the keywords IS NULL. Your WHERE clause would look like this:

```
WHERE salary IS NULL;
```

If you write it using the equals sign, it won't find anything:

```
WHERE salary = NULL;
```

Let's take a look at some examples to explain this.

Examples of Working with NULL

You'll see some examples of working with NULL values in a database. First, you'll need to add some NULL values to your table so you can write SELECT queries that work with them.

Adding More Data

Your table currently looks like this:

ID	LAST_NAME	SALARY
1	JONES	20000
2	SMITH	35000
3	KING	40000
4	SIMPSON	52000
5	ANDERSON	31000

You should add a new row into the table which has a NULL value for the salary column, and another row that has a NULL value for both last_name and salary columns.

ID	LAST_NAME	SALARY
1	JONES	20000
2	SMITH	35000
3	KING	40000
4	SIMPSON	52000
5	ANDERSON	31000
6	COOPER	NULL
7	NULL	NULL

Let's add this to our table.

1. Open SQL Developer and connect to the database, using the steps shown in the previous chapters, if you haven't done so already.

2. Click on the arrow next to the connection name, then click on the arrow next to "Tables (Filtered)" to expand it, and click on EMPLOYEE, as shown in Figure 8-1.

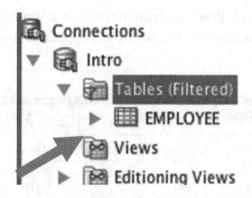

Figure 8-1. *The Connections list including the table name*

3. Click on the Data tab on the window that appears on the main section of the screen, as shown in Figure 8-2.

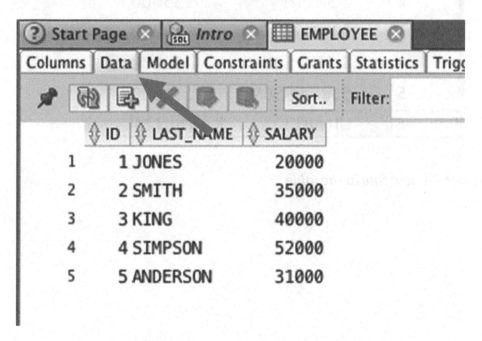

Figure 8-2. *The Employee table data*

4. Click on the Insert Row button on the toolbar. It should be the
   third button from the left. A new row will appear, as shown in
   Figure 8-3.

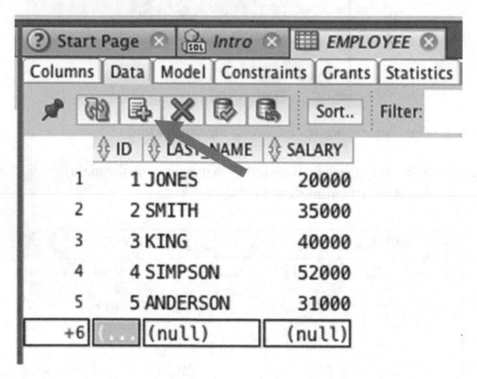

Figure 8-3. *A new row in the table*

5. In the new row, enter an ID of 6 and a last_name of
    COOPER. Leave the salary value as (null), as shown in Figure 8-4.

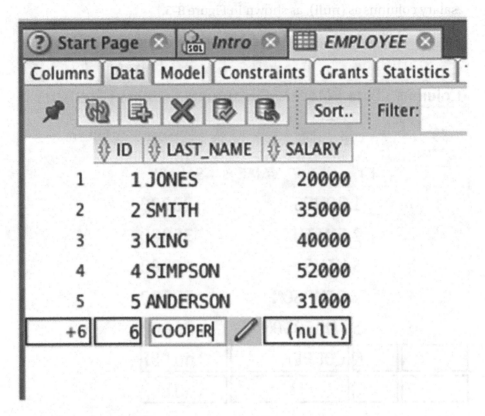

Figure 8-4. *Entering the data*

6. Click on the Insert Row button again, to insert a new row.

7. Enter an ID of 7 for the new row, and leave the last_name and salary columns as (null), as shown in Figure 8-5.

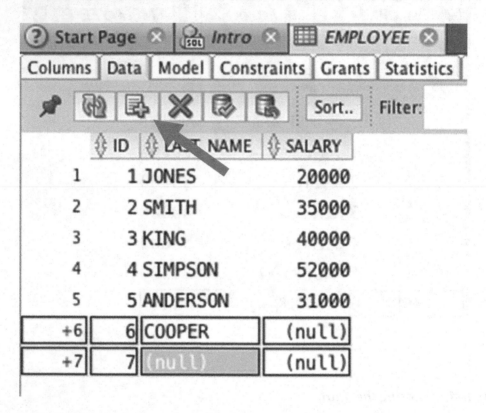

Figure 8-5. *Two new rows in the table*

8. Click the Commit Changes button to save this data to the database. The Commit Changes button is the grey shape with the green tick, to the right of the red cross, as shown in Figure 8-6.

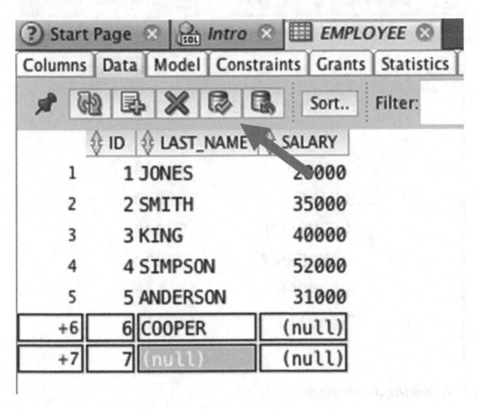

Figure 8-6. The Commit Changes button

Your screen should look like Figure 8-7.

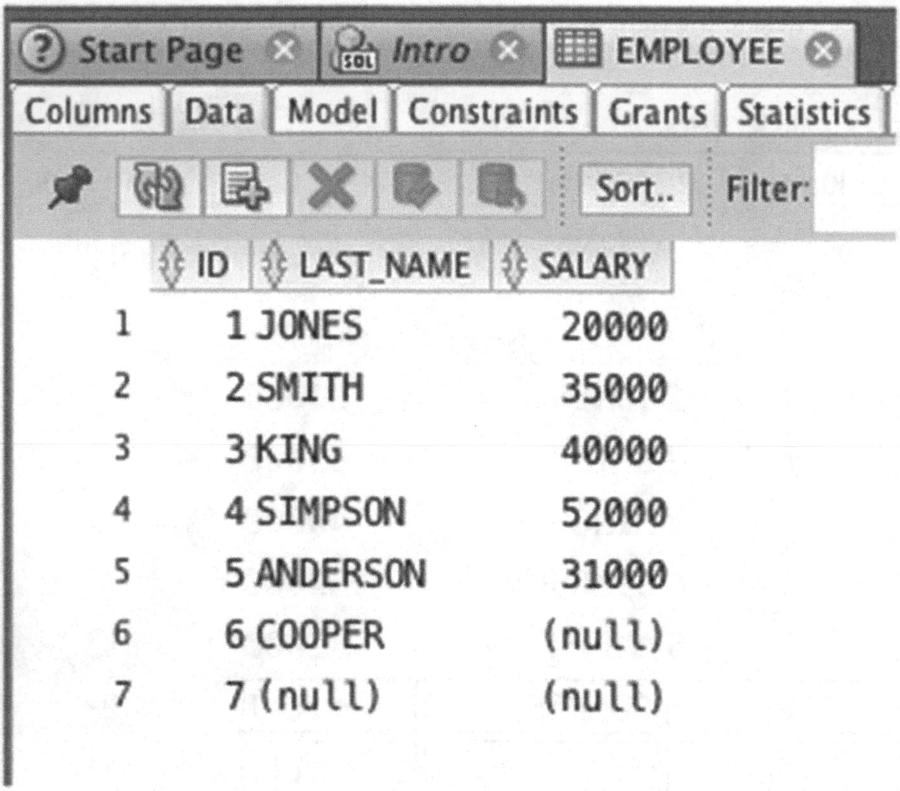

Figure 8-7. *Saving the changes*

Selecting the Records

You can check that the new data is in the table by running a SELECT statement, just like you have done in earlier chapters. To do this:

1. Open a new SQL file or use an existing file you have open.

    In the earlier chapters we looked at how to do this, and we'll go through that again now. If you have a window open already, you can skip the next few steps.

2. To open a new SQL file, click on the New Worksheet button.

3. Select a Connection, as shown in Figure 8-8.

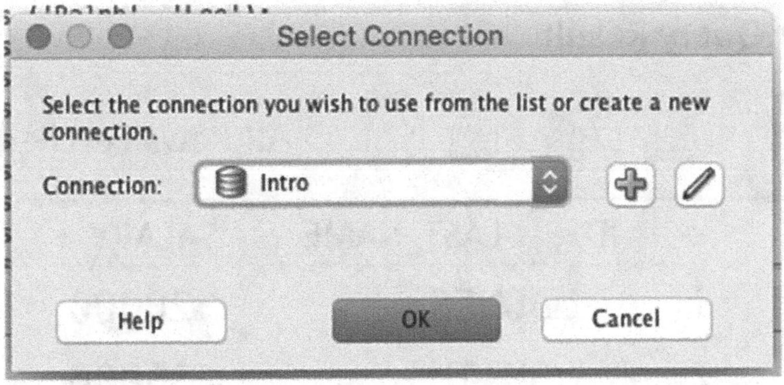

Figure 8-8. *The Select Connection window*

A new SQL worksheet is shown.

4. Run the following query:

```
SELECT id, last_name, salary
FROM employee;
```

The results should look like Figure 8-9.

119

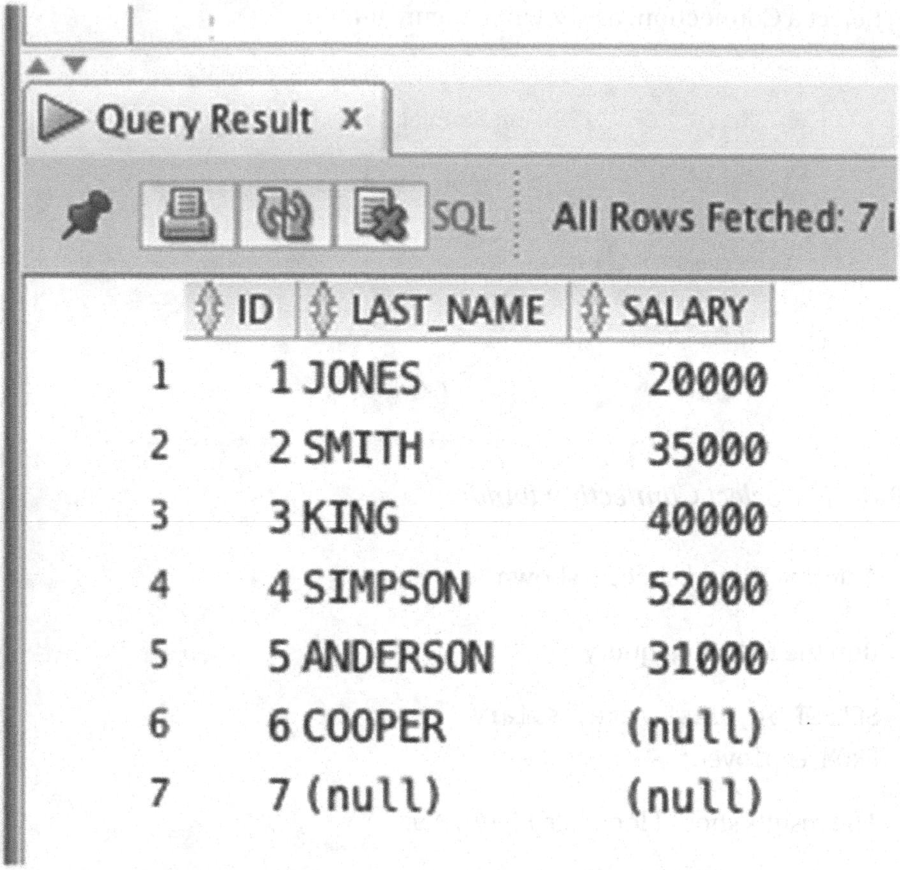

Figure 8-9. *The SELECT query on the employee table*

As you can see, the NULL values are displayed in this table. In SQL Developer, they are displayed as (null) so we can see that they are NULL values. However, if the results of this query are used in an application, they will be NULL and need to be treated accordingly.

Restricting the NULL Values

You can see the NULL values in the table. What if you wanted to exclude them from our results? Earlier I mentioned that you can't use the "equals to" sign. Let's see what happens when you do this. You can run this query:

```
SELECT id, last_name, salary
FROM employee
WHERE salary = NULL;

No results found.
```

120

SQL Developer would display no results, as shown in Figure 8-10.

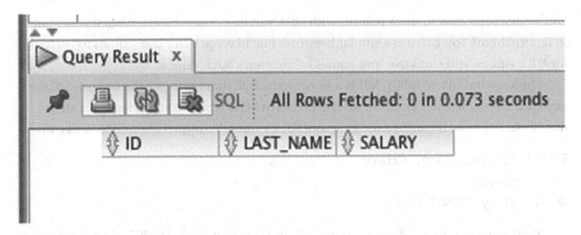

Figure 8-10. *No results found*

You need to use the IS NULL keyword. To do this, you can adjust your query so it looks like this:

```
SELECT id, last_name, salary
FROM employee
WHERE salary IS NULL;
```

Your results will look like this:

```
ID    LAST_NAME    SALARY
6     COOPER       NULL
7     NULL         NULL
```

It only shows the rows that have a NULL salary value. You can try the same thing for the last_name column:

```
SELECT id, last_name, salary
FROM employee
WHERE last_name IS NULL;
```

The results are:

```
ID    LAST_NAME    SALARY
7     NULL         NULL
```

This will only show records where the last_name column is NULL.

Hiding Null Values

You've just seen how to show records with NULL values in your results. What if you want to ignore them? You can use a similar keyword. Just like you can't use "equals to" to look for NULL values, you can't use "not equals to" to ignore NULL values.

The keyword to use is NOT. NOT is a keyword in SQL that performs the opposite of the keyword it is used on. It's used in several places in SQL, which you will learn about in this book. For now, it can be used to ignore NULL values. Your query would look like this:

```
SELECT id, last_name, salary
FROM employee
WHERE salary IS NOT NULL;
```

Notice that you have added the word NOT after IS, so it reads IS NOT NULL. This means that all records where the salary is not NULL will be shown. Your results are:

ID	LAST_NAME	SALARY
1	JONES	20000
2	SMITH	35000
3	KING	40000
4	SIMPSON	52000
5	ANDERSON	31000

These results do not include those records where the salary is NULL. You can do the same thing for the last_name column:

```
SELECT id, last_name, salary
FROM employee
WHERE last_name IS NOT NULL;
```

The results would be:

ID	LAST_NAME	SALARY
1	JONES	20000
2	SMITH	35000
3	KING	40000
4	SIMPSON	52000
5	ANDERSON	31000
6	COOPER	NULL

You can see that ID 7 is not shown because the last_name is NULL. The record with ID 6 is shown, because the last_name is populated. The salary is NULL, but your query did not mention the salary.

You can exclude records where either of these two columns are NULL by using the AND keyword.

```
SELECT id, last_name, salary
FROM employee
WHERE last_name IS NOT NULL
AND salary IS NOT NULL;
```

The results of this query are:

ID	LAST_NAME	SALARY
1	JONES	20000
2	SMITH	35000
3	KING	40000
4	SIMPSON	52000
5	ANDERSON	31000

You can see that the two records with NULL values are not shown.

Multiple Queries in One SQL Window

In this chapter, and earlier chapters, you ran several SQL queries on the same data. You may have run your queries by deleting all of the SQL code that you already had in the window and entering the new code.

However, SQL Developer (and many other programs) make it easier to write many queries and run just the query you want. This is also where the semicolon character ";" comes in, which we mentioned earlier in the book.

You can write many different SQL statements in an SQL window. If they are separated by semicolon characters, they are treated as separate queries, and can be run separately.

For example, your window may look like Figure 8-11.

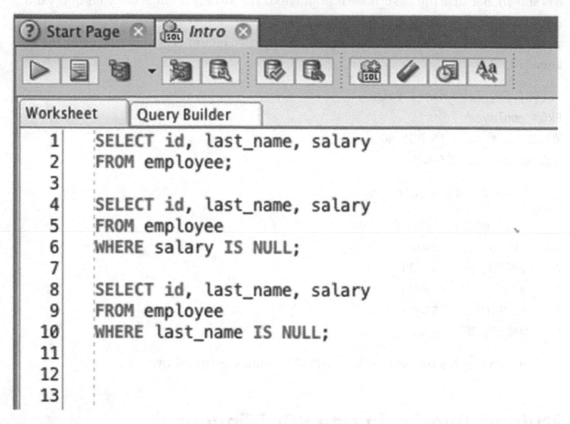

Figure 8-11. *Multiple queries in the one window*

This includes three SQL queries. They are separated by a blank line to make it easier to read. More importantly, they each end with a semicolon to indicate where the statement ends.

You can run an individual query in SQL Developer by clicking anywhere inside the query, before the semicolon, and clicking the green Run Statement button. This will run only the query that the cursor is in, as shown in Figure 8-12.

```
    Start Page  ⊗   🔲 Intro  ⊗

    ▷  🔲  🐚  ▾  🐉  🔩    🔩  🔩    🔩  ✎

    Worksheet      Query Builder
     1    SELECT id, last_name, salary
     2    FROM employee;
     3
     4    SELECT id, last_name, salary
     5    FROM employee
     6    WHERE salary IS NULL;
     7
     8    SELECT id, last_name, salary
     9    FROM employee
    10    WHERE last_name IS NULL;
    11
```

Figure 8-12. *Running a single query*

You can click inside any other query and run that query as well. This means you can write as many queries as you want in the one file and run only the query that you want. It's very helpful for the exercises in this book, as you can write one set of code after the other and go back and run any previous queries.

Summary

Missing values in SQL are captured as NULL values, which represent unknown values. This is different to an empty string or a zero. SQL queries can use the keyword IS NULL to check if a value is NULL. They can also use IS NOT NULL to look for values that aren't NULL.

CHAPTER 9

Removing Duplicate Results

When you store data in a table, as you have learned so far, you can just enter the values and save it. The data is then saved into the table. As long as the values you enter match the type of column, then it should work. This means you can't enter a text value into a number column, for example.

Your sample data looks like this so far:

```
ID   LAST_NAME    SALARY
1    JONES        20000
2    SMITH        35000
3    KING         40000
4    SIMPSON      52000
5    ANDERSON     31000
6    COOPER       NULL
7    NULL         NULL
```

Looking at this table, you may assume a few things:

- The ID number is sequential, starting at 1 and going up.
- The last_name values are all in upper case.
- The salary has some kind of minimum and maximum value.
- All of the last_name values are different.

You haven't defined anything on this table to make any of those statements facts. They're just assumptions at this stage. This means that each of these could be false. ID numbers may not be sequential. The last_name values may not be in upper case.

© Ben Brumm 2019
B. Brumm, *Beginning Oracle SQL for Oracle Database 18c*,
https://doi.org/10.1007/978-1-4842-4430-2_9

The salary may not have a minimum and maximum range. All of the last_name values might not be different.

Add New Records

For this example, let's add some new values to the table. You can follow the same steps that you did earlier in this book.

1.   Open SQL Developer and expand the Connection on the left side of the window.

2.   Expand "Tables (Filtered)" and click the EMPLOYEE table.

3.   In the SQL Window that appears, click the Data tab, as shown in Figure 9-1.

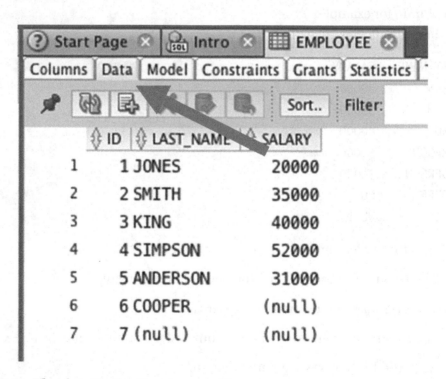

Figure 9-1. *The data in the Employee table*

4. Click the Add Row button

5. Enter a new row into the table with an ID of 8, last_name of
    SMITH, and a salary of 62000.

6. Click the Add Row button again and enter a new row into the table
    with an ID of 9, last_name of PATRICK, and a salary of 40000.
    Your screen should look like Figure 9-2.

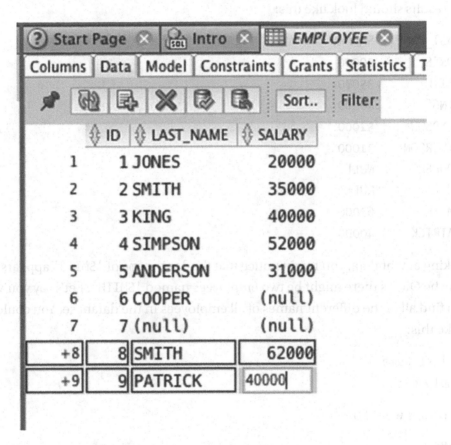

Figure 9-2. *New data in the Employee table*

7. Click Commit.

You have now added new data into the employee table. These new records will be
used to demonstrate how Oracle handles duplicate data.

Select the Data

Now the data is in the table, let's see what it looks like. Open a new or existing SQL window and run the following query, which shows all columns and rows from the table:

```
SELECT id, last_name, salary
FROM employee;
```

The results should look like this:

ID	LAST_NAME	SALARY
1	JONES	20000
2	SMITH	35000
3	KING	40000
4	SIMPSON	52000
5	ANDERSON	31000
6	COOPER	NULL
7	NULL	NULL
8	SMITH	62000
9	PATRICK	40000

Looking at that data, you might notice that the last_name of 'SMITH' appears twice. This may be OK, as there might be two employees named 'SMITH'. Let's say you've been asked to find all of the different names of all employees in the database. You could run a query like this:

```
SELECT last_name
FROM employee;
```

The results would be:

```
LAST_NAME
JONES
SMITH
KING
SIMPSON
ANDERSON
COOPER
```

```
(null)
SMITH
PATRICK
```

Once you show this to your manager or your team, they might ask, "Why does SMITH appear twice? I only need to see each name once." You might be wondering how to do this. Do you delete the record? Do you ignore record 8, which is the second 'SMITH' value? You can't delete the data, as it might be valid. You could try to ignore record 8 though:

```
SELECT last_name
FROM employee
WHERE id <> 8;
```

```
LAST_NAME
JONES
SMITH
KING
SIMPSON
ANDERSON
COOPER
(null)
SMITH
PATRICK
```

With the query you just ran, you knew what ID was duplicated and how to remove it. What if there are many records that have this issue, or hundreds, or thousands of records? You can't possibly know the ID values for all of them. There is a better way you can do this.

What is DISTINCT?

There is a keyword in SQL called *DISTINCT*, which allows you to remove duplicate rows from your results. The DISTINCT keyword doesn't delete data from the database. It just identifies any records that are the same when you run a SELECT query and removes any duplicate rows from your results. The DISTINCT keyword goes after the SELECT keyword:

```
SELECT DISTINCT columns
FROM table...
```

This DISTINCT keyword will apply to the entire query. You can't specify DISTINCT for each column, because it removes duplicate records from the result, not duplicate values from each column. This is an important distinction, and you'll see some examples of this soon.

Note   The DISTINCT keyword removes duplicate rows from your results, not duplicate values from each column.

Finding Unique Last Name Values

You can use the earlier example of finding all unique last_name values without using the ID in the WHERE clause. Your query would look like this:

```
SELECT DISTINCT last_name
FROM employee;
```

The results will look like this:

```
LAST_NAME
JONES
SMITH
KING
SIMPSON
ANDERSON
COOPER
(null)
SMITH
PATRICK
```

You can see that the duplicate record (the second last_name of SMITH) is not showing. This is what the DISTINCT keyword does.

Finding Unique Salary Values

Let's try another example. Let's say you had to find all of the unique salary values in the table. This will show that the DISTINCT keyword can work on number values and not just text values. Your query could start looking like this:

```
SELECT salary
FROM employee;
```

The results of this query are:

```
SALARY
20000
35000
40000
52000
31000
(null)
(null)
62000
40000
```

This shows you two things. First, there are two NULL values in this column. Second, the salary of 40000 is repeated, as two employees have the same salary. You can resolve this with DISTINCT.

```
SELECT DISTINCT salary
FROM employee;
```

The results of this query are:

```
SALARY
20000
35000
40000
52000
31000
(null)
62000
```

Using DISTINCT has eliminated one of the NULL values and one of the 40000 values. What if you did not want to include NULL values? You can combine the DISTINCT keyword with a WHERE clause that you learned in a previous chapter.

```
SELECT DISTINCT salary
FROM employee
WHERE salary IS NOT NULL;
```

Your results would look like this:

```
SALARY
20000
35000
40000
52000
31000
62000
```

This shows all unique salary values, excluding NULL values.

Finding Unique Combinations of Values

Let's have a look at another example. Let's say you've been asked to find all unique last_name and salary values in this table. Your query would look like this:

```
SELECT DISTINCT last_name, salary
FROM employee;
```

Notice that the DISTINCT keyword only appears once. You have defined it for our query, and don't need to define it for each column. If you run the query, the results look like this:

LAST_NAME	SALARY
JONES	20000
SMITH	35000
KING	40000
SIMPSON	52000
ANDERSON	31000
COOPER	(null)

134

```
(null)      (null)
SMITH       62000
PATRICK     40000
```

You might be wondering why 'SMITH' appears twice. And why does the salary of 40000 appear twice? This is because they might be duplicate values, but they are not duplicate rows. The row of 'SMITH' with a salary of 35000 is a different row to 'SMITH' with a salary of 62000, so the row stays in the results.

The same can be said for the row of 'KING' with a salary of 40000 and the row of 'PATRICK' with the salary of 40000. Even though the salary is the same, the last_name is different, so the row is different.

DISTINCT is not designed to remove duplicate values from different columns in different rows. If it did this, then the data in each row would be mixed up and wouldn't be correct. If you need to find unique results in your query by eliminating duplicates, then DISTINCT is the way to do that.

How can you tell that the two 'SMITH' employees are different? You can look at the ID column. Alternatively, you can add a new column that defines more information about them, which you will learn about in a later chapter.

Summary

SQL does not eliminate duplicate records from your result automatically. You can do this in your queries by adding the keyword DISTINCT after the SELECT keyword. It removes duplicate records, and not duplicate columns, which are quite different concepts.

CHAPTER 10

Applying Filters on Lists and Ranges of Values

In previous chapters, you learned about the WHERE clause and how you could use it to restrict the results you see. You can do this using a variety of symbols, called *operators*, such as "equal to" and "less than." You can also specify multiple criteria using the AND/OR keywords.

Working with lists of values presents an interesting challenge in that a large list can result in a large number of AND and OR keywords in a query. This chapter introduces some syntax that's helpful when working with large lists. You'll also learn about some syntax for ranges too.

Too Many Conjunctions

Writing a query with a long list of equality conditions in the WHERE clause can become tedious. Let's work through an example that will help set the stage for the syntax you'll learn about next.

First, our sample data looks like this so far:

ID	LAST_NAME	SALARY
1	JONES	20000
2	SMITH	35000
3	KING	40000
4	SIMPSON	52000
5	ANDERSON	31000
6	COOPER	(null)
7	(null)	(null)
8	SMITH	62000
9	PATRICK	40000

137

© Ben Brumm 2019
B. Brumm, *Beginning Oracle SQL for Oracle Database 18c*,
https://doi.org/10.1007/978-1-4842-4430-2_10

If you wanted to find all records where the salary was equal to a 5,000 or 10,000 increment, you could have a query like this:

```
SELECT id, last_name, salary
FROM employee
WHERE salary = 20000
OR salary = 35000
OR salary = 40000;
```

If you run the query, this is the result you get:

ID	LAST_NAME	SALARY
1	JONES	20000
2	SMITH	35000
3	KING	40000
9	PATRICK	40000

We are ignoring records with a salary of 52000, 31000, and other values. You get the results you want, but our WHERE clause includes three checks on the same column:

```
WHERE salary = 20000
OR salary = 35000
OR salary = 40000;
```

What if you had more values in our table and wanted to check five or ten different values? You could use a few more OR keywords but it would make our query look a little messy:

```
WHERE salary = 20000
OR salary = 35000
OR salary = 40000
OR salary = 45000
OR salary = 50000
OR salary = 55000
OR salary = 60000
OR salary = 65000;
```

There is a way to improve this repetition of so many OR keywords: use the IN keyword.

The IN Keyword

The IN keyword allows you to specify multiple values in a single comparison. This keyword works in the same way as using multiple OR keywords. The IN clause looks like this:

```
WHERE column IN (value1, value2... value_n)
```

The IN keyword is used instead of an "equal to" operator. You then specify an open bracket "(" and include all of the values inside the brackets that you want to check for, each of which are separated by a comma. Finally, you close the brackets.

Example of Using IN

You can specify a long list of values inside the IN keyword here (up to 1,000 in fact). That ability to specify a list is great for the example you were looking at. Instead of having a query like this:

```
SELECT id, last_name, salary
FROM employee
WHERE salary = 20000
OR salary = 35000
OR salary = 40000;
```

You can have a query like this:

```
SELECT id, last_name, salary
FROM employee
WHERE salary IN (20000, 35000, 40000);
```

This second version looks neater and is easier to read, as all of the criteria for the salary are together. The results of this query are:

ID	LAST_NAME	SALARY
1	JONES	20000
2	SMITH	35000
3	KING	40000
9	PATRICK	40000

These results are the same as from the query with the separate OR statements.

A Longer Value List

Your example earlier included three values inside the IN clause. What if you wanted to include more? Using several OR statements, your query could look like this:

```
SELECT id, last_name, salary
FROM employee
WHERE salary = 10000
OR salary = 20000
OR salary = 30000
OR salary = 40000
OR salary = 50000
OR salary = 60000
OR salary = 70000
OR salary = 80000
OR salary = 90000
OR salary = 100000;
```

This query checks for salary values at 10,000 increments. There are separate OR keywords for each value. This query shows the following results:

```
ID    LAST_NAME    SALARY
1     JONES        20000
3     KING         40000
9     PATRICK      40000
```

The query result shows only three records, as there are only three salary values that match values from the list provided. Even though there were ten values in the list, rows do not exist for many of those, so only three rows are returned.

You can rewrite the query using the IN clause:

```
SELECT id, last_name, salary
FROM employee
WHERE salary IN (
    10000, 20000, 30000, 40000, 50000,
    60000, 70000, 80000, 90000, 100000);
```

Once again, the IN clause looks a lot neater than separate OR keywords and is easier to read. The results of this query are also the same:

```
ID   LAST_NAME   SALARY
1    JONES       20000
3    KING        40000
9    PATRICK     40000
```

Using IN with Text Values

The IN keyword can also be used with text values. Let's say you had a list of names you wanted to filter on. Your query with OR keywords could look like this:

```
SELECT id, last_name, salary
FROM employee
WHERE last_name = 'SIMPSON'
OR last_name = 'COOPER'
OR last_name = 'ANDERSON';
```

This query can be written using an IN keyword:

```
SELECT id, last_name, salary
FROM employee
WHERE last_name IN ('SIMPSON', 'COOPER', 'ANDERSON');
```

Each of the text values need to be enclosed in single quotes, just like you've seen in other WHERE clauses. The text values are also all inside the brackets, separated by commas, just like the query with salary values.

The results for this query are:

```
ID   LAST_NAME   SALARY
4    SIMPSON     52000
5    ANDERSON    31000
6    COOPER      NULL
```

You can see that the results show the records with the last_name values you specified. This type of query works no matter how many values you specify inside the IN keyword, and the query is a lot easier to type and read than separate OR statements

Using IN with Other Clauses

You've seen some queries that had one WHERE clause that looked for a few different values in a column. You can combine that approach with other criteria as well, such as another AND or OR clause.

Let's say you want to find all employees that have a salary of 20000, 25000, 30000, 35000, or 40000, and also had a last_name of SMITH. Your query could look like this:

```
SELECT id, last_name, salary
FROM employee
WHERE salary IN (20000, 25000, 30000, 35000, 40000)
AND last_name = 'SMITH';
```

This query uses the IN keyword to look for salary values, and it uses an equality comparison to check for the last_name value. This technique of combining the IN keyword with other clauses is perfectly valid SQL. When you run this query, the results should be:

```
ID    LAST_NAME    SALARY
2     SMITH        35000
```

These results show a single record, as there is only one record in the table that matches the specified salary values and has the given last_name value.

IN with AND?

You've learned that specifying values in an IN clause is the same as writing out several OR clauses. Why is an IN clause not like several AND clauses? What happens when you have several AND clauses?

Here is the earlier query that uses OR:

```
SELECT id, last_name, salary
FROM employee
WHERE salary = 20000
OR salary = 35000
OR salary = 40000;
```

Now, think about replacing all the OR keywords with AND, because a common mistake is to think in terms of "I'm interested in salary values of 20000, 35000, and 40000." It's easy to make the mistake of seizing upon the "and" from the thought as written in English, and to translate that conjunction into the keyword AND in a query. For example:

```
SELECT id, last_name, salary
FROM employee
WHERE salary = 20000
AND salary = 35000
AND salary = 40000;
```

However, this query won't give you what you need. It's essentially saying, "show me records where the salary is equal to 20000 AND 35000 AND 40000".

A column can't be equal to more than one value at a time. If a salary value is equal to 20000 it can't also be equal to 35000. This query will return zero rows. That's why the IN keyword is comparable to the OR keyword and not to the AND keyword.

IN with LIKE?

In a previous chapter, you learned how to use the LIKE keyword to perform partial matches. For example, to find all records where the last_name starts with "S," our query would be:

```
SELECT id, last_name, salary
FROM employee
WHERE last_name LIKE 'S%';
```

What if you wanted to find all records where the last_name started with "S" or "P"? Could you use an IN keyword for this? Could you write something like this?

```
SELECT id, last_name, salary
FROM employee
WHERE last_name IN ('S%', 'P%');
```

Unfortunately, this use of IN won't give you the results you need. The IN clause does an "equals to" on all of the values inside the brackets, and not a LIKE. So, the IN clause won't be able to perform a partial match on the values in the list. It will return records where the last_name exactly matches the characters "S%" or "P%", of which there are none.

When you have multiple LIKE conditions, you can combine them using OR keywords. For example:

```
SELECT id, last_name, salary
FROM employee
WHERE last_name LIKE 'S%'
OR last_name LIKE 'P%';
```

This query will show the following results:

ID	LAST_NAME	SALARY
2	SMITH	35000
4	SIMPSON	52000
8	SMITH	62000
9	PATRICK	40000

Filtering on Ranges of Values

You've learned how to use operators such as "equal to" and "greater than" to filter data using a WHERE clause. Sometimes you may need to find data that falls within a range of values. There is a better way to filter on a range of values than using a combination of greater than and less than operators.

Filtering on a range of values could be done using your employee table. You may want to filter on a range of salary values. The employee table looks like this:

ID	LAST_NAME	SALARY
1	JONES	20000
2	SMITH	35000
3	KING	40000
4	SIMPSON	52000
5	ANDERSON	31000
6	COOPER	NULL
7	NULL	NULL
8	SMITH	62000
9	PATRICK	40000

Let's say your manager wants to know who is being paid a salary in a certain range. You have been asked for the details of all people who have a salary between 20,000 and 40,000 inclusive.

How would you do this? You can use a WHERE clause that uses:

- A greater than or equal to symbol, for salaries of 20,000

- A less than or equal to symbol, for salaries of 40,000

- The AND keyword to ensure records meet both criteria

Your query could look like this:

```
SELECT id, last_name, salary
FROM employee
WHERE salary >= 20000
AND salary <= 40000;
```

This query will find records where the salary is greater than or equal to 20000 and the salary is less than or equal to 40000. Your results would look like this:

ID	LAST_NAME	SALARY
1	JONES	20000
2	SMITH	35000
3	KING	40000
5	ANDERSON	31000
9	PATRICK	40000

These results show records that have a salary equal to 20000, 40000, and everything in between. There's an alternative way to write the same logic into a query: using an operator called BETWEEN.

The BETWEEN Operator

In SQL, BETWEEN is an operator that lets you specify an upper and lower limit for a particular column, and the rows must match that criteria to be included. BETWEEN is the same as using a "greater than or equal to" and a "less than or equal to." The syntax for using BETWEEN looks like this:

```
WHERE column BETWEEN low_value AND high_value
```

This means:

- It starts with the WHERE column, which is the column whose values you want to look up.

- You then specify the BETWEEN operator.

- Next comes the low_value, or the lower value in the range.

- Then you have the AND keyword.

- Finally, you have the high_value, or the higher value in the range.

Using Between with Two Salary Values

You can rewrite your earlier example into a query that uses BETWEEN.

The first example was this query:

```
SELECT id, last_name, salary
FROM employee
WHERE salary >= 20000
AND salary <= 40000;
```

You can rewrite this using the BETWEEN keyword like this:

```
SELECT id, last_name, salary
FROM employee
WHERE salary BETWEEN 20000 AND 40000;
```

This query has a little less typing, and is arguably easier to read. The results are the same:

```
ID    LAST_NAME    SALARY
1     JONES        20000
2     SMITH        35000
3     KING         40000
5     ANDERSON     31000
9     PATRICK      40000
```

Using BETWEEN When Values Don't Match

The BETWEEN operator can also be used on data that does not exactly match the upper and lower values you specify. To find the employee records with salary values between 50,000 and 100,000, you would write a query like this:

```
SELECT id, last_name, salary
FROM employee
WHERE salary BETWEEN 50000 AND 100000;
```

The results of this query are:

ID	LAST_NAME	SALARY
4	SIMPSON	52000
8	SMITH	62000

You'll notice a few things. First, there are no values that are exactly 50,000 or 100,000, but that's OK. The values that are in this range are shown. Also, the NULL values are not shown. NULL is considered an unknown, so the database is unable to tell if those NULL values are within this range.

Using BETWEEN with Text Values

You can also use text values with a BETWEEN keyword. Let's say you wanted to find all last_name values that were between ANDERSON and MOON. You would write a query that looks like this:

```
SELECT id, last_name, salary
FROM employee
WHERE last_name BETWEEN 'ANDERSON' AND 'MOON';
```

Our results would display like this:

ID	LAST_NAME	SALARY
1	JONES	20000
3	KING	40000
5	ANDERSON	31000
6	COOPER	NULL

This result is determined by checking the characters in each last_name value to see if they come after 'ANDERSON' and before 'MOON' if they were sorted alphabetically. All three of these values do.

An Example of an Inclusive and Exclusive Check

Here's an example of something that won't work as a BETWEEN clause. Let's say that you need to find all employee records that have a salary of 20000 or greater, and employee records that have a salary of less than 40000. If they have a salary of 40000, they should not be included. Your query without BETWEEN could look like this:

```
SELECT id, last_name, salary
FROM employee
WHERE salary >= 20000
AND salary < 40000;
```

Notice that the first WHERE condition uses ">=" to reflect "greater than or equal to 20000". The second condition uses "<" to reflect "less than 40000". This query will return the following results:

ID	LAST_NAME	SALARY
1	JONES	20000
2	SMITH	35000
5	ANDERSON	31000

If you write this using a BETWEEN, it will look the same as the earlier query and show different results.

```
SELECT id, last_name, salary
FROM employee
WHERE salary BETWEEN 20000 AND 40000;
```

The results are different:

ID	LAST_NAME	SALARY
1	JONES	20000
2	SMITH	35000
3	KING	40000
5	ANDERSON	31000
9	PATRICK	40000

This is something to be aware of. If you need to use "greater than or equal to" and "less than or equal to," then BETWEEN can work, otherwise it won't work. Could you just say BETWEEN 20000 and 39999?

You could, but what's to say there isn't a salary of 39999.50? How can you effectively work out the highest value that is less than 40000? You can't do that very easily. The same issue can be found with date fields, which you'll look at later in this book.

Should You Use BETWEEN?

You've seen the BETWEEN keyword as something that can be used as an alternative to "greater than or equal to" and "less than or equal to" logic (otherwise known as "inclusive"). Which method should you use?

Here's what I would recommend: if you are truly looking for a range of values, and your rule says it needs to be inclusive, then you can use BETWEEN. If you aren't, then I would suggest using the other symbols. Table 10-1 provides an at-a-glance summary of this rule.

Table 10-1. *When to Use the BETWEEN Operator*

Looking for a range of values?	Inclusive of values specified?	Use BETWEEN or Operators
Yes	Yes	BETWEEN
Yes	No	Operators
No	Yes	Operators
No	No	Operators

Summary

The IN keyword allows you to specify several values to perform an "equal to" check on. It's easier to type and easier to read than using multiple OR keywords, and it can be used with any data type.

The BETWEEN keyword is a helpful concept that allows you to specify a WHERE clause for a value that must be within two other values. It's an easy to write and easy to understand combination of "greater than or equal to" and "less than or equal to," but cannot be modified to use "greater than" or "less than" if required.

CHAPTER 11

Ordering Your Data

In this chapter, you'll learn how to sort your results in a specific order. In SQL, the data you select from a table is not guaranteed to be shown in a particular order. If you want to show it in a particular order, there is a command you can use.

Results Are Not Ordered

When you run a SELECT query on a table, the data in the table is displayed for you to sees. If you run a SELECT query to get all rows, for example, you see all of the rows.

```
SELECT id, last_name, salary
FROM employee;
```

ID	LAST_NAME	SALARY
1	JONES	20000
2	SMITH	35000
3	KING	40000
4	SIMPSON	52000
5	ANDERSON	31000
6	COOPER	(null)
7	(null)	(null)
8	SMITH	62000
9	PATRICK	40000

If you look at the results, you'll see that they are ordered by the ID field in ascending order, which is from lowest to highest. This ordering didn't happen as part of your query though. Oracle does not order your results in a certain way when you run a query, which means you can't guarantee that data will be ordered this way.

151

© Ben Brumm 2019
B. Brumm, *Beginning Oracle SQL for Oracle Database 18c*,
https://doi.org/10.1007/978-1-4842-4430-2_11

The reason the data has been ordered by ID number in the prior example is because the data is often ordered by when you added it to the database. However, there are many factors that can change that behavior, such as:

- Deleting data from a table

- Adding new data into a table

- Updating existing data in a table

- Other database administrator tasks

- Parallel data access such as in high-performance systems

So, if Oracle can't guarantee that your data will be ordered in a certain way, what can you do? You can specify the order you want your data to appear in when you write the query.

Warning!   Developers will sometimes argue a specific case, saying that there is no way the database engine will return rows out of order. Ignore such arguments. They are always wrong, and will become wrong at the worst possible time, such as at 2:00 AM when you least want to be paged back to the office to solve a problem.

Ordering Results with ORDER BY

There's a clause in SQL called ORDER BY. This allows you to specify the order that you want the rows in your result to appear in. The ORDER BY clause looks like this:

```
ORDER BY expression [ASC|DESC]
```

This syntax includes:

- An ORDER BY keyword to indicate what is being done.

- An expression, which specifies how you want to order your results

- ASC or DESC, which are optional, and specify whether to order your data in ascending or descending order.

You can also order by more than one column:

```
ORDER BY expression [ASC|DESC], expression [ASC|DESC], expression [ASC|DESC]...
```

You can just keep adding expressions to the end of the clause, separated by commas. You'll see examples of this being done later in this chapter.

The expression can be any of:

- A column name or expression including the column

- A number which represents the position of a column in the SELECT clause

- A column alias (which you will learn later in this book)

You'll have examples of these in the chapter as well.

ORDER BY Examples

Let's see some examples of ordering your data. You can see this ORDER BY clause in action in SQL queries, and see how it impacts the results.

Order by a Text Value

You'll start by ordering your data by the last_name, so you can see all of the records in alphabetical order. To do this, you add an ORDER BY to your SELECT query. For example:

```
SELECT id, last_name, salary
FROM employee
ORDER BY last_name;
```

You've just added in ORDER BY and then the last_name column. You can specify either ASC or DESC, but doing so is optional and the default is ASC.

Your results will look like these:

ID	LAST_NAME	SALARY
5	ANDERSON	31000
6	COOPER	(null)
1	JONES	20000
3	KING	40000
9	PATRICK	40000
4	SIMPSON	52000
2	SMITH	35000
8	SMITH	62000
7	(null)	(null)

These results are sorted by last_name in ascending order. The NULL value appears at the bottom. If you want to be clear about your ordering, you can specify the keyword ASC in the query:

```
SELECT id, last_name, salary
FROM employee
ORDER BY last_name ASC;
```

Your results would then be the same:

```
ID   LAST_NAME   SALARY
5    ANDERSON    31000
6    COOPER      (null)
1    JONES       20000
3    KING        40000
9    PATRICK     40000
4    SIMPSON     52000
2    SMITH       35000
8    SMITH       62000
7    (null)      (null)
```

So, if the results are the same, should you add in the ASC keyword? I think that you should, because it makes it clear that data is ordered in a specific way. When writing SQL, it's usually better to avoid any ambiguity and specify exactly what needs to be done. However, it is common to omit ASC, so be prepared to encounter queries in other people's code in which ASC is omitted because it is the default.

Order by a Number Value

Let's look at an example on the salary column. You can sort the results based on the highest and then on the lowest salary values.

First, let's sort the data based on the lowest salary values. Our query will look like this:

```
SELECT id, last_name, salary
FROM employee
ORDER BY salary ASC;
```

This query will sort the employee records by the salary column in ascending order. The results will look like these:

```
ID  LAST_NAME   SALARY
1   JONES       20000
5   ANDERSON    31000
2   SMITH       35000
3   KING        40000
9   PATRICK     40000
4   SIMPSON     52000
8   SMITH       62000
6   COOPER      (null)
7   (null)      (null)
```

As you can see, the lowest salary is at the top and the highest is at the bottom. You can also sort any column, such as the salary, in descending order. You can do this by changing the ASC to DESC:

```
SELECT id, last_name, salary
FROM employee
ORDER BY salary DESC;
```

The results will now be sorted in the reverse order:

```
ID  LAST_NAME   SALARY
6   COOPER      (null)
7   (null)      (null)
8   SMITH       62000
4   SIMPSON     52000
3   KING        40000
9   PATRICK     40000
2   SMITH       35000
5   ANDERSON    31000
1   JONES       20000
```

You can see that the highest salary is at the top of the list.

Order by a Column Not in the SELECT Clause

When you order by a column, you don't have to specify that column in the SELECT clause. This means you don't need to see the column to be able to order by it.

You can use the query from the earlier example and change it to remove the salary column from the SELECT clause. It's still in the ORDER BY clause.

```
SELECT id, last_name
FROM employee
ORDER BY salary DESC;
```

The results are shown as:

ID	LAST_NAME
6	COOPER
7	(null)
8	SMITH
4	SIMPSON
3	KING
9	PATRICK
2	SMITH
5	ANDERSON
1	JONES

As you can see, the salary column isn't shown. However, the order of the results is the same as the earlier example, which was by salary in descending order.

Order by a Number

Another way to order your results is to specify a number, rather than the name of the column. The number you specify is the number of the column in the SELECT clause.

You could have a query like this:

```
SELECT id, last_name, salary
FROM employee;
```

To order by the id column, you can specify an ORDER BY clause:

```
ORDER BY 1 ASC;
```

This will order by the ID column, because the number 1 indicates the first column in the SELECT clause, which is ID.

```
SELECT id, last_name, salary
FROM employee
ORDER BY 1 ASC;
```

```
ID  LAST_NAME  SALARY
1   JONES      20000
2   SMITH      35000
3   KING       40000
4   SIMPSON    52000
5   ANDERSON   31000
6   COOPER     (null)
7   (null)     (null)
8   SMITH      62000
9   PATRICK    40000
```

The data is ordered by the ID column. To change this to the last_name column, you can change the number 1 to 2.

```
SELECT id, last_name, salary
FROM employee
ORDER BY 2 ASC;
```

```
ID  LAST_NAME  SALARY
5   ANDERSON   31000
6   COOPER     (null)
1   JONES      20000
3   KING       40000
9   PATRICK    40000
4   SIMPSON    52000
2   SMITH      35000
8   SMITH      62000
7   (null)     (null)
```

The column number works in the same way as specifying the column name. So why would you use the number instead of the name? The column number is easier to type and can be used in once-off SQL scripts you write. However, I recommend using the full column name when writing code that will be used by other people or applications, as it's easier to understand which column is being ordered, and it's less prone to errors from changes in the database.

ORDER BY and NULLs

You might have noticed in the earlier examples that some NULL values appeared. By default, the NULL values appear at the bottom of results when they are ordered in ascending order, and at the top of results when ordered in descending order.

In Oracle SQL, you can change this behavior for your query if you like. You can specify one of two optional keywords at the end of your ORDER BY clause to indicate how you want NULL values to be treated:

- NULLS FIRST: NULL values are shown at the **top** of the list, regardless of how it is ordered.

- NULLS LAST: NULL values are shown at the **bottom** of the list, regardless of how it is ordered.

For example, if you wanted to order by salary in descending order, but have the NULL values shown at the bottom instead of the top, your query would look like this:

```
SELECT id, last_name, salary
FROM employee
ORDER BY salary DESC NULLS LAST;
ID   LAST_NAME    SALARY
8    SMITH        62000
4    SIMPSON      52000
3    KING         40000
9    PATRICK      40000
2    SMITH        35000
5    ANDERSON     31000
1    JONES        20000
7    (null)       (null)
6    COOPER       (null)
```

The salary values are ordered in descending order, and the NULL values are shown at the end. To sort with NULL values at the top:

```
SELECT id, last_name, salary
FROM employee
ORDER BY salary DESC NULLS FIRST;
```

The results are:

```
ID  LAST_NAME  SALARY
6   COOPER     (null)
7   (null)     (null)
8   SMITH      62000
4   SIMPSON    52000
3   KING       40000
9   PATRICK    40000
2   SMITH      35000
5   ANDERSON   31000
1   JONES      20000
```

Order by Multiple Columns

In our examples, you've seen how to sort by a single column. What if you wanted to sort by two columns, or more? You can do that in SQL. To sort by more than one column, just add a comma, then the name or number of the column, then the direction to sort (either ASC or DESC).

For example, to sort by the last_name column and then the salary column:

```
SELECT id, last_name, salary
FROM employee
ORDER BY last_name ASC, salary DESC;
```

```
ID  LAST_NAME  SALARY
5   ANDERSON   31000
6   COOPER     (null)
1   JONES      20000
3   KING       40000
9   PATRICK    40000
```

```
4    SIMPSON    52000
8    SMITH      62000
2    SMITH      35000
7    (null)     (null)
```

The results are sorted by last_name in ascending order, and then salary in descending order. This means that the results are sorted by the last_name value, and if there are any rows that have the same last_name, they are then sorted by the salary in descending order.

You've sorted by two columns in this query. You've also sorted by these columns in a different way: one ascending, and one descending. There are no rules to say they both have to be in the same order. You can use the same kind of syntax to sort by three columns:

```
SELECT id, last_name, salary
FROM employee
ORDER BY last_name ASC, salary ASC, id ASC;
```

```
ID   LAST_NAME   SALARY
5    ANDERSON    31000
6    COOPER      (null)
1    JONES       20000
3    KING        40000
9    PATRICK     40000
4    SIMPSON     52000
2    SMITH       35000
8    SMITH       62000
7    (null)      (null)
```

The data will be ordered in the way you have specified. With such a small table, it can be hard to tell how the data is ordered, but with a larger table it will be clearer.

You don't have to order all of your columns in the same way. For example, you can order one column in ascending order and another column in descending order:

```
SELECT id, last_name, salary
FROM employee
ORDER BY last_name ASC, salary DESC;
```

The results are:

ID	LAST_NAME	SALARY
5	ANDERSON	31000
6	COOPER	(null)
1	JONES	20000
3	KING	40000
9	PATRICK	40000
4	SIMPSON	52000
8	SMITH	62000
2	SMITH	35000
7	(null)	(null)

You'll notice the difference here on the rows where the last_name is SMITH. The values are still ordered by last_name in ascending order, but when the last_name is the same, the salary is sorted in descending order. The rows for SMITH are sorted so that the salary of 62000 comes above the salary of 35000.

Do You Really Need to Order Your Data?

You've seen how to order the results from a query. Doing so can make it easier to view the data and understand what's in the table.

However, it's not always necessary to order the data. Using the ORDER BY clause can be quite an intensive process. It might not have much of an impact on a table of ten records, but when you're working with hundreds or thousands of results, having an ORDER BY clause can slow a query down.

If you really need to show your results in a particular order, then feel free to use the ORDER BY clause. Because you need what you need, and the database engine is there to do the work for you. However, if the order of the results does not matter to you or to the application, then don't order them.

Some examples of queries where you may want to order results are:

- All orders for a particular customer, sorted by the order date, so the customer can view the list

- All products in a category, sorted by the name, so they can be displayed on your website

Some examples of queries where you may not want to order results are:

- A list of students enrolled in a class, as you may want to leave the ordering up to the users, or may not want to order them at all

- A unique list of status values that are going to be used in a drop-down box on a page.

Summary

The results of your query can be shown in a specific order using the ORDER BY clause. You can specify either the name of the column, or the position it appears in the SELECT clause. Results can be ordered by a column in either ascending or descending order. You can specify multiple columns to order the results by, and each of these can be ordered in ascending or descending order.

CHAPTER 12

Applying Table and Column Aliases

In all of the chapters so far, you've learned how to view data from our database tables. You've learned how to choose the columns and rows you want to display using many different methods.

In this final chapter of Part II, we'll look at two techniques you can use to improve your SQL queries and make them easier to write and easier to understand the results of. The first of these techniques is called a "table alias."

What is a Table Alias?

A *table alias* is an alternative name you can apply to your table as part of your SQL query. This alias applies only to your query, and no permanent changes are made to the database.

Why would you want to use a table alias in your query?

- It can make it easier and faster to refer to columns in your query.

- It's easier to work with queries involving two or more tables (which you will learn about later in this book).

- There are some types of queries that need to use table aliases, which you'll learn about later in this book.

What does a table alias look like? It's a short word after your table name in the FROM clause:

```
SELECT columns
FROM table_name alias_name;
```

© Ben Brumm 2019
B. Brumm, *Beginning Oracle SQL for Oracle Database 18c*,
https://doi.org/10.1007/978-1-4842-4430-2_12

The `alias_name` is a name you provide. You write the table name, then a space, then the `alias_name`. The `alias_name` can be as short or as long as you like. You can write a short alias, such as a single letter, or a long alias.

Once you have done this, you can then use the alias as a prefix to any column you refer to in your query.

Let's take a look at an example of this.

Example of a Table Alias

We'll start with our query on the `employee` table that we looked at in earlier chapters. This was our query:

```
SELECT id, last_name, salary
FROM employee;
```

You can add a table alias to this query by adding a space and then a name after the table name:

```
SELECT id, last_name, salary
FROM employee e;
```

In this example, I've used an alias of "e". This is helpful because:

- It's easy to type, as it's a single character.

- It's shorter than the full table name of "employee."

- It starts with the same letter, so when you read the query you can see that "e" is short for "employee."

With our table alias set, we can now update our `SELECT` clause to use this table alias. There are a few reasons to do this, which we've mentioned earlier in this chapter (faster to type, helpful for queries with multiple tables). One way that it's faster is the use of a feature called "Intellisense" or "AutoComplete"

Intellisense or AutoComplete

Intellisense, or AutoComplete as it's often called, is a feature in many software development tools that allow you to write code faster. It's available in SQL Developer, and easily accessible when you use table aliases. Let's see an example of this.

1. Open SQL Developer and connect to your database, in the same way that you have done for earlier chapters. Your screen should show a new SQL window, as shown in Figure 12-1.

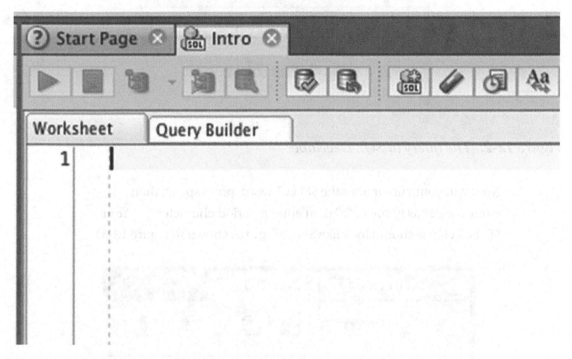

Figure 12-1. *The new SQL window*

2. Enter in part of the query:

```
SELECT
FROM employee e;
```

3. Your screen should look like that shown in Figure 12-2. If a red underline appears, you can ignore that for now. It's just letting you know that the query is incomplete, as you have not specified any columns.

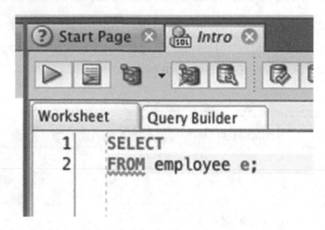

Figure 12-2. *The query in SQL Developer*

4. Now, put your cursor after the SELECT word, press space, then enter your alias name of "e", then enter a period character " . " Your SELECT clause should look like SELECT e. (as shown in Figure 12-3).

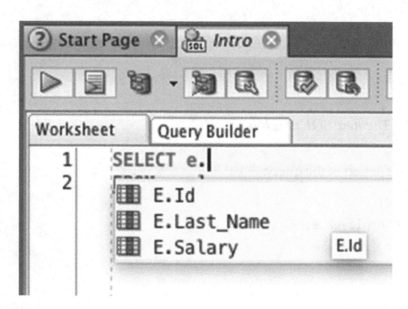

Figure 12-3. *The AutoComplete options*

5. The popup that appears shows all of the columns available in the
   employee table. You can select a column by pressing the up and
   down arrow keys, typing in part of the column name, or clicking
   on the name in the list.

6. Repeat these steps until you have entered all of the columns you
   want to show in your query.

This popup that appears is called Intellisense or AutoComplete. It's easy to trigger
when a table alias is used. Simply enter the alias name and a period to trigger it. This
feature allows you to easily select a column from the table to include in your query,
saving time and preventing errors from mistyping the column name.

If you run the query with the table aliases, you'll get the same results as without the
table aliases:

```
SELECT e.id, e.last_name
FROM employee e;
```

```
ID    LAST_NAME
1     JONES
2     SMITH
3     KING
4     SIMPSON
5     ANDERSON
6     COOPER
7     (null)
8     SMITH
9     PATRICK
```

Longer Table Aliases

You don't have to use a single letter for a table alias. Many examples of SQL code online
will use a single letter, and many others will use more letters. The disadvantage of using
a single letter is it's not immediately obvious what table it refers to, when there are
multiple tables in a query that may start with the same letter.

For example, let's say your database has a table called "product" that stored details about products that it sold. You may also have a table called "pay_rate", which included the different pay rates for employees. If you had a query that used a table alias of "p", would you be able to easily tell that it referred to the product table rather than the pay_rate table?

In some instances, especially with longer queries, you may want to use a longer table alias name. The longer the name is, the harder it is to type, so you would need to have a balance between a name that's too short to be informative and a name that's too long to be an effective alias.

I usually try to keep my aliases to four or five characters at most. You can make a more descriptive alias for the employee table by using an alias name of "emp".

```
SELECT emp.id, emp.last_name, emp.salary
FROM employee emp;
```

This is short enough that it's easier to type, and long enough to describe what the table is.

What If I Don't Use a Table Alias?

All of this effort to add a table alias, which is just another name for a table, to make things easier to type? What if you don't want to use a table alias?

You don't have to. In many of the queries I write, I don't use aliases. It's an optional feature, and not used that often in smaller queries. But it's good to know that the feature is there, both in SQL and in the SQL Developer software.

What Is a Column Alias?

Another feature of SQL that's helpful for writing queries is a *column alias*. A column alias is a name that you give to a column that's shown in your results.

There are a few reasons for using column aliases:

- To make the heading of the output easier to read by users

- To make the heading of the output easier to use by applications

- To make the column available in other parts of the query

Just like a table alias, a column alias is an optional feature. There's nothing built into SQL Developer to take advantage of column aliases, unlike a table alias.

To use a column alias, you add a name after the column name in your query:

```
SELECT column_name [AS] column_alias
FROM table;
```

There's a keyword in the middle called "AS", which is used to define a column alias. However, it's an optional keyword: a column alias will work with or without it.

Let's take a look at an example.

Example of a Column Alias

We can start with our query from earlier in this chapter:

```
SELECT id, last_name, salary
FROM employee;
```

If you run this query, you get the following output:

ID	LAST_NAME	SALARY
1	JONES	20000
2	SMITH	35000
3	KING	40000
4	SIMPSON	52000
5	ANDERSON	31000
6	COOPER	(null)
7	(null)	(null)
8	SMITH	62000
9	PATRICK	40000

SQL Developer, and many other integrated development environments (IDEs) will show the column names from the SELECT clause as the column headings here.

What if you wanted to have a different name for your heading? You could adjust your table, but that would mean all other queries using this table would need to be updated, otherwise they would no longer work.

A better way to do this would be to use column aliases. Let's say you wanted to display your last_name column as "surname". You can adjust your query:

```
SELECT id, last_name AS surname, salary
FROM employee;
```

If you run the query, your results will look like this:

ID	SURNAME	SALARY
1	JONES	20000
2	SMITH	35000
3	KING	40000
4	SIMPSON	52000
5	ANDERSON	31000
6	COOPER	(null)
7	(null)	(null)
8	SMITH	62000
9	PATRICK	40000

The column heading is now called surname. No changes have been made to the employee table (just your query), so other areas of your database or applications won't be affected. If you don't want to include the AS keyword, because it's optional, your query would look like this:

```
SELECT id, last_name surname, salary
FROM employee;
```

The results of this query would be the same.

ID	SURNAME	SALARY
1	JONES	20000
2	SMITH	35000
3	KING	40000
4	SIMPSON	52000
5	ANDERSON	31000
6	COOPER	(null)
7	(null)	(null)
8	SMITH	62000
9	PATRICK	40000

The AS Keyword

If the AS keyword for column aliases is optional, should you use it or not? Surely the less typing you need to do, the better? I would recommend that you include the AS keyword whenever you use a column alias. Here's why.

Let's say you had a query like the preceding one:

```
SELECT id, last_name surname, salary
FROM employee;
```

If you look closely at this query, you can see it includes three columns, and the last_name column has an alias of surname. However, the surname may look like an extra column. How do you know, by looking at this query, if the surname is meant to be a column alias, or the person who wrote it forgot to add the comma after the last_name column, and surname is actually a different column?

It's not easy to tell the difference. In this example, the query will run, as it did earlier. However, let's say you have a query like this:

```
SELECT id, last_name salary
FROM employee;
```

This looks like you want to select three columns: id, last_name, and salary. This is what we've seen a lot during this book. However, when you run the query, this is what you'll see.

ID	SALARY
1	JONES
2	SMITH
3	KING
4	SIMPSON
5	ANDERSON
6	COOPER
7	(null)
8	SMITH
9	PATRICK

Why is the `last_name` column called `salary`? Or why is the `salary` column showing text values that look like names? If you look closely at your query, you can see the issue:

```
SELECT id, last_name salary
FROM employee;
```

A comma is missing between the end of the `last_name` column and the start of the `salary` column. The Oracle database doesn't know what you meant; it just knows what it's told, so it looks at the `last_name` column and calls it "salary".

If you specify the AS keyword for every column alias you use, it's immediately clear that this is supposed to be a column alias, and not a column that's missing a comma. Sometimes in SQL it's better to use the slightly longer version of a statement to make it clearer to the reader, than to use the short version to save time but cause more issues later.

Note   Using the AS keyword when specifying column aliases is helpful for you and other developers to know that the following word is supposed to be a column alias and not a mistyped query.

Mathematical Operations and Column Aliases

Another feature of SQL is the ability to perform *mathematical operations* on columns. This includes the basic operations of addition, subtraction, multiplication, and division. These are done using the following symbols:

- + for addition
- - for subtraction
- * for multiplication
- / for division

To perform one of these operations, enter a column or value, then one of these symbols, then another column or value.

Addition

For example, our `salary` column indicates the annual salary for each employee. To show what the value would be if you increased it by 10000, our query would be:

```
SELECT id, last_name, salary + 10000
FROM employee;
```

The results would be:

ID	LAST_NAME	SALARY+10000
1	JONES	30000
2	SMITH	45000
3	KING	50000
4	SIMPSON	62000
5	ANDERSON	41000
6	COOPER	(null)
7	(null)	(null)
8	SMITH	72000
9	PATRICK	50000

The values are showing 10000 more than the original `salary` value. How can you be sure? How do you know what the earlier `salary` value was?

You can add that to your query. There's no rule to say you can't select a column more than once. To see the old `salary` value as well, you can run this query:

```
SELECT id, last_name, salary, salary + 10000
FROM employee;
```

The results would be:

ID	LAST_NAME	SALARY	SALARY+10000
1	JONES	20000	30000
2	SMITH	35000	45000
3	KING	40000	50000
4	SIMPSON	52000	62000
5	ANDERSON	31000	41000
6	COOPER	(null)	(null)

7	(null)	(null)	(null)
8	SMITH	62000	72000
9	PATRICK	40000	50000

You can see the old and the new value. All salary values have increased by 10000, except for those with a NULL salary. This is because NULL means unknown and adding 10000 to an unknown value is still an unknown value.

What does this have to do with column aliases? If you look at the results, you can see that the column heading for the "salary plus 10000" column is "SALARY+10000". By default, Oracle will label your column headings like this, by combining any operators and removing spaces. This isn't very readable by your or by any applications that use this value, so we can give it a column alias.

Let's say you wanted to label our new column new_salary. Our query would be:

```
SELECT id, last_name, salary, salary + 10000 AS new_salary
FROM employee;
```

Your results would look like this

ID	LAST_NAME	SALARY	NEW_SALARY
1	JONES	20000	30000
2	SMITH	35000	45000
3	KING	40000	50000
4	SIMPSON	52000	62000
5	ANDERSON	31000	41000
6	COOPER	(null)	(null)
7	(null)	(null)	(null)
8	SMITH	62000	72000
9	PATRICK	40000	50000

This column heading of NEW_SALARY is a lot easier to read and a lot easier for applications to work with than SALARY+10000.

Subtraction

You can perform subtraction in our SQL code in the same way as you performed addition. For example, to subtract 5000 from our salary values, your query would look like this:

```
SELECT id, last_name, salary, salary - 5000
FROM employee;
```

The results of this query are:

ID	LAST_NAME	SALARY	SALARY-5000
1	JONES	20000	15000
2	SMITH	35000	30000
3	KING	40000	35000
4	SIMPSON	52000	47000
5	ANDERSON	31000	26000
6	COOPER	(null)	(null)
7	(null)	(null)	(null)
8	SMITH	62000	57000
9	PATRICK	40000	35000

You can give this new column a column alias:

```
SELECT id, last_name, salary, salary - 5000 AS low_salary
FROM employee;
```

The results of this query are:

ID	LAST_NAME	SALARY	LOW_SALARY
1	JONES	20000	15000
2	SMITH	35000	30000
3	KING	40000	35000
4	SIMPSON	52000	47000
5	ANDERSON	31000	26000
6	COOPER	(null)	(null)
7	(null)	(null)	(null)
8	SMITH	62000	57000
9	PATRICK	40000	35000

This shows the salary value minus 5000, with a label of LOW_SALARY.

175

Multiplication

You can multiply a value by another value in the same way as addition and subtraction, by using the "*" symbol. Let's say you wanted to multiple our salary value by 5 to see the cost of the salary over 5 years. Our query would look like this:

```
SELECT id, last_name, salary, salary * 5
FROM employee;
```

The results of this query are:

ID	LAST_NAME	SALARY	SALARY*5
1	JONES	20000	100000
2	SMITH	35000	175000
3	KING	40000	200000
4	SIMPSON	52000	260000
5	ANDERSON	31000	155000
6	COOPER	(null)	(null)
7	(null)	(null)	(null)
8	SMITH	62000	310000
9	PATRICK	40000	200000

You can see that the salary has been multiplied by 5 to show the new value. A column alias can also be applied to this value to make it more readable:

```
SELECT id, last_name, salary, salary * 5 AS five_year_salary
FROM employee;
```

The results of this query are:

ID	LAST_NAME	SALARY	FIVE_YEAR_SALARY
1	JONES	20000	100000
2	SMITH	35000	175000
3	KING	40000	200000
4	SIMPSON	52000	260000
5	ANDERSON	31000	155000
6	COOPER	(null)	(null)
7	(null)	(null)	(null)
8	SMITH	62000	310000
9	PATRICK	40000	200000

176

The alias in this case is FIVE_YEAR_SALARY. This might seem strange, as it's longer than the SALARY column name, but it's easier to read and easier for applications to use than SALARY*5.

Division

Finally, you can apply division to values in SQL with the "/" symbol. It works in the same way as the other symbols. Let's say you wanted to see the monthly salary for each employee. You could divide our existing annual salary by 12 to get the monthly salary.

```
SELECT id, last_name, salary, salary / 12
FROM employee;
```

The results from this query are:

ID	LAST_NAME	SALARY	SALARY/12
1	JONES	20000	1666.666667
2	SMITH	35000	2916.666667
3	KING	40000	3333.333333
4	SIMPSON	52000	4333.333333
5	ANDERSON	31000	2583.333333
6	COOPER	(null)	(null)
7	(null)	(null)	(null)
8	SMITH	62000	5166.666667
9	PATRICK	40000	3333.333333

All of the values shown are now in decimals, because none of them are neatly divisible by 12. You'll learn how to round these numbers in a later chapter.

If you wanted to give your column an alias, you can do that as well:

```
SELECT id, last_name, salary, salary / 12 AS monthly_salary
FROM employee;
```

The results from this query are:

ID	LAST_NAME	SALARY	SALARY/12
1	JONES	20000	1666.666667
2	SMITH	35000	2916.666667
3	KING	40000	3333.333333

4	SIMPSON	52000	4333.333333
5	ANDERSON	31000	2583.333333
6	COOPER	(null)	(null)
7	(null)	(null)	(null)
8	SMITH	62000	5166.666667
9	PATRICK	40000	3333.333333

The column now has a new heading in these results. Using column aliases is especially useful when working with mathematical operations, as you've seen.

Column Aliases with Table Aliases

You've learned about column aliases and table aliases in this chapter, in separate queries. They can actually be used in the same query to make your query even more readable.

You can use the query to find the monthly salary from earlier in the chapter.

```
SELECT id,
last_name,
salary,
salary / 12 AS monthly_salary
FROM employee;
```

This query uses a column alias to rename salary / 12 to monthly_salary. You can use a table alias with this query:

```
SELECT e.id,
e.last_name,
e.salary,
e.salary / 12 AS monthly_salary
FROM employee e;
```

In this query, every time we have referred to a column from the employee table, we've used the table alias of "e". As we mentioned before, this might seem like too much work for a simple query like this, but it's an important tip to learn for when you move on to more complicated queries.

Summary

Table aliases and column aliases are both optional features in SQL that you can use in your queries. Table aliases allow you to give another name to your table for your query, which is usually shorter than the real name. They help when you are working with more complicated queries and they allow you to use the Intellisense or AutoComplete feature of your IDE.

Column aliases allow you to give another name or label to your column in the output, making it more readable by users and easier for other applications to process.

Mathematical operations allow you to add, subtract, multiply, and divide values in SQL, and these are common targets for using column aliases. Finally, you can use both column aliases and table aliases in a single query. As you move on to more complicated queries, you'll find these features more useful.

PART III

Adding, Updating, Deleting Data

CHAPTER 13

Understanding the Data Types

In this chapter, you'll learn what data types are, why you need them, and how the Oracle database handles different data types.

What is a Data Type?

A *data type* is the format that a piece of information is stored in a database. Each column in a table has a data type, which is defined when you create the table and specify the column names.

If you've done any programming before, such as .Net or Java, you'll know that there are different data types available in these languages. Database development, and SQL, are no different. Data types are available for specifying how data is stored.

Do you remember earlier in this book when you created the employee table? We asked you to select a data type for the ID, last_name, and salary columns (Figure 13-1).

© Ben Brumm 2019
B. Brumm, *Beginning Oracle SQL for Oracle Database 18c*,
https://doi.org/10.1007/978-1-4842-4430-2_13

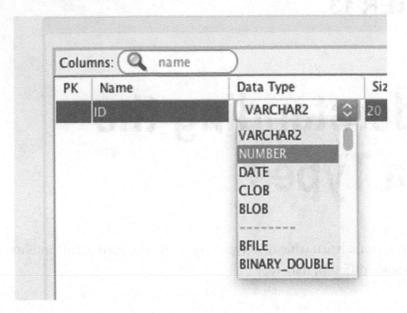

Figure 13-1. *Selecting a data type when adding columns to a table*

This step was where the data type for each column was specified. You specified that:

- The ID column is some kind of number.

- The last_name column is a text value.

- The salary column is also a number.

Why Do We Have Different Data Types?

When you create a table, you specify the column names. That should be all you need to do, right? Why do we care what the data type is? There are a few reasons that different data types exist.

First, it allows the database to be more efficient with storing data. If you define every column in every table as a text value of up to 10,000 characters, then the database will need to allow for that much storage space for those situations where you want to store 10,000 characters (no matter how rare those situations are). Defining an appropriate data type for each of your columns will mean the database can store the data efficiently.

It also means your queries will be faster. Storing values that are supposed to be numbers as a "number" data type will mean the database can search for specific values easier (as it knows the limits of the field, such as numbers and not letters). It also means mathematical calculations can be performed easier and faster, if values should be stored as numbers rather than text.

Using an appropriate data type also prevents invalid data. One of the major benefits of using a database to store your data is the restrictions you can place on storing the data. For example, storing an "order date" could be stored as a text value, but that means you may get values like this:

- 30/01/2018

- 01/30/2018

- 30-Jan 2018

- 40 Jan 2018

- 124/Abc/1000

Some of these values are OK, but others are not. However, if we stored this "order date" as a date value, then we can use the databases in-built validation to check for invalid dates. The Oracle database will know that "40 Jan 2018" is not a valid date, so it will not store the value. This ensures the quality of your data remains high and prevents errors.

So, in summary, data types are used to store data efficiently, to improve the performance of queries, and to prevent invalid data.

What Are the Different Data Types?

We've covered what data types are and why they are used. What kind of data types exist, and how can you use them?

The data types in the Oracle database (and in many other databases and programming languages) can be broken down into three groups: text, number, and date. Each of these groups has a range of data types you can use for your columns.

Text Data Types

The text data types in Oracle are those that are used to store text values. They can be used to store alphabet characters, numbers, and many special characters.

There are many different data types available in Oracle for storing text values, and each of them has their own use. Let's take a look at each of them.

CHAR

Oracle has a data type called CHAR, which is short for "character." It stores strings, which is a programming word that means "text values." This data type stores data in a fixed length, which means the value takes up the same amount of space regardless of the actual value being stored.

When you specify a CHAR column, you need to specify a length value. This represents the number of characters to store in the field and must be between 1 and 2000. You can store any text value inside this column, as long as its length is equal to or shorter than this number. For example, a CHAR column with a length of 10 can store the value of "Car" and "Fast Car" but not "Red Sports Car", because "Red Sports Car" is longer than 10 characters.

The main thing to remember about CHAR is that values that are less than the length you define have space characters added to the right of the value to meet the length. This means if you store a value of "Fast Car" in a CHAR column with a length of 10, the value that is actually stored is "Fast Car . Two spaces have been added to the end to bring the length to 10.

To define a column as a CHAR with a length, you use the word CHAR and then the length inside brackets:

```
CHAR(10)
```

You can change the number that is inside the brackets to the length that you would like to use. For a CHAR value with a length of 150, use this code:

```
CHAR(150)
```

Note   Values added to CHAR columns have space characters added to the right of the value to bring the length of the value up to the defined length of the CHAR column.

VARCHAR2

The VARCHAR2 data type in Oracle also stores strings, or text values, like the CHAR data type. VARCHAR is short for "variable character." A maximum length is specified when you define a VARCHAR2 column, which must be between 1 and 4000, and represents the number of characters. However, the length is variable. This means that the values you store do not have space characters added to the end to meet the length you define.

For example, if you declare a VARCHAR2 column with a length of 10 bytes, then you can store a value of "Car" or "Fast Car." When you store these values, spaces are not added, so the value of "Fast Car" is stored exactly as you enter it.

VARCHAR2 is one of the most common data types in my experience, so it's one you'll be using a lot.

Why is it called VARCHAR2 and not VARCHAR? This is because VARCHAR is an SQL standard data type and isn't used in Oracle SQL. When Oracle wanted to implement their own version of VARCHAR, they created VARCHAR2 rather than changing the way that VARCHAR works. This also means that they can implement the VARCHAR standard at some point in the future.

Defining a VARCHAR2 is similar to CHAR, where you specify the length inside brackets:

VARCHAR2(20)

This means a VARCHAR2 data type is defined with a maximum length of 20 bytes. The difference between bytes and characters is subtle but important. A character is stored as bytes, and in many cases one byte is one character. However, there are some characters that require multiple bytes to be stored.

NCHAR

The NCHAR data type is short for "Unicode character." It's very similar to the CHAR data type, as it stores character data of a fixed length and adds spaces for shorter values to bring the value up to the length you have specified.

However, it's used for storing text values that contain Unicode characters. Unicode characters are a set of special characters that can be used in software. They have their own data type in Oracle, as they can often require more than one byte to store the character. Some examples of Unicode characters are:

- Mathematical characters, such as the Greek symbol that represents "sum": Σ

- Many characters with accents: for example, â

The standard characters that we are used to, such as the alphabet and symbols visible on a keyboard, can be stored in a single byte of data per character. This makes it possible to store in a CHAR data type, where one byte equals one character.

187

For Unicode characters, it's possible that a character needs to be stored in multiple bytes, so a special data type is needed. This means that if you want to store these special Unicode characters, and you need to store them in a fixed length, use NCHAR instead of CHAR.

To define an NCHAR data type, specify the length in bytes inside brackets, just like the CHAR data type.

NCHAR(30)

This defines an NCHAR data type with a length of 30 bytes.

NVARCHAR2

NVARCHAR2 is the Unicode version of VARCHAR2. Just like the NCHAR data type, it allows for Unicode characters to be stored, but it uses the variable-length concept of VARCHAR2, which means you can store the value you want without having to add extra space characters to it.

To define an NVARCHAR2 data type, specify the length inside brackets, just like the VARCHAR2 data type.

NVARCHAR2(200)

This defines an NVARCHAR2 data type with a length of 200 bytes.

This table summarizes the different data types we've just looked at.

	Fixed Length (padded with spaces)	Variable Length (maximum length)
Standard characters	CHAR	VARCHAR2
Unicode characters	NCHAR	NVARCHAR2

If you're wondering which data type you should use, I'll explain some recommendations later in this chapter.

LONG

The LONG data type can be used to store text values up to 2GB in length. VARCHAR2 had a maximum length of 4000 bytes, which represents 4KB. LONG is much larger than that.

However, I don't recommend creating columns with the LONG data type, as it has been deprecated by Oracle. This means that Oracle has determined it's not something they will support in future releases and is only included in recent releases to ensure customers using old code with LONG data types won't have their databases break.

If you want to store a large amount of data in a single field, it's recommended to use LOB data types, such as CLOB or BLOB. I'll explain those later in this chapter.

RAW

The RAW data type is similar to VARCHAR2, as it stores a variable-length string. However, it stores data in a raw format, which means it does not get converted when exporting to another type of database.

It's not a data type I would recommend using. If you're doing a lot of conversion between systems, then perhaps you can use it, but there are other text data types that are more suitable.

LONG RAW

The LONG RAW data type is a mix between the LONG data type and the RAW data type. It allows for a large amount of data to be stored (like the LONG data type), and it ensures characters are not converted when exporting data to other systems.

However, like the LONG data type, the LONG RAW data type is deprecated, so you shouldn't use it. The BLOB data type should be used instead.

Number Data Types

There are many data types that can be used to store number values in Oracle. While you can store numbers in text-based data types such as VARCHAR2, it's better to use number data types if you're storing just numbers because:

- You can perform arithmetic on them (e.g., dividing annual salary by 12).

- You can round them to a different number of decimal places.

- You can aggregate them using sum, average, and other features.

Let's take a look at the number data types.

NUMBER

The NUMBER data type in Oracle is used to store numbers. It can store either whole numbers or decimal numbers, positive or negative numbers. The range of a value stored as a NUMBER data type is from -9×10^{125} to 9×10^{125}, which means numbers that are about 125 digits, positive or negative.

When you define a NUMBER data type, you can define two things: a precision and a scale.

- Precision is the total number of digits in the number.

- Scale is the number of digits to the right of the decimal point.

Using different combinations of values for precision and scale allows you to store positive and negative decimals and whole numbers.

You can define a NUMBER data type by specifying the precision and scale inside brackets (p stands for precision, s stands for scale):

NUMBER(p, s)

For example, to define a number that has ten total digits, with three decimal places, you would write this:

NUMBER(10, 3)

This means there are seven digits to the left of the decimal and three to the right (e.g., 1234567.123).

INTEGER

The INTEGER data type is an SQL standard data type, which means it is in all SQL databases. However, in Oracle, it's the same as defining a NUMBER(38) data type, which is a NUMBER with 38 digits and 0 decimal places.

Because the INTEGER data type is actually translated to a NUMBER(38) data type, it's better to use NUMBER. It allows you more freedom with the size of the value, if you don't want a 38-digit number. It's also clearer what it represents.

FLOAT

Oracle includes a FLOAT data type, which is an ANSI standard data type (meaning it is available in all types of SQL). However, just like INTEGER, the FLOAT data type is translated internally by the Oracle database to NUMBER.

So, rather than using the FLOAT data type, which is translated to NUMBER, I would suggest just using NUMBER.

DECIMAL

Just like the FLOAT data type, Oracle includes a DECIMAL data type that is also an ANSI standard data type. It's also translated to a NUMBER data type by the Oracle database. I would recommend using the NUMBER data type instead of DECIMAL for this reason.

BINARY_FLOAT

The BINARY_FLOAT data type is used for storing floating-point numbers, which are numbers that contain decimal places. It's similar to "float" data types in other programming languages.

There are a few differences between BINARY_FLOAT and the NUMBER data type:

- BINARY_FLOAT can often perform arithmetic calculations faster than NUMBER.

- BINARY_FLOAT is often smaller to store than NUMBER.

- BINARY_FLOAT is an approximate definition, where NUMBER is an exact definition

When a BINARY_FLOAT value is stored, an approximate value is stored. This can cause rounding issues if you're using many calculations on this number. However, it's good for storing large decimal or floating-point numbers.

BINARY_DOUBLE

The BINARY_DOUBLE data type is very similar to the BINARY_FLOAT data type:

- They both store floating-point numbers.

- They both store numbers in an approximate way, rather than the exact way that NUMBER does.

However, BINARY_FLOAT is a 32-bit precision value and BINARY_DOUBLE is a 64-bit precision value. This means it can store many more decimal places than BINARY_FLOAT. If you need to store a large decimal number, and BINARY_FLOAT cannot handle it, then BINARY_DOUBLE may be a good option.

Date Data Types

The final main category of data types is date data types. These data types are used to store anything that relates to dates and times.

DATE

The DATE data type allows you to store a date and time value. Yes, even though it's called DATE, it stores both a date and a time. It stores year, month, day, hours, minutes, and seconds. There is no DATETIME data type in Oracle SQL.

This data type is useful if you want to store date and time values, and don't need to store time zones or fractions of seconds (which the other date data types do).

One thing to remember with the DATE data type is that the default display format of this data type only shows the date (year, month, and day), and not the time. This may seem confusing, as the values only show a date and the data type is called DATE but it does include a time. We'll see some examples of this later in this book.

TIMESTAMP

The TIMESTAMP data type in Oracle is similar to the DATE data type, except you can store fractions of a second. You can store up to a precision of 9, which means 9 decimal places within a second.

TIMESTAMP allows for more granular recording of time than the DATE data type. For example, if you're recording data in a log file to see exactly when certain events happen, perhaps fractions of a second is important to you.

TIMESTAMP WITH TIME ZONE

The TIMESTAMP WITH TIME ZONE data type is like the TIMESTAMP data type, but also includes a time zone. This means it includes year, month, day, hours, minutes, seconds, fractional seconds, and time zone.

An example of a TIMESTAMP WITH TIME ZONE value is: "2018-04-21 07:41:03.152 -7:00." This is the 21st of April 2018, at 7:41:03.152 in the morning. It also indicates that the value is -7 hours from GMT/UTC.

Dealing with time zones in databases and in software can be hard. Using this data type can help with storing the data in the right way.

TIMESTAMP WITH LOCAL TIME ZONE

The TIMESTAMP WITH LOCAL TIME ZONE is similar to the TIMESTAMP WITH TIME ZONE, in that it stores a date, time, and time zone. However, when you SELECT a value from this type of column, the value is displayed in the user's time zone, instead of the database's time zone like the TIMESTAMP WITH TIME ZONE data type.

This makes it easier to convert data to a different time zone depending on the user that's viewing it. It might seem like a very specific case, but if you're working on a system that is used around the world, then this data type can be very useful.

INTERVAL YEAR TO MONTH

The date data types we have looked at so far are used to store a "point in time": a specific date and a specific time. However, there is sometimes a need to store a "period of time" such as "4 years" or "2 months." There are a few ways this could be done.

You could store it in a NUMBER data type, which represents the number of months you want to store. However, what if you also want to store years, or days? You could create a few different columns to store each value (e.g., a year column and a month column). This would mean a lot of extra columns. It would also mean you could store some invalid data.

This is where the INTERVAL data types come in. They are used to store a period of time.

The INTERVAL YEAR TO MONTH data type is used to store a number of years and months. The value is separated by a dash, so a value of "03-06" represents 3 years 6 months.

The advantages of using this data type are:

- You can store the data in a single column, and not two columns, saving time with your queries and saving space on the database.

- It ensures only valid values are allowed.

So, if you need to store a period of time involving years and months, this data type is useful.

INTERVAL DAY TO SECOND

The INTERVAL DAY TO SECOND is another data type used to store a "period of time." It allows you store days, hours, minutes, and seconds.

For example, a value of 213 days, 14 hours, 28 minutes and 17 seconds is displayed as "213 14:28:17."

Just like the INTERVAL YEAR TO MONTH data type, it allows you to store all of this information in a single column. It also ensures you store only valid data.

Other Data Types

There are a few other data types that don't fit into the text/number/date data types. The two more common data types are BLOB and CLOB.

BLOB

The BLOB data type stands for "binary large object." It's used to store unstructured binary objects.

This means it's useful for storing images or audio files that can't be stored in text columns. It stores data for a single file, but it can't store character data. It has a maximum size of 4GB.

CLOB

The CLOB data type stands for "character large object." It's similar to BLOB, but unlike BLOB it stores character data and not binary data.

It also has a maximum size of 4GB. It's useful for storing large character values, but if you want to store images or audio or other files, then a BLOB would be used.

Data Type Recommendations

You've seen all of the major data types available in Oracle SQL. How do you know which ones you should use, especially for data types that are similar?

Here are some recommendations for different data types:

- Don't use LONG or LONG RAW, as these are deprecated. Use BLOB or CLOB instead.

- VARCHAR2 can be used instead of CHAR. I don't know of a reason to use CHAR instead of VARCHAR2.

- NUMBER should be used instead of INTEGER, FLOAT, or DECIMAL.

- Consider the advantages and disadvantages of the binary number types, to decide whether or not BINARY_FLOAT or NUMBER should be used.

- Always specify the size or precision. Most data types allow you to specify this but have a default value. It's better to be specific with the size you want rather than rely on defaults.

In the next few chapters, you'll see some examples of these data types being used.

Summary

There are many different data types in Oracle SQL, which allow you to store different kinds of values. The three main groups of data types are text, number, and date. There are many data types in each of these groups, which are all used for specific reasons and have their own advantages and disadvantages.

CHAPTER 14

Creating a Table

Earlier in this book, you created a new table called `employee` and added data to it. You did this using the menu options within SQL Developer. There is another way to create tables, which we will learn about in this chapter.

Creating Tables Using SQL Code

An alternative to creating tables using the menu options is to use SQL code. The SQL code you've learned so far allows you to read data from an existing table using the `SELECT` statement. There is a range of different SQL statements that can be used, and one of them is for creating a table.

Why would you create a table using SQL code instead of using the menu options? There are a few reasons.

You may not have access to SQL Developer. While it was a simple program to download and set up, if you're working for a company on their database, you may not have access to this program. The only way to create a table would be to run an SQL statement.

Another reason is if creating a table is a step within a larger process. Multiple SQL statements can be run, one after the other, without you having to press a "Run" button for each statement. This is common when you're working as a database developer or database administrator. Using SQL code to create a table allows you to do this.

You may also be using a different program for running SQL. I recently looked into how many different IDEs exist that work on Oracle database and found over thirty! There's a subset of those that are more commonly used by companies, and using menu options may not be available in each of them. Using an SQL statement to create a table is accepted in all of these programs.

So how can you create a table using an SQL statement? You use the `CREATE TABLE` statement.

197

© Ben Brumm 2019
B. Brumm, *Beginning Oracle SQL for Oracle Database 18c*,
https://doi.org/10.1007/978-1-4842-4430-2_14

The CREATE TABLE Statement

SQL has a statement called CREATE TABLE, which lets you create a new table on the database. As with many SQL statements, it's simple to use for creating a basic table, but it has a lot of advanced options you may want to use in the future. In this chapter, we'll focus on creating a basic table.

A CREATE TABLE statement looks like this:

```
CREATE TABLE tablename (
column_1 data_type,
column_2 data_type,
...
column_n  data_type
);
```

You might have noticed it looks quite different to a SELECT statement. There are a few things to note about the CREATE TABLE statement:

- It starts with CREATE TABLE. It can be written in lower case, but in order to keep to the code standards I recommend putting SQL keywords in upper case.

- You then specify the table name. This can be up to 30 characters.

- You then have an open bracket.

- Inside the open brackets is where you specify the columns you want the table to have.

- For each column, you specify a name and a data type. A comma is used to separate each column specification.

- After adding all of the columns, you end with a closing bracket and a semicolon.

Once you write one of these statements, you run the statement, and the table is then created on the database. We'll look at a few examples of this statement.

Our Employee Table

In the earlier chapters, we created a new table called employee. We used the menu options inside SQL Developer for this, as shown in Figure 14-1.

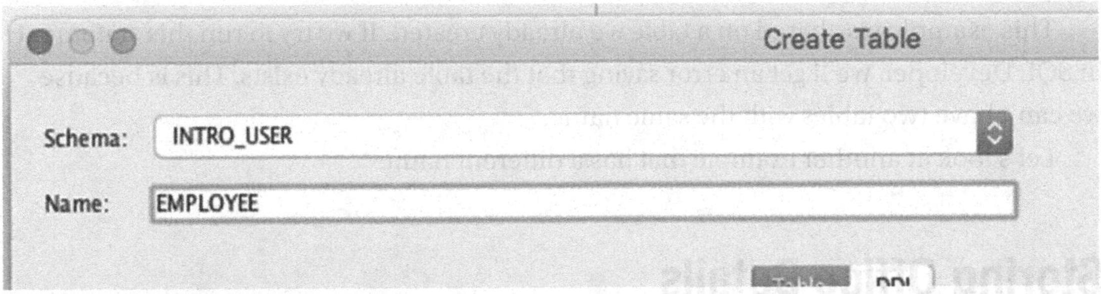

Figure 14-1. *The employee table*

What would this look like as a CREATE TABLE statement? If we wanted to create this employee table using the CREATE TABLE statement instead, it would look like this:

```
CREATE TABLE employee (
id NUMBER,
last_name VARCHAR2(20),
salary NUMBER
);
```

The table has been named employee. It's written in lowercase, as that's the standard I like to stick to (writing table names in lowercase). Oracle actually stores the table names in upper case, so according to the database you'll have the same result if you write employee or EMPLOYEE.

The first column shown is id. I also prefer to write column names in lower case. The data type of this was NUMBER, and then a comma is added because we want to add another column to this table.

The second column is last_name. This has a data type of VARCHAR2, which is a text data type that we covered in the last chapter. This VARCHAR2 has a 20 in brackets after it. This is how you specify length or size or precision for many data types, and for VARCHAR2 data types this number represents the maximum number of characters allowed in this column. So, for the last_name in this table, you can store up to 20 bytes.

Finally, we have the `salary` column, which is also a number. You can see that both the `id` and `salary` columns just say NUMBER with no value in brackets. By not including a value, a default value is used, which means the value is stored as you enter it. The default size of a NUMBER data type is 38. It's usually better to specify a size for each variable so it's clear how big you expect it to be.

This example was based on a table we already created. If we try to run this statement in SQL Developer, we'll get an error saying that the table already exists. This is because we can't have two tables with the same name.

Let's look at another example that has a different name.

Storing Office Details

Let's say we wanted to expand our database to store more information. We want to store data about the different offices that our company has, where they are located, and which employees work in them. To do this, we will create a new table.

Why can't we just store this information in the `employee` table? Let's try that and see what happens.

In SQL, you can alter existing tables to add new columns, which we will learn about in a later chapter. Let's say that we have added a new column to our `employee` table called `office`, which looks like this:

ID	LAST_NAME	SALARY	OFFICE
1	JONES	20000	
2	SMITH	35000	
3	KING	40000	
4	SIMPSON	52000	
5	ANDERSON	31000	
6	COOPER	(null)	
7	(null)	(null)	
8	SMITH	62000	
9	PATRICK	40000	

Now, you can try to add data to this table, by adding information to this office column.

ID	LAST_NAME	SALARY	OFFICE
1	JONES	20000	123 Main Street
2	SMITH	35000	45 Smith Street
3	KING	40000	Level 2, 10 Clark Street
4	SIMPSON	52000	205 Capital Road
5	ANDERSON	31000	123 Main Street
6	COOPER	(null)	12 Main Street
7	(null)	(null)	Level 2, 10 Clark Street
8	SMITH	62000	Level 1, 10 Clark Street
9	PATRICK	40000	123 Main St

This might seem OK. We store the address, and sometimes a building level, in this column. We can see some employees work in the same office as other employees.

However, look at the records with an ID of 5, 6, and 9.

ID	LAST_NAME	SALARY	OFFICE
5	ANDERSON	31000	123 Main Street
6	COOPER	(null)	12 Main Street
9	PATRICK	40000	123 Main St

The office values look similar. Are they the same? Is COOPER's office of 12 Main Street the same as ANDERSON's office of 123 Main Street and they just mistyped the street number? Is PATRICK's office the same as ANDERSON's office, but typed St instead of Street? It's easy to get confused with this kind of setup.

Another issue can arise when we update data. Let's say we have updated the office for SMITH from 45 Smith Street to be 123 Main Street.

ID	LAST_NAME	SALARY	OFFICE
1	JONES	20000	123 Main Street
2	SMITH	35000	123 Main Street
3	KING	40000	Level 2, 10 Clark Street
4	SIMPSON	52000	205 Capital Road
5	ANDERSON	31000	123 Main Street
6	COOPER	(null)	12 Main Street
7	(null)	(null)	Level 2, 10 Clark Street
8	SMITH	62000	Level 1, 10 Clark Street
9	PATRICK	40000	123 Main St

What does this mean? Does it mean that SMITH has moved from the 45 Smith Street office to the 123 Main Street office? If so, does the 45 Smith Street office still exist in the company? According to this table, it doesn't, as it's not listed in that column.

This is called a *delete anomaly* and is an issue when designing databases that should be avoided. A delete anomaly is where you update a row to refer to a different value, and all record of the previous value existing is lost. This is something we want to avoid.

Another issue that may appear is called an "update anomaly." Let's say we changed ANDERSON's office from 123 Main Street to 123 Main Street South.

ID	LAST_NAME	SALARY	OFFICE
1	JONES	20000	123 Main Street
2	SMITH	35000	123 Main Street
3	KING	40000	Level 2, 10 Clark Street
4	SIMPSON	52000	205 Capital Road
5	ANDERSON	31000	123 Main Street South
6	COOPER	(null)	12 Main Street
7	(null)	(null)	Level 2, 10 Clark Street

ID	LAST_NAME	SALARY	OFFICE
8	SMITH	62000	Level 1, 10 Clark Street
9	PATRICK	40000	123 Main St

Does this mean that ANDERSON has moved to a new office at 123 Main Street South? Or, does it mean that the 123 Main Street office no longer exists and has moved to 123 Main Street South? Or, does it mean that the city council has renamed Main Street to Main Street South, but it's actually the same office and location for the company?

We can see there are several other employees with the 123 Main Street office, which may or may not be correct. If you intended to update all occurrences of this office, but some have been missed, then there can be a problem. This is called an *update anomaly* and should be avoided.

There's an area of software development called *database design*, or *relational database design*, which introduces a process called *normalization*. This process is followed to ensure your database is structured in an efficient way to avoid these errors.

For our example, we can avoid all of these issues if we store the details of our office in a separate table. This is because we actually want to store two different things:

- A list of all offices in the company

- A record of which employees work at which offices

These are captured in two different ways.

The Office Table

Let's create our office table. We want the office table to include an ID and an address.

Our CREATE TABLE statement would look like this:

```
CREATE TABLE office (
id,
address
);
```

Before we can create this, we need to specify data types and sizes. For our ID column, this will be a whole number. We can use the NUMBER data type, and for our example we can use a size of 5. This will handle numbers from 0 to 99999, which should be enough for us.

For the address field, this will be a text field, because we want to store the street number and street name. We can use 200 characters for our example, and we will use VARCHAR2.

Our CREATE TABLE statement would then look like this:

```
CREATE TABLE office (
id NUMBER(5),
address VARCHAR2(200)
);
```

To run this statement:

1. Open SQL Developer and create a new SQL file (or use one you already have opened), like you have done in earlier chapters.

2. Enter the CREATE TABLE statement shown previously into the SQL window, as shown in Figure 14-2.

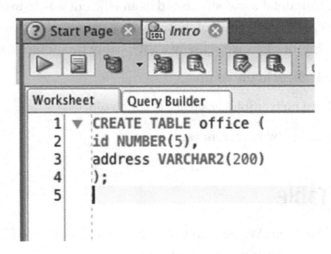

Figure 14-2. *The CREATE TABLE statement in SQL Developer*

3. Click the Run Statement button (the big green triangle) on the toolbar, as you've done when running earlier statements. Running a CREATE TABLE statement is done in the same way as a SELECT statement.

Once the statement is run, a message will appear at the bottom of the screen to let you know that the table was created successfully, as shown in Figure 14-3.

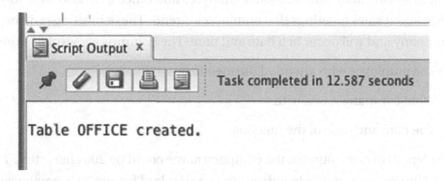

Figure 14-3. *Table successfully created*

If an error message appears, it could be for a few reasons:

- The table name is already being used by another table. The table name must be unique in the database, so if you have already created this table, you can't create it again. You'll learn how to delete tables later in this book.

- Make sure there is a comma after the id NUMBER(5) statement, as this lets the database know you want to specify a second column. If there is no comma, you'll get an error.

- Make sure there are spaces in the same places as shown, such as between CREATE and TABLE, between the name of the column (id, or address) and the data type (NUMBER or VARCHAR2).

- Make sure there is no space in VARCHAR2. It's a single word.

You have now created a second table in the database! Let's create a third table that uses different data types.

The Sales Meeting Table

In addition to storing information about employees and offices, we also want to store information about sales meetings that employees attend. These meetings will be with a certain company and will occur at a date and time. The columns we want to store are:

- The employee who attended the meeting

- What company it was with

- The date and time of the meeting

For the length of our columns, the company name could be 200 characters. The date and time value does not need a length, as it's in a standard format. Our employee name will be the same as the `employee` table, which was 20 characters.

Our `CREATE TABLE` statement will look like this:

```
CREATE TABLE sales_meeting (
id NUMBER(5),
employee VARCHAR2(200),
company VARCHAR2(200),
meeting_date DATE
);
```

Before we run this statement, there are a couple of concepts that you should know about.

Primary Key

You might have noticed that all tables we have created so far include a column called `id`, and this column has a data type of `NUMBER`. The reason for using this field is so you can identify the record in your queries.

What does this mean? Well, let's look at our `employee` table.

ID	LAST_NAME	SALARY
1	JONES	20000
2	SMITH	35000
3	KING	40000
4	SIMPSON	52000
5	ANDERSON	31000
6	COOPER	(null)
7	(null)	(null)
8	SMITH	62000
9	PATRICK	40000

This has an `id` and a `last_name` column. Let's say you wanted to find all of the information for the employee JONES. This would be simple, as you can just look up the table where `last_name` is JONES.

However, what if you needed to find the information for SMITH? You could look up the record where the `last_name` is SMITH, but there are two records with SMITH. Which one would you use? They have the same `last_name` but different `salary` values. They may also have different `offices`. There needs to be a way to uniquely identify the records in this table.

This is what the `id` column is for. It's a column that stores a unique number for the `employee` record in the table. Whenever the database or the system needs to find a particular record, it can use this ID.

The same concept can be found in many different systems:

- Your tax ID number, such as a Social Security Number (in the United States) or the Tax File Number (in Australia)

- Your e-mail address

- Any username you have when logging on to a system

- Membership or account numbers for insurance or phone or internet companies

Using this kind of ID or unique identifier is helpful because:

- There's always a way to find the record you want if you know this ID.

- Any other information on the record can change, as long as the ID is the same. For example, people can change names, but the record is still the same record.

- It's easy to search and relate to other records (which we'll learn more about in this book).

The concept of a unique identifier for each record in a table is called a *primary key*. A primary key on a table is more than just adding an ID field. Oracle (and many other databases) allow you to specify one or more columns as the primary key. This means:

- The database ensures that the values are unique. If you try to enter a value that is already used by another record, you'll get an error.

- The database will make it easier to search on this field, which we'll cover later in this book.

It's good database design to ensure that tables have a primary key. It improves the quality of your data, prevents duplicate rows, and improves the performance of your tables.

When we wrote the CREATE TABLE statement for the sales_meeting table, we asked you not to run the statement yet. This is because we wanted to add the "primary key" to this table. Let's do that now.

To add a primary key to a table, you can add the words PRIMARY KEY after the column name and data type. As you can see in the following statement, it goes after the data type but before the comma. Before you run this statement to create the table, there's another concept to explain, and another change to make to this statement.

```
CREATE TABLE sales_meeting (
id NUMBER(5) PRIMARY KEY,
employee VARCHAR2(200),
company VARCHAR2(200),
meeting_date DATE
);
```

Recording the Employee Again

Our sales_meeting table had a column called employee, which stores the last_name of the employee who is involved in the sales_meeting. Let's say our sales_meeting table would look like this:

```
ID   EMPLOYEE   COMPANY             MEETING_DATE
1    ANDERSON   ABC Construction    10 August 2018
2    SMITH      BW Signage          21 August 2018
```

You can see the first record is a meeting with ANDERSON and the company ABC Construction. The second record, however, is with SMITH. Which SMITH record? There are two employees called SMITH.

If you try to store the employee's name in this table, this can cause a few problems:

- You can't tell which employee it actually relates to if there are two records with the same name.

- If you change the employee's last name in the employee table, you have to change it here as well. If you forget, then the record in this table won't match the employee table.

- If you add an employee name to this table, then you'll need to ensure there is a record in the employee table as well, otherwise you know nothing about the employee involved in the sales meeting.

There is a solution to this issue. The solution is a concept called a "foreign key."

Foreign Key

When you are creating your sales_meeting table, you need to store information about the employee that the meeting is with. However, you don't necessarily need to store the employee's name. You just need to know which employee it was with. This can be done by referring to the record in the employee table.

This is the employee table:

```
ID   LAST_NAME   SALARY
1    JONES       20000
2    SMITH       35000
3    KING        40000
```

```
4    SIMPSON     52000
5    ANDERSON    31000
6    COOPER      (null)
7    (null)      (null)
8    SMITH       62000
9    PATRICK     40000
```

This is our `sales_meeting` table:

```
ID   EMPLOYEE    COMPANY             MEETING_DATE
1    ANDERSON    ABC Construction    10 August 2018
2    SMITH       BW Signage          21 August 2018
```

Rather than storing the employee's last name in the employee column (e.g., ANDERSON, SMITH), you can store the ID number of the employee, which is the primary key. This means:

- Our sales_meeting record will relate to only one employee, so you avoid the issue of two employees with the same last_name.

- There's always an employee record that exists. You can't store the ID of 10 because there is no employee with an ID of 10.

- If you change the last_name, you only change it in one place. The related records in the sales_meeting table don't have the last_name, so they don't need to know about the change.

So instead of storing ANDERSON and SMITH in the `sales_meeting` table, you would store their ID numbers:

```
ID   EMPLOYEE    COMPANY             MEETING_DATE
1    5           ABC Construction    10 August 2018
2    2           BW Signage          21 August 2018
```

This way you can see the first record has an `employee` value of 5, which refers to the employee ID of 5 in the `employee` table. You can also see that the second record has an `employee` value of 2, which refers to an `employee` record with the `last_name` of SMITH. It's clear which of the two SMITH records it refers to.

The concept of using a database column to store the primary key of another table is called a *foreign key*. In this example, the employee column in the sales_meeting table is a foreign key.

Just like using a primary key, a foreign key is a good database design technique, and avoids all of the issues mentioned earlier. How do we specify a foreign key when creating our table?

Currently, our CREATE TABLE statement for the sales_meeting table looks like this:

```
CREATE TABLE sales_meeting (
id NUMBER(5) PRIMARY KEY,
employee VARCHAR2(200),
company VARCHAR2(200),
meeting_date DATE
);
```

First, you need to change the data type of the employee column from a VARCHAR2 to a NUMBER type, so it matches the ID in the employee table. You can also change the name from employee to employee_id, so it's clear that it refers to the id of the employee table.

```
CREATE TABLE sales_meeting (
id NUMBER(5) PRIMARY KEY,
employee_id NUMBER(5),
company VARCHAR2(200),
meeting_date DATE
);
```

Now, you need to add some code to this to specify the foreign key. You can leave the statement the way it is, which will allow you to add the employee ID into this table. However, you want to add something called a *foreign key constraint* to actually specify that it is a foreign key and to use a few benefits of the database.

A *constraint* is something you can add to a table to specify rules around the data that can be added. This means you won't be able to add numbers to the employee_id table that don't have a record in the employee table, which improves the quality of your data.

We'll look at adding a foreign key constraint in a later chapter, because each foreign key needs a corresponding primary key, and we haven't yet added a primary key to the employee table.

The final code for creating the sales_meeting table looks like this:

```
CREATE TABLE sales_meeting (
id NUMBER(5) PRIMARY KEY,
employee_id NUMBER(5),
company VARCHAR2(200),
meeting_date DATE
);
```

You can now run this query in SQL Developer. The table should be created like it was for the office table. In a later chapter we'll learn how to get data from both tables.

Summary

Creating a table in SQL can be done using an SQL command called CREATE TABLE. Using the SQL command is helpful when you don't have access to SQL Developer, and if you run this statement as part of a larger set.

A primary key is a database feature that you can apply to a column, and it ensures that the column value is unique and identifies the row in the table. A foreign key is another database feature applied to a column, which stores the primary key of another table and prevents storing the same data twice.

CHAPTER 15

Adding Data to a Table

The database we have been working on so far has three tables: employee, office, and sales_meeting. Only one of these tables has any data in it: the employee table. Adding data to a table is a separate step to creating the table.

Earlier in the book, when you added data to the employee table, you used the menu options within SQL Developer. You did this when you set up the table, and when you added more data to the table. However, just as we learned that creating a table can be done with a statement, adding data can also be done with an SQL statement.

The reasons for using an SQL statement to add data to a table are the same as using the CREATE TABLE statement for creating a table:

- You can use it when you are using a different IDE or don't have access to SQL Developer.

- It's faster.

- It can be used as part of a larger set of steps.

In Oracle SQL, you can add data to a table using the INSERT statement.

The INSERT Statement

The INSERT statement is an SQL statement that lets you add data to a table. You specify the table, the columns, and the values you want to add, and when you run the statement the data is added to the table. The INSERT statement looks like this:

```
INSERT INTO tablename (columns) VALUES (values_to_insert);
```

It starts off with INSERT INTO, which are SQL keywords that indicate you want to insert data. You then specify the tablename, which is the table that the data is to be inserted into. Next, you specify the columns, which are the specific columns you want

213

© Ben Brumm 2019
B. Brumm, *Beginning Oracle SQL for Oracle Database 18c*,
https://doi.org/10.1007/978-1-4842-4430-2_15

to add data to. After that, you have the keyword VALUES, then inside brackets the values that you want to insert into the table.

The reason you specify the columns when inserting data into a table is because not every column might be needed. You may want to leave some columns blank. It's also used so the database knows which values are meant for each column.

When you write an INSERT statement, it often has multiple columns:

```
INSERT INTO tablename (col1, col2, col3) VALUES (val1, val2, val3);
```

You need to specify the same number of columns from the table (the first brackets) as the VALUES section (the second brackets). In this example, val1 will be added to column col1, val2 is added to column col2, and val3 is added to column col3.

Let's see an example. Let's say you wanted to add a new record to the office table. The office table had columns for the id and address. Our INSERT statement would start like this:

```
INSERT INTO office (id, address) VALUES (
```

Next, you need to specify the values to insert. We want to insert our first record, so we have an ID of 1 and an address of '123 Smith Street'. Our statement looks like this:

```
INSERT INTO office (id, address) VALUES (1, '123 Smith Street');
```

We have two columns and two values. The values are separated by a comma. The first value represents the id and the second value represents the address. The id value is a number, so it does not need to be enclosed in single quotes. The address value is a text value, so it needs to be inside single quotes.

Running an INSERT Statement

You can run this statement in the same way as any other SQL statement.

1. Open SQL developer and open a new SQL file.

2. Enter the INSERT statement mentioned earlier into the code area, as shown in Figure 15-1.

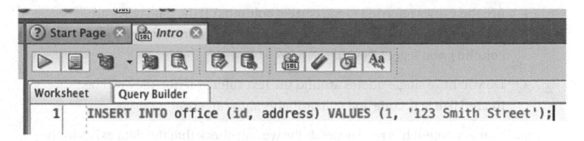

Figure 15-1. *The INSERT statement in SQL Developer*

    3.   Click the Run button.

Once the statement has run, you'll see the output of the statement at the bottom of the screen, as shown in Figure 15-2.

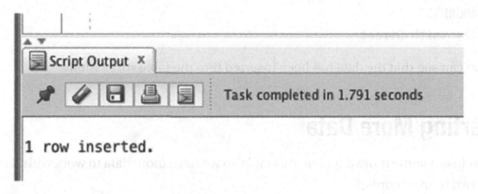

Figure 15-2. *The output of the INSERT statement*

It will display "1 row inserted." This means that the record is inserted. It won't show you what the record is; to do that, you'll need to run a SELECT statement on the table.

If you see an error message, you should check a few things in your INSERT statement:

- Is the table spelled correctly? The table name must already exist in the database, and I've encountered many errors where I have misspelled the table name slightly.

- Have you specified the same number of columns as the number of values? If the number of columns is different, you'll get an error.

- Are the values referring to the correct columns? If the data types are different (for example, you attempt to enter the address into the id column), you'll get an error.

- Do you have single quotes around the text values? If not, they will be treated like SQL code and will probably show an error.

Once your statement has run successfully, we can check that the data exists in the table. To do this, run a SELECT statement on the table:

```
SELECT *
FROM office;
```

Because we are just checking that the data exists, it's OK to use SELECT *. If you run this statement, you'll get the following results:

```
ID    ADDRESS
1     123 Smith Street
```

You can see that the data has been inserted into the table successfully.

Inserting More Data

We can insert some more data into this table so we have more data to work with. Let's insert two more records:

- 45 Main Street, with an ID of 2

- 10 Collins Road, with an ID of 3

The INSERT statements would look like this:

```
INSERT INTO office (id, address) VALUES (2, '45 Main Street');
INSERT INTO office (id, address) VALUES (3, '10 Collins Road');
```

We can run these two statements in SQL Developer. Instead of running them separately, you can run them one after the other.

1. Add these two statements into your SQL Developer window, as shown in Figure 15-3.

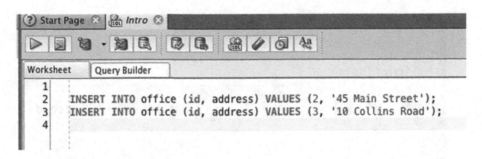

Figure 15-3. *Two INSERT statements*

2. Select both of the statements so they are highlighted, as shown in Figure 15-4.

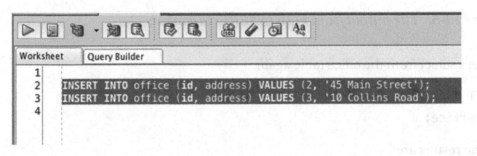

Figure 15-4. *Selecting both INSERT statements*

3. Click on the Run button. Both statements will be run, one after the other.

The output at the bottom of the screen should show two separate lines of "1 row inserted," just like Figure 15-5.

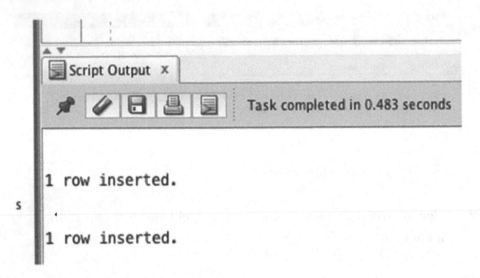

Figure 15-5. *The output from both INSERT statements*

Let's select from the office table again.

```
SELECT *
FROM office;
```

The results are:

```
ID    ADDRESS
1     123 Smith Street
2     45 Main Street
3     10 Collins Road
```

You can see that all three of the records appear in the table. Let's see some examples of inserting date values.

Inserting Date Values

Adding date values into a table requires special treatment, because the default date format can differ in parts of the world.

The Oracle database determines the date format for all dates when you install the database (Oracle Express). This is relevant because it determines how we can add date values to the database.

Let's add some data to the sales_meeting table. If you remember from the earlier chapter where you created the table, it had a few columns:

- id

- employee_id

- company

- meeting_date

Both the id and employee_id columns were numbers. The company column is a text value, and meeting_date is a date. Our INSERT statement would look like this:

```
INSERT INTO sales_meeting (id, employee_id, company, meeting_date) VALUES
(1, 5, 'ABC Construction', 'Aug 10 2018');
```

This would insert a record with an id of 1, an employee_id of 5, a company of 'ABC Construction', and a meeting_date of 'Aug 10 2018'.

However, if you try to run this statement in SQL Developer, you will likely get an error, as shown in Figure 15-6.

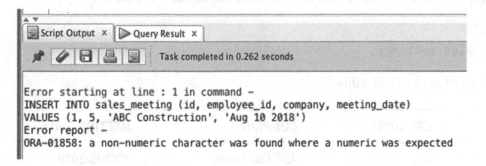

Figure 15-6. *An error message from inserting a date*

This error happens because the database does not recognize "Aug 10 2018" as a valid date. To you and me it might seem valid, but to the database it doesn't. The database needs dates in a certain format, depending on your location in the world.

However, there is an ANSI-standard way you can insert dates into the database. You can use a date literal, which is a keyword (the word "DATE") that specifies a date in a specific format of "YYYY-MM-DD". This means:

- A four-digit value for the year, followed by a dash

- Then a two-digit value for the month, followed by a dash

- Then a two-digit value for the day

So, to write the date of "Aug 10 2018" in this format, it needs to be written as DATE 2018-08-10.

Note   The default date format is set when you install the Oracle database and could be different depending on where you are in the world.

Let's try that INSERT statement again with this new format:

```
INSERT INTO sales_meeting (id, employee_id, company, meeting_date)
VALUES (1, 5, 'ABC Construction', DATE '2018-08-10');
```

If you run this statement in SQL Developer, you'll get a successful message of "1 row inserted."

You can view the data in this table by running a SELECT statement:

```
SELECT *
FROM sales_meeting;
```

The output looks like this.

ID	EMPLOYEE	COMPANY	MEETING_DATE
1	5	ABC Construction	10/AUG/2018

The meeting_date column here is a DATE data type. Oracle will display this date in a different format depending on your part of the world and your database settings. The format shown above is "DD/MON/YYYY", but your format may be "DD-MON-YYYY" or "MM/DD/YYYY", for example.

Let's insert a second record into this table, which was used in the previous chapter:

```
INSERT INTO sales_meeting (id, employee_id, company, meeting_date) VALUES
(2, 2, 'BW Signage', DATE '2018-08-21');
```

Once you run this statement, the record is in the table. You can run the SELECT query again to see the results in the table:

```
SELECT *
FROM sales_meeting;
```

ID	EMPLOYEE	COMPANY	MEETING_DATE
1	5	ABC Construction	10/AUG/2018
2	2	BW Signage	21/AUG/2018

Saving and Undoing Changes

There's a database concept that is relevant and helpful to know when making changes to your data. When you use a program on your computer, you make changes to a file and see the changes. However, these changes are not permanently stored on the file until you save the file. If you don't want to save your changes, you can exit the program without saving.

Oracle databases have a similar concept, called COMMIT and ROLLBACK. These are two keywords in Oracle SQL:

- COMMIT will save any changes you have made permanently to the database. This is similar to pressing the Save button within a word processor.

- ROLLBACK will undo all changes made to the database. This is similar to closing a word processor without saving changes.

These two statements apply to data inserted, updated, or deleted since you connected to the Oracle database or since the last time you ran one of these statements.

Why do you need to know this? Because unless you run either of these two commands, the data you just inserted using the INSERT statements will not be saved in the database. You'll get a warning if you exit SQL Developer about committing your changes, but it's good to be able to commit while you're using SQL Developer.

You can COMMIT or ROLLBACK in SQL developer in two ways: by running the statement or clicking a button inside SQL Developer. To run the statement, type the command COMMIT; into SQL Developer, as shown in Figure 15-7.

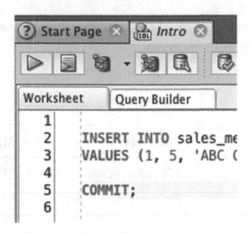

Figure 15-7. *The COMMIT command*

Then, click the Run button. The output panel should show "Commit completed."

If you want to ROLLBACK instead, enter the command ROLLBACK and click the Run button. For now, though, you just need to COMMIT and not ROLLBACK.

Alternatively, you can use the button in SQL Developer to commit. This button is a gray cylinder with a green tick and it's available on the SQL window, as shown in Figure 15-8. The ROLLBACK button is next to it.

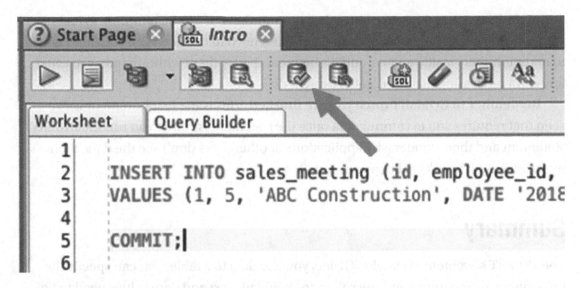

Figure 15-8. *The COMMIT button in SQL Developer*

So, once you have finished inserting data into your database tables, it's good to commit the data. You'll get asked if you exit SQL Developer, but committing the data yourself is a good habit to get into.

Best Practices for Inserting Data

You've learned how to insert data into an Oracle database in this chapter. There are some "best practices" or tips that I can suggest when doing this.

Specify the columns you are inserting. The INSERT statement lets you specify the columns in the table you're adding data to. This is the part inside the first set of parentheses:

```
INSERT INTO table (col1, col2, col3) VALUES (val1, val2, val3)
```

In SQL, this part is optional. You don't actually need to specify the columns to run an INSERT statement. If you don't specify them, the values are inserted into the order that the columns are defined in the database. This is risky, as the columns are not guaranteed to stay in the same order. If you don't specify the columns, then your INSERT statement may fail in the future. It's a good idea to always specify the columns when running an INSERT statement.

Include text and dates in quotes, but not numbers. It can be tempting to include all values inside quotes because text and date values need to be. However, you don't need to enter numbers inside quotes, and it's better to specify them without quotes to avoid any extra processing that the database might do.

Remember to COMMIT once you are finished. This is the first statement we've seen that requires you to commit data once the statement is run. If you run the INSERT statement and then wonder why applications or other users don't see the data, then it's likely because it hasn't yet been committed.

Summary

The INSERT statement in Oracle SQL lets you add data to a table. You can specify the table name, the columns, and the values to be added. Text and date values need to be inside single quotes, but numbers do not.

After inserting data, for it to be permanently saved to the database, it needs to be committed with the COMMIT command. If you decide you don't want to commit the data, you can run the ROLLBACK command to undo these changes.

CHAPTER 16

Updating and Removing Data

In the last chapter, you learned how to add data to a table. SQL allows you to make changes to data that's already in a table, and we'll learn how to do that in this chapter.

Why would you want to update data after it's been added? Perhaps you made a mistake with the data when running the INSERT statement, such as spelling a name wrong or adding the wrong date. Or perhaps part of an application makes a change and needs to update the data. Or perhaps a user of the application changes some data and wants to save it. Each of these will involve an update to the data in the database.

The good news is that you don't have to delete the record and insert it as a new record. SQL provides a command that lets you make changes to existing data.

The UPDATE Statement

There's a statement in SQL called *UPDATE*, which allows you to make changes to data that already exists in a table. The UPDATE statement works in a similar way to the SELECT and INSERT statements where you specify some keywords and some data and run the statement.

The UPDATE statement looks like this:

```
UPDATE tablename
SET col1 = val1 [, col2 = val2…]
[WHERE condition];
```

225

© Ben Brumm 2019
B. Brumm, *Beginning Oracle SQL for Oracle Database 18c*,
https://doi.org/10.1007/978-1-4842-4430-2_16

There are a few parts to this statement:

- First, we start with an UPDATE keyword, which lets the database know what statement you're running.

- We then specify the table name that contains the data you want to update. In Oracle SQL, you can only update one table at a time.

- We then have a SET keyword, which is where you specify what is being changed.

- After the SET keyword, we specify combinations of columns and values. This includes the column name, an equals sign, and the new value you want to apply to that column. You can specify multiple combinations of columns and values if you want to update more than one column in the same table.

- Finally, we have a WHERE clause, which lets you filter the table to only the rows you want to update.

The square brackets represent optional parts of the statement. For the UPDATE statement, extra columns to update are optional. The WHERE clause is also optional. This means it's possible to update every record in the table: either deliberately or accidentally!

Note   In an UPDATE statement, the WHERE clause is optional. If you don't want to update every record in your table, make sure you add a WHERE clause.

Let's take a look at some examples of the UPDATE statement.

Update to a New Value

For our first example, we're going to update the employee table. This table currently looks like this:

ID	LAST_NAME	SALARY
1	JONES	20000
2	SMITH	35000
3	KING	40000
4	SIMPSON	52000

```
5     ANDERSON    31000
6     COOPER      (null)
7     (null)      (null)
8     SMITH       62000
9     PATRICK     40000
```

Let's say that the employee KING, with an id of 3, has gotten a promotion and needs to have their salary updated. Their current salary is 40000 and their new salary is 45000.

Our UPDATE statement starts like this:

```
UPDATE employee
```

We are updating the employee table, so we've specified it here. Then we need to specify what columns and values we are updating:

```
UPDATE employee
SET salary = 45000
```

Now, how does the database known which salary we are updating? We need to specify a WHERE clause. This will include criteria that identify the record. We can do this in two ways:

- Match on the id = 3

- Match on the last_name = KING

As we learned in previous chapters, there's a chance that some data may be duplicated (such as two employees with the same last_name). For this reason, it's better to use an id or primary key column when updating individual records. In this example, both conditions will find the same record, but we will use the id column to get into the habit. So, add this to your query:

```
UPDATE employee
SET salary = 45000
WHERE id = 3;
```

Our UPDATE statement is complete. To run this, enter it into an SQL Developer window, just like the other statements we've learned so far, and click the Run button. You won't see the changes that were made to the table, but you'll see an output at the bottom of the screen that says "1 row(s) updated." This means the update was successful.

If you get an error here, ensure that your table name and column names are spelled correctly. Many times, I've gotten errors in SQL that were caused by me mistyping a table name, such as "emplyoee" instead of "employee."

You can see the changes that were made by selecting the data from the employee table:

```
SELECT *
FROM employee;
```

These are the results that are shown:

ID	LAST_NAME	SALARY
1	JONES	20000
2	SMITH	35000
3	KING	45000
4	SIMPSON	52000
5	ANDERSON	31000
6	COOPER	(null)
7	(null)	(null)
8	SMITH	62000
9	PATRICK	40000

Checking an Update Statement Before Running It

When you ran the UPDATE statement, there was no way of seeing what data was going to be updated before it happened. It might be easy to work out if you're updating a single record using an id field, but what if your WHERE clause is more complicated?

You can see what data is being updated by the UPDATE statement by running a SELECT statement with the same table and WHERE clause before running the UPDATE statement.

Look at the example you ran earlier:

```
UPDATE employee
SET salary = 45000
WHERE id = 3;
```

You can convert this to a SELECT query by selecting all columns from the employee table, using the same WHERE clause:

```
SELECT *
FROM employee
WHERE id = 3;
```

If you run the SELECT statement before running the UPDATE statement, you can see the exact record that will be impacted by the UPDATE statement. You don't need to run a SELECT statement before running the UPDATE statement, but if you want to be sure you're updating the correct records, then it's a good idea.

Update a NULL Value

Another reason to update a table is to add a value where a NULL value existed previously. In our employee table, we have a record with an id of 7 that had no last_name. You can run an UPDATE statement to add a last_name to this record. However, instead of finding this value based on the id, you'll find it based on the last_name being NULL.

Let's say our last_name value is supposed to be "ADAMS." You can update the employee table with this statement:

```
UPDATE employee
SET last_name = 'ADAMS'
WHERE last_name IS NULL;
```

In the WHERE clause, you are using IS NULL to check for records where the last_name has a NULL value. NULL values being checked with an = sign won't work in SQL. The WHERE clause is also run before the data is updated, so there is no issue with this statement looking for a NULL value and updating that value to something else.

This table only has one record with a NULL last_name. If there was more than one record with a NULL value, then this query would update all of those records. This might not be something you want to do, so it's good to be sure of your WHERE clause before you run the query.

If you run this statement, you should get a message "1 row(s) updated." You can now select the data from this table to check it has been updated:

```
SELECT *
FROM employee;
```

The results of this query are:

ID	LAST_NAME	SALARY
1	JONES	20000
2	SMITH	35000

3	KING	45000
4	SIMPSON	52000
5	ANDERSON	31000
6	COOPER	(null)
7	ADAMS	(null)
8	SMITH	62000
9	PATRICK	40000

You can see that the employee with a `last_name` of NULL was updated to "ADAMS."

Update Based on Existing Value

Sometimes you may want to update your data based on data that's already in the table. One example we'll look at is updating a salary to increase it by a certain amount.

Let's say that the employee JONES (id = 1) has been performing well and has been awarded a salary increase of 10000. There are two ways we can update this data:

- Run a query to find the current salary, write a query to update the current salary to 10000 more than what it is, and run that query.

- Or, write a query that updates the current salary to add 10000, and run that query.

The second option is preferable. We won't need to run two separate queries. We can run a single query that does this. Our UPDATE query would look like this:

```
UPDATE employee
SET salary = salary + 10000
WHERE id = 1;
```

This query is similar to the earlier queries. However, in the SET clause, it says SET salary = salary + 10000. This means "set the salary to the current salary value plus 10000." It allows you to increase the value without knowing what the existing value is.

If you run this query, you'll see the familiar message of "1 row(s) updated." You can select from the table to see what the data now looks like.

```
SELECT *
FROM employee;
```

The results of this query are:

```
ID   LAST_NAME   SALARY
1    JONES       30000
2    SMITH       35000
3    KING        45000
4    SIMPSON     52000
5    ANDERSON    31000
6    COOPER      (null)
7    ADAMS       (null)
8    SMITH       62000
9    PATRICK     40000
```

You can see that the salary for JONES is now 30000, which is 10000 more than the original 20000.

Update a Date Value

Writing and running an UPDATE statement using a date value is similar to updating text or numeric values. You should use the date literal we learned about in the previous chapter on inserting data.

This is the sales_meeting table from the earlier chapter:

```
ID   EMPLOYEE_ID   COMPANY            MEETING_DATE
1    5             ABC Construction   10/AUG/2018
2    2             BW Signage         21/AUG/2018
```

Let's say that the meeting with BW Signage needs to have the date updated from 21 August to 25 August. You can do this using an UPDATE statement:

```
UPDATE sales_meeting
SET meeting_date = DATE '2018-08-25'
WHERE id = 2;
```

In this WHERE clause, you could write it in several ways:

- Company = BW Signage, but there may be more meetings with the same company that we don't want to change.

- Meeting_date = 21 Aug 2018, but there could be other meetings on the same date

You should use id = 2 because that's the only way to guarantee that this is the only record you want to update. If you run this query, you'll get the message about 1 row being updated. To see the changes, run a SELECT statement:

```
SELECT *
FROM sales_meeting;
```

The results are:

```
ID   EMPLOYEE_ID   COMPANY            MEETING_DATE
1    5             ABC Construction   10/AUG/2018
2    2             BW Signage         25/AUG/2018
```

You can see the data has been updated with the correct date. The date format depends on your location, but it can be changed.

Viewing and Updating the Date Format

The Oracle database displays date formats in a certain way, depending on the location specified when installing the database. You can see what the format is set to, and change it, by looking at the parameters of the database. These parameters are stored in a table called nls_session_parameters:

```
SELECT * FROM nls_session_parameters
WHERE parameter = 'NLS_DATE_FORMAT';
```

Your output would look similar to this:

```
PARAMETER          VALUE
NLS_DATE_FORMAT    DD/MON/RRRR
```

The value column specifies the format that the date is shown in. In this example, "DD" stands for a two-digit day, "MON" is a three-letter month, and "RRRR" is a four-digit year. If you run this query, you may get a different value, such as "DD-MON-RRRR" or "MM-DD-RRRR."

You can update your date format to a format you prefer by using the ALTER SESSION command. Simply change the date format in this command to one you prefer, and run it:

```
ALTER SESSION SET NLS_DATE_FORMAT = 'YYYY/MM/DD';
```

This will update the format to show the dates as a year/month/day format, such as 2018/08/25 for 25th August 2018.

Update Two Columns

The UPDATE statement in SQL lets you update more than one column. There may be situations where this is needed, such as developing an application where more than one field on a web page can be changed.

To do this, add your second and further columns to the SET clause separated by a comma. All of the updates will be applied to the rows that match the WHERE clause. For example, to update the sales_meeting table to change the employee and date of the meeting with BW Signage, you can run this query:

```
UPDATE sales_meeting
SET employee_id = 6, meeting_date = DATE '2018-08-22'
WHERE id = 2;
```

When you run this statement, you'll see that one row was updated. It doesn't tell you how many columns were updated. However, just like the earlier examples, you can run a SELECT statement to see the changes.

```
SELECT *
FROM sales_meeting;
```

ID	EMPLOYEE_ID	COMPANY	MEETING_DATE
1	5	ABC Construction	10/AUG/2018
2	6	BW Signage	22/AUG/2018

The update was made to both columns that meet the WHERE clause. If you want to update separate columns based on different criteria, you'll have to write separate UPDATE statements.

Update Without WHERE Clause

Earlier in this chapter, I mentioned that the WHERE clause is optional in an UPDATE statement. This means it's possible to update every record in the table, either deliberately or accidentally. Let's see what happens when we do this.

First, commit any changes you have already made by clicking on the Commit button in SQL Developer or running a COMMIT command in the SQL window. This will ensure you can rollback any commands you run from now on, and not lose anything you've done in this chapter.

Now, let's run an UPDATE statement to update the salary value in the employee table. We want this to be updated where the salary is NULL, but let's say you forget to add the WHERE clause:

```
UPDATE employee
SET salary = 25000;
```

When you run this query, you'll get a message of "9 row(s) updated." Oh no! Nine rows! You only wanted to update one or two! You can run a SELECT query on the table and see what has changed:

```
SELECT *
FROM employee;
```

ID	LAST_NAME	SALARY
1	JONES	25000
2	SMITH	25000
3	KING	25000
4	SIMPSON	25000
5	ANDERSON	25000
6	COOPER	25000
7	(null)	25000
8	SMITH	25000
9	PATRICK	25000

You can see that every record in the table has been updated to the same `salary`. The information for each employee's `salary` has been lost.

If you didn't mean to do this, that's OK. You can undo these changes by running a `ROLLBACK` command or clicking the Rollback button in SQL Developer. A message should appear that says "Rollback successful."

You can then run a `SELECT` command to see the data in the employee table again.

```
SELECT *
FROM employee;
```

ID	LAST_NAME	SALARY
1	JONES	30000
2	SMITH	35000
3	KING	45000
4	SIMPSON	52000
5	ANDERSON	31000
6	COOPER	(null)
7	(null)	(null)
8	SMITH	62000
9	PATRICK	40000

So, be careful with your UPDATE statements. Make sure you have a WHERE clause on them unless you're very sure you want to update every record in the table! This might be OK for smaller tables such as this, but when you're working with tables that contain thousands or millions of records, it can be problematic!

Removing Data from a Table

There may be a time you want to delete data from a table. Perhaps it's while you're learning SQL and have made a mistake when inserting data, or it's to remove data that is no longer needed. In SQL, there is a way to do that, and it involves using the DELETE statement.

The DELETE statement allows you to delete data from a table. It works similar to the update statement, where you specify the table name and the criteria for the records that will be deleted. The DELETE statement looks like this:

```
DELETE FROM tablename
[WHERE condition];
```

The statement starts with DELETE FROM, and then you mention the table name to delete the data from. You then can specify a WHERE clause. This WHERE clause is used to identify which records you want to delete.

Just like the UPDATE statement, the WHERE clause on the DELETE statement is optional. This means it's easy to delete all of the records in your table if you're not careful! Before running a DELETE statement, make sure you have a WHERE clause unless you really want to delete all the records in the table.

Note: The WHERE clause on a DELETE statement is optional. If you exclude it, all records in the table will be deleted.

Deleting a Record

Let's delete a record from the office table. The office table currently looks like this.

ID	ADDRESS
1	123 Smith Street
2	45 Main Street
3	10 Collins Road

We want to delete the record for "10 Collins Road" from this table. To do that, you can write a statement like this:

```
DELETE FROM office
WHERE address = '10 Collins Road';
```

This will find all records in the office table that have an address of "10 Collins Road" and delete them from the table.

If you run this statement in SQL Developer, the output panel at the bottom of the screen will show "1 row deleted." Just like the INSERT and UPDATE statements, the DELETE statement doesn't show you what records were deleted.

You can run a SELECT statement on the table to see what the table looks like after the DELETE statement:

```
SELECT *
FROM office;
```

ID	ADDRESS
1	123 Smith Street
2	45 Main Street

You can see the record for "10 Collins Road" is no longer in the table.

When you added data with the INSERT statement or updated data with the UPDATE statement, the data wasn't permanently saved in the database until you either ran a COMMIT statement to save it or a ROLLBACK statement to undo it. The same functionality applies to a DELETE statement: the data is not permanently deleted until you run a COMMIT statement or undo the delete with a ROLLBACK.

We want to commit this statement, so run a COMMIT statement or click on the COMMIT button to save your changes.

Check What Records Will Be Deleted

The DELETE statement doesn't tell you what records will be deleted before you run the statement. There's no "Are you sure?" dialog box that appears, asking you to confirm these records.

However, you can make a slight change to your DELETE statement to see what records are impacted before you run it. You can simply change the DELETE to a SELECT *.

For example, your statement might look like this:

```
DELETE FROM office
WHERE address = '10 Collins Road';
```

To see what records will be deleted before you run the DELETE statement, replace the word DELETE with SELECT *.

```
SELECT *
FROM office
WHERE address = '10 Collins Road';
```

237

You can run this SELECT query to see the records that meet the WHERE clause criteria. Changing this statement back to a DELETE will then delete those records. This is helpful with simple queries like this and even queries with more complicated WHERE clauses.

Delete All Records in a Table

If you want to delete all records in a table, you can also use the DELETE statement. This is helpful for resetting a table or removing all of its data, so you can reinsert it.

To delete all records in a table, write a DELETE statement that has no WHERE clause.

```
DELETE FROM office;
```

This will delete all records in the table. You can also have the same effect by running a DELETE statement that has a WHERE clause that meets all criteria. For our example, these queries will delete all data:

```
DELETE FROM office
WHERE id >= 1;
```

```
DELETE FROM office
WHERE address IS NOT NULL;
```

You can run these queries, and all records will be removed from your table. If you want to insert the records again, you can run the INSERT statements from the earlier chapter.

Summary

The UPDATE statement in SQL allows you to update data that already exists in a table. You don't need to remove and reinsert the data to correct it. You can update one or many columns in a table that meet certain criteria using a WHERE clause, which works in the same way as a SELECT statement.

You can remove records from a table using the DELETE statement. This statement has an optional WHERE clause that lets you specify which records to delete, and if you leave this out, all records are deleted.

CHAPTER 17

Updating or Deleting a Table

You've learned how to work with tables and data in the last few chapters. Specifically, you've learned how to:

- Create a table
- Add data to a table
- Update data in a table
- Delete data from a table

There are two more operations relating to tables that you'll learn about: how to update the structure of a table, and how to delete a table.

Why Update the Structure of a Table?

In SQL, you can update the structure of your table. This means you can add or remove columns, rename columns, rename tables, change data types of columns, and more. Why would you want to do this? There are a few reasons.

In the world of software development, once something is developed, there is no guarantee it will stay that way forever. This applies to an application as a whole, all the way down to the code and the tables that it works with.

You may need to alter a table to add a new column to capture some more information. This wasn't known about when you created the table originally, as it's a new request.

Another scenario is if a column was created but needs to be renamed for some reason, such as matching with another table or to reflect what it's really used for.

© Ben Brumm 2019
B. Brumm, *Beginning Oracle SQL for Oracle Database 18c*,
https://doi.org/10.1007/978-1-4842-4430-2_17

Why wouldn't you just delete the table and recreate it? Sometimes that's easier, but most of the time it's easier to alter the table. This is because you don't always have the SQL to create the table, and if you remove the table you'll lose all of the data inside it.

We'll go through some examples for making changes to tables to demonstrate how this is done.

The ALTER TABLE Statement

The way to make changes to the structure of a table is to use a statement called ALTER TABLE. This will alter the structure of the table, as opposed to the UPDATE statement, which changes the data inside the table.

There are quite a few things that the ALTER TABLE statement can do:

- Add one or more columns to a table

- Change the data type of a column

- Add a constraint to a column (such as a primary key or a foreign key)

- Remove a column from a table

- Rename a column

- Rename a table

The ALTER TABLE statement looks like this:

```
ALTER TABLE table_name alter_table_clause;
```

This includes a few things:

- It starts with ALTER TABLE.

- You then specify the name of the table you want to alter.

- Finally, you specify an alter_table_clause. This describes the changes you are making.

Let's take a look at some examples of altering a table.

Example: Adding a Column

You can add a new column to an existing table using the ALTER TABLE statement. This type of statement would look like this:

```
ALTER TABLE table_name
ADD column_name column_definition;
```

This includes the name of the table, the name of the new column, and the details of the new column you want to add such as the data type.

Let's say you want to add a new column for the employee's job title to the employee table. This is a text value, and 100 characters should be enough to capture it. Your ALTER TABLE statement would look like this:

```
ALTER TABLE employee
ADD job_title VARCHAR2(100);
```

This statement will add a new column called job_title to the employee table, with a data type of VARCHAR2 and a maximum size of 100 bytes. The names of columns have a limit of 128 bytes (as of version 12.2). While a longer column name might be more descriptive, there's a balance between having a column name that's descriptive enough without being too long.

To run this statement, simply enter it into an SQL Developer window as you've been doing for other statements and click the Run button. You'll get a message in the output panel that says, "Table EMPLOYEE altered."

If you add a new column to a table with data in it already, what will the values in this column be? Let's find out. You can see what's in the table, including your new column, by running a SELECT statement:

```
SELECT *
FROM employee;
```

Your table should look something like this, depending on if you ran the UPDATE statements in previous chapters or not:

ID	LAST_NAME	SALARY	JOB_TITLE
1	JONES	30000	(null)
2	SMITH	35000	(null)
3	KING	45000	(null)
4	SIMPSON	52000	(null)
5	ANDERSON	31000	(null)
6	COOPER	(null)	(null)
7	ADAMS	(null)	(null)
8	SMITH	62000	(null)
9	PATRICK	40000	(null)

The new job_title column has a value of NULL for every record. This is because it's not possible to know what the value would be for each record when we add the column, so it is set to NULL. You can run an UPDATE statement to update existing records with a new job_title value.

Example: Change a Data Type

Another thing you can do with the ALTER TABLE statement is to change the data type of a column. This is useful for situations such as:

- You need to make a column larger, such as increasing the size of a NUMBER or VARCHAR2 field.

- You are changing a column from a text value to a number value, as it is going to refer to a primary key in another table.

- You need to capture additional parts of a date and time value.

Changing a data type of a column with data already in it may cause issues, so it's something to be careful with. Depending on the change you make, the data may be kept, or you may get an error. If you do want to change the data type of a column, your statement would look like this:

```
ALTER TABLE table_name
MODIFY column_name data_type;
```

As an example, if you want to change the `job_title` column from a `VARCHAR2(100)` to an `NVARCHAR2(250)`, your statement would look like this:

```
ALTER TABLE employee
MODIFY job_title NVARCHAR2(250);
```

You only need to specify the new data type, not the old data type. If you run this statement on your database in SQL Developer, you'll get a "Table EMPLOYEE altered" message.

Example: Add a Primary Key

In an earlier chapter, we explained the concept of a primary key (one or more columns in a table that are used to uniquely identify a row). You added a primary key for the `sales_meeting` table when you created it. You can also use the `ALTER TABLE` statement to add a primary key to a table that already exists.

The `ALTER TABLE` statement to add a primary key would look like this:

```
ALTER TABLE table_name
ADD CONSTRAINT constraint_name constraint_type;
```

This statement uses the word "*constraint.*" A constraint is a type of object in the database that is used to apply rules to columns in a table. A primary key is a type of constraint. The rules that apply to a primary key are:

- It must be unique.

- It cannot contain any NULL values.

- There can only be one primary key per table.

- It can apply to one or more columns.

Our employee table does not have a primary key, but you can add one now. The statement to do this would be:

```
ALTER TABLE employee
ADD CONSTRAINT pk_emp_id PRIMARY KEY (id);
```

This statement includes:

- The ALTER TABLE employee to identify which table is being changed

- ADD CONSTRAINT to specify what is being added on the table

- The constraint name of "pk_emp_id," which is a name for the new constraint

- PRIMARY KEY, which specifies that this is a primary key constraint

- The column name id, which means the id column on the employee table is the primary key

Why did we give the primary key a name? The primary key is something that is stored on the database, and therefore it needs a name. When you create a table, you can add the words PRIMARY KEY after the column that you want to be the primary key without specifying the name of the primary key constraint. However, Oracle will automatically set the name of the primary key when it is created, and it will be a long combination of letters and numbers. Using your own name makes it easier to identify in the future.

The primary key name that I used in this example is pk_emp_id. I like to follow a standard naming format when naming constraints, such as primary keys. This means you can easily know what it is just by looking at the name. This naming format includes:

- The type of constraint in the first two letters ("pk"), then an underscore

- An abbreviated name of the table ("emp" is short for employee), then an underscore

- The name of the column, possibly abbreviated if it's a long name (the id column)

- The name I used is pk_emp_id, which means it's a primary key on the employee table using the id column.

If you haven't already, you should run this ALTER TABLE statement on the database. You'll need it for the next example.

Example: Add a Foreign Key

A foreign key is one or more columns that refer to a primary key in another table. Foreign keys are a part of a good database design. Oracle allows you to add foreign key constraints, which enforce the rules of a foreign key, ensuring that a record exists in the table that is being referred to.

For example, our `sales_meeting` table has an `employee_id` column, and looks like this:

```
ID   EMPLOYEE_ID   COMPANY            MEETING_DATE
1    5             ABC Construction   10/AUG/2018
2    2             BW Signage         21/AUG/2018
```

The `employee_id` column is the foreign key, and it refers to the employee table's id column. We can use the `ALTER TABLE` command to add a foreign key constraint to this table:

```
ALTER TABLE sales_meeting
ADD CONSTRAINT fk_sm_empid FOREIGN KEY (employee_id) REFERENCES
employee(id);
```

This statement includes:

- ALTER TABLE sales_meeting to identify the table we are altering

- ADD CONSTRAINT fk_sm_emp_id, which gives the new constraint a name

- FOREIGN KEY (employee_id) means it is a foreign key constraint, and the employee_id is the column in this table that it applies to.

- REFERENCES employee (id) means that the column in this table refers to the id column in the employee table.

If you run this statement, you'll get the message "Table SALES_MEETING altered." This means the foreign key has been applied to this table. It ensures:

The `employee_id` in the `sales_meeting` table matches a record in the employee's `id` column. If you add a `sales_meeting` for `employee_id` 15, but no employee record exists with that `id`, you'll get an error.

Employee records that have a related `sales_meeting` can't be deleted. A setting can be changed to allow them to be deleted, but by default they can't be. You can't delete the employee with an `id` of 5 as they have a `sales_meeting` record.

If you run this statement and the referring table (the `employee` table in this example) does not have a primary key on the `id` column, you'll get this error message:

```
Error starting at line : 21 in command -
ALTER TABLE sales_meeting
ADD CONSTRAINT fk_sm_empid FOREIGN KEY (employee_id) REFERENCES
employee(id)
Error report -
ORA-02270: no matching unique or primary key for this column-list
02270. 00000 -  "no matching unique or primary key for this column-list"
*Cause:    A REFERENCES clause in a CREATE/ALTER TABLE statement
           gives a column-list for which there is no matching unique or
           primary key constraint in the referenced table.
*Action:   Find the correct column names using the ALL_CONS_COLUMNS
           catalog view
```

This means that the `employee` table does not have a primary key on the `id` column.

Example: Rename a Column

To rename a column in a table, you can use the `ALTER TABLE` statement. The statement looks like this:

```
ALTER TABLE table_name
RENAME COLUMN column_name TO new_column_name;
```

Let's say you wanted to rename our new column from `job_title` to `position_title`. The statement to do this would be:

```
ALTER TABLE employee
RENAME COLUMN job_title TO position_title;
```

If you run this statement, you'll get the "Table EMPLOYEE altered" just like earlier examples. You can also see the change has been applied by running a SELECT statement on the employee table:

```
SELECT *
FROM employee;
```

ID	LAST_NAME	SALARY	POSITION_TITLE
1	JONES	30000	(null)
2	SMITH	35000	(null)
3	KING	45000	(null)
4	SIMPSON	52000	(null)
5	ANDERSON	31000	(null)
6	COOPER	(null)	(null)
7	ADAMS	(null)	(null)
8	SMITH	62000	(null)
9	PATRICK	40000	(null)

None of the values in the column have been changed with this statement.

Example: Remove a Column

To remove a column from a table, you can also use the ALTER TABLE statement:

```
ALTER TABLE table_name
DROP [COLUMN] column_name
[CASCADE CONSTRAINTS];
```

There are a few things to note about this statement:

- It uses the DROP keyword, which is the word used when removing objects from the database.

- The word COLUMN is optional. If you omit the word COLUMN, the column names must be within brackets.

- The words CASCADE CONSTRAINTS are optional, and we'll cover what this means shortly.

Let's remove the new column on the employee table, which is called position_title. To do this, our statement would be:

```
ALTER TABLE employee
DROP COLUMN position_title;
```

Alternatively, this statement would also work:

```
ALTER TABLE employee
DROP (position_title);
```

If you run either of these statements, the column will be removed from the table. You can confirm this by running a SELECT statement:

```
SELECT *
FROM employee;
```

ID	LAST_NAME	SALARY
1	JONES	30000
2	SMITH	35000
3	KING	45000
4	SIMPSON	52000
5	ANDERSON	31000
6	COOPER	(null)
7	ADAMS	(null)
8	SMITH	62000
9	PATRICK	40000

What does CASCADE CONSTRAINTS mean? If you try to drop a column from a table that has constraints applied, such as the employee_id column on the sales_meeting table, you'll get an error saying you can't remove a column that has constraints. To avoid this error if you want to remove the column and any constraints, you can specify CASCADE CONSTRAINTS. This means the column and any constraints will be removed.

Example: Rename a Table

The last operation we will look at for the ALTER TABLE statement is renaming a table. You may want to rename a table if there's a better name for the table, or if you are making changes to the software that require the table name to be changed.

To do this, the ALTER TABLE statement would look like this:

```
ALTER TABLE table_name
RENAME TO new_table_name;
```

Let's say the company for which we are creating our database has determined that the meetings with customers should represent more than just sales. This means that we should rename our sales_meeting table to something more descriptive, such as customer_meeting.

Your ALTER TABLE statement would look like this:

```
ALTER TABLE sales_meeting
RENAME TO customer_meeting;
```

When you run this statement, the table name will be updated on the database. If you try to run a SELECT statement on the old table name, you'll get an error that says the table does not exist. If you run a SELECT statement on the new table name, you'll see the results from the table.

Removing a Table with DROP TABLE

So far in this chapter you have learned how to make changes to a table and its columns. There's one thing we haven't looked at yet, and that is removing a table from the database.

You may want to remove a table if you don't need it anymore. It's better to remove tables that aren't used, rather than leave them in the database, because removing them will save space on the database and will cause less confusion for others who need to write queries on the database.

Removing a table from the database is called "*dropping*" a table. The word drop is used to describe the process of deleting objects from the database, and a table is a type of object.

The DROP TABLE statement is used to drop a table, and it looks like this:

```
DROP TABLE table_name;
```

It's a short statement, and the only thing you need to do is add the table name. For example, let's say you need to remove the office table. To do this, your statement would be:

```
DROP TABLE office;
```

If you run this statement, the table will be deleted from the database. If you want to recreate the table, you can use the CREATE TABLE statement mentioned in the earlier chapter.

Note   Both the ALTER TABLE and DROP TABLE automatically perform a COMMIT, which means you can't undo the statement by running a ROLLBACK.

Summary

A lot of adjustments can be made to existing tables using the ALTER TABLE statement, such as adding, removing, and dropping columns, and renaming the table. Constraints such as primary keys and foreign keys can also be added to existing tables using the ALTER TABLE statement. Tables can be removed from the database with the DROP TABLE statement.

PART IV

Joining Tables

CHAPTER 18

Inner Join

Earlier in this book, we learned what a database was, and that it had several advantages over other ways of storing data. In this chapter, we'll learn how to make the most of one of those advantages: the ability to view data from multiple tables at once.

Multiple Tables

In earlier chapters we created an employee table to store information about employees. We then created an `office` table and a `sales_meeting` table. The `sales_meeting` table was then renamed to `customer_meeting`. There were several reasons for creating these other two tables:

- Ensure data is only stored in one place
- Improve the quality of the data we store
- Save time when making changes to the data

Our tables are shown below.

This is the employee table:

```
ID   LAST_NAME   SALARY    JOB_TITLE
1    JONES       30000     (null)
2    SMITH       35000     (null)
3    KING        45000     (null)
4    SIMPSON     52000     (null)
5    ANDERSON    31000     (null)
6    COOPER      (null)    (null)
7    (null)      (null)    (null)
8    SMITH       62000     (null)
9    PATRICK     40000     (null)
```

253

© Ben Brumm 2019
B. Brumm, *Beginning Oracle SQL for Oracle Database 18c*,
https://doi.org/10.1007/978-1-4842-4430-2_18

This is the office table:

ID	ADDRESS
1	123 Smith Street
2	45 Main Street
3	10 Collins Road

This is the customer_meeting table:

ID	EMPLOYEE_ID	COMPANY	MEETING_DATE
1	5	ABC Construction	10/Aug/2018
2	2	BW Signage	21/Aug/2018

You've seen some SELECT queries that show you all of the records in the employee table, or all of the records in the office table, or all of the records in the customer_meeting table. What if you want to see a list of employees and the customer_meeting records that they are related to? You could write separate queries to get this data and use your application code to link the data together.

However, having your application code match up related records is not very efficient and may result in quite a bit of code. One of the strengths of databases and the SQL language is being able to process data from multiple tables. The feature of SQL that allows you to do so is called a *join*.

What is a Join?

A join is a feature of SQL that allows you to view the columns from two or more tables in a single query. Data in a database is stored in separate tables, where each table stores a certain type of information. A join allows you to write a query that gets information from two or more tables and view the columns in a single set of results. Joins are often written in SELECT queries, but can also be done in other queries such as an UPDATE.

In SQL, you can add a join by specifying a keyword in your query. There are several different types of joins, each of which has their own keyword. We'll learn about these types of joins later in this book. For now, we'll start with a simple join.

A join in SQL involves a few things:

- Two tables

- A JOIN keyword

- Conditions that specify how the two tables are joined

The SQL looks like this:

```
SELECT columns
FROM table1
JOIN table2 ON criteria;
```

The two tables are table1 and table2, for which you can substitute the two tables you want to use in your query. The JOIN keyword specifies that you are joining the two tables together for your query. The ON keyword lets you specify the criteria, which is how the tables are joined.

An Example of a Join

Let's take a look at an example. Let's say you need to show the customer_meeting data, such as the meeting date and company name, along with the name of each employee who is attending a meeting.

The employee names are available in the employee table, and the sales meeting data is in the customer_meeting table. You need to write a query to show data from two tables.

First, you can start with the columns. Let's show all of the columns from the customer_meeting table:

```
SELECT id, employee_id, company, meeting_date
FROM customer_meeting;
```

You also want to see the names of the employees. Let's add in that column:

```
SELECT id, employee_id, company, meeting_date, last_name
FROM customer_meeting;
```

If you run this query as it is, you'll get an error. You'll get an error because there is no last_name column in the customer_meeting table. You need to include the employee table in your query, which is done using a join.

```
SELECT id, employee_id, company, meeting_date, last_name
FROM customer_meeting
JOIN employee
```

You'll need to do more than just specify JOIN employee in the query. The keyword JOIN says that we want to get data from the customer_meeting and the employee tables. But how does the Oracle database know which employee is related to which customer_meeting? How do *you* know?

This is where foreign keys are used. In an earlier chapter, we explained what a foreign key was and added them to our tables. A foreign key is a column in one table that refers to the primary key in another table. Foreign keys are mainly used to define how two tables are related, which is exactly what we need to know right now.

In the customer_meeting table, there is a column called employee_id. This column refers to the id in the employee table. Referring to the data in the employee_id column is how we can join the two tables together. The query needs to say that the records are related if the customer_meeting's employee_id column matches the employee's id column

You can update your query to include this criterion:

```
SELECT id, employee_id, company, meeting_date, last_name
FROM customer_meeting
JOIN employee ON customer_meeting.employee_id = employee.id;
```

The criterion of "the records are related if the customer_meeting's employee_id column matches the employee's id column" is written as ON customer_meeting. employee_id = employee.id. The line that has the JOIN keyword on it is called the *join clause*, and the join criteria always specifies two columns with an operator (such as "=") in the middle.

This query will show the customer_meeting information, along with the last_name column of the employee, in the same result set. Let's run the query.

```
ORA-00918: column ambiguously defined
00918. 00000 -  "column ambiguously defined"
*Cause:
*Action:
Error at Line: 1 Column: 8
```

If you run this query, you'll get an error about a "column ambiguously defined." What does this mean? It means that the id column mentioned in the SELECT clause could come from either the customer_meeting table or the employee table, and the database doesn't know which one you want, so it displays an error. It's unclear, or ambiguous, which column is needed.

You can resolve this error by specifying the table that the column comes from. You can do this by adding the table name and a period before the column name:

```
SELECT customer_meeting.id, employee_id, company, meeting_date, last_name
FROM customer_meeting
JOIN employee ON customer_meeting.employee_id = employee.id;
```

If you run the query now, you should get some results:

ID	EMPLOYEE_ID	COMPANY	MEETING_DATE	LAST_NAME
1	5	ABC Construction	10/Aug/2018	ANDERSON
2	2	BW Signage	21/Aug/2018	SMITH

Congratulations! You've just written and run your first SQL query that joins two tables together!

Joins, Formatting, and Table Aliases

In the earlier example, we added the customer_meeting table name to the id column so it was clear which column we meant in the SELECT clause. This meant that one column had the table name specified, but the others did not. The query ran, but looking at the query, it may not be easy to know which table each column comes from.

```
SELECT customer_meeting.id, employee_id, company, meeting_date, last_name
FROM customer_meeting
JOIN employee ON customer_meeting.employee_id = employee.id;
```

There is a way you can improve the query. You can specify each table name along with the column name. Adding the table name is quite a lot of code to write, but the added code makes it clear which column comes from which table. For example:

```
SELECT customer_meeting.id, customer_meeting.employee_id, customer_meeting.
company, customer_meeting.meeting_date, employee.last_name
FROM customer_meeting
JOIN employee ON customer_meeting.employee_id = employee.id;
```

Another thing to note is the formatting. When reading this query in the book, it may be easy to read. However, if we write the query in an IDE such as SQL Developer, the SELECT clause extends far to the right, as shown in Figure 18-1.

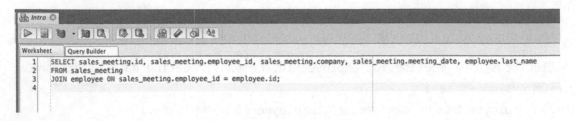

Figure 18-1. *A query that has a long line*

Having the query extend far to the right makes the query hard to read, and you may need to scroll to the right to see the rest of the query. The good news is that SQL does not treat white space, such as new lines and spaces, any differently. This means that it's commonly preferred to have each column in the SELECT clause on its own line, as in:

```
SELECT
customer_meeting.id,
customer_meeting.employee_id,
customer_meeting.company,
customer_meeting.meeting_date,
employee.last_name
FROM customer_meeting
JOIN employee ON customer_meeting.employee_id = employee.id;
```

Writing a query like this takes up more lines than normal. However, it makes it easier to read the list of columns that are included. It also makes it easier to maintain, as you can add and remove columns easier. You also don't need to scroll left and right in SQL Developer. Figure 18-2 shows how the query fits the window more nicely.

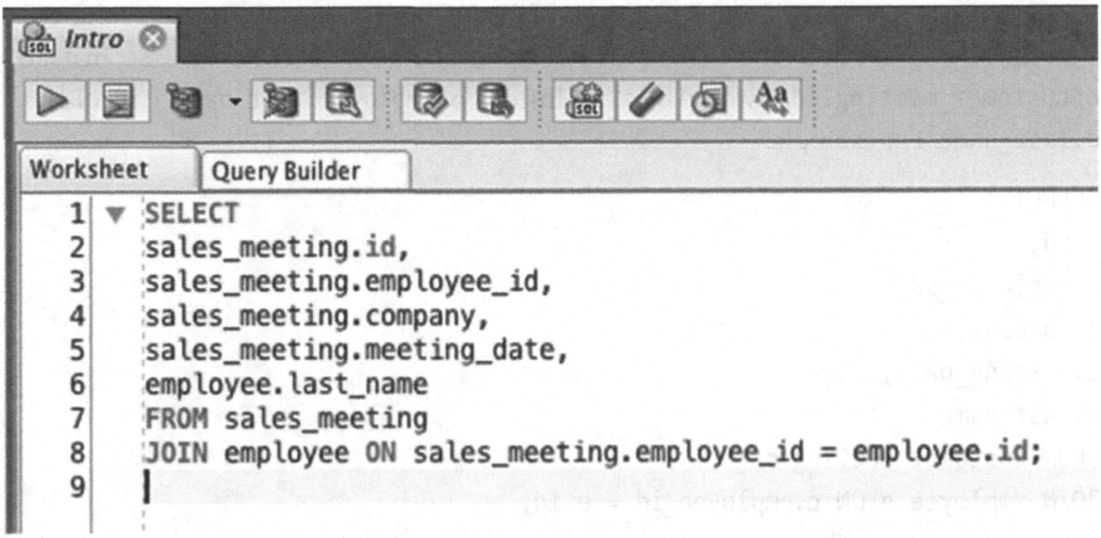

```
 1 ▼  SELECT
 2      sales_meeting.id,
 3      sales_meeting.employee_id,
 4      sales_meeting.company,
 5      sales_meeting.meeting_date,
 6      employee.last_name
 7      FROM sales_meeting
 8      JOIN employee ON sales_meeting.employee_id = employee.id;
 9
```

Figure 18-2. *The same query on separate lines*

There is one more improvement you can make to our query. Earlier in this book we learned about table aliases, which are names you can give to your tables in a query. A great place to use them is in queries that have joins.

You can apply table aliases to both the customer_meeting table and the employee table. For example, you can give the customer_meeting table an alias of "s" and the employee table an alias of "e". Here's the version of the query showing how to alias the table names as I've just described:

```
SELECT
customer_meeting.id,
customer_meeting.employee_id,
customer_meeting.company,
customer_meeting.meeting_date,
employee.last_name
FROM customer_meeting s
JOIN employee e ON customer_meeting.employee_id = employee.id;
```

The next step is to replace the mentions of the full table name next to each column with the alias. You can do this in both the join criteria and the SELECT clause. So, instead of `customer_meeting.id`, it would be `c.id`. Instead of `employee.last_name`, it would be `e.last_name`. For example:

```
SELECT
c.id,
c.employee_id,
c.company,
c.meeting_date,
e.last_name
FROM customer_meeting c
JOIN employee e ON c.employee_id = e.id;
```

This query is much smaller and easier to write than the earlier query. It's also clear which table each column comes from, as you can see that the c table is `customer_meeting` and the e table is `employee`. It also avoids the ambiguous column error we saw earlier.

If you run this query in SQL Developer, you'll get these results:

ID	EMPLOYEE_ID	COMPANY	MEETING_DATE	LAST_NAME
1	5	ABC Construction	10/Aug/2018	ANDERSON
2	2	BW Signage	21/Aug/2018	SMITH

You see the same results as earlier, but the query is a lot easier to read and write. Just to recap, after writing a query with a join, it's a good idea to:

- Specify the columns in the SELECT clause on separate lines

- Add table aliases, and refer to those aliases in the JOIN criteria and the SELECT clause

An INNER JOIN

There are several different types of joins in SQL. The join type we just saw is an *inner join*. This means that the query we wrote only returns results that are related in both tables. The results did not include:

- Any customer_meetings that did not have an employee record (there were none in the table anyway)

- Any employees that did not have a sales meeting

An inner join only returns results that match in both tables. Your SELECT query could have also used the INNER JOIN keyword instead of the JOIN keyword. Following is the same query, because JOIN is the same as INNER JOIN in Oracle SQL.

```
SELECT
c.id,
c.employee_id,
c.company,
c.meeting_date,
e.last_name
FROM customer_meeting c
INNER JOIN employee e ON c.employee_id = e.id;
```

So, if INNER is an optional keyword, should you specify it? I recommend that you do, because it makes it clear that you are asking for an INNER JOIN and not one of the other join types we'll cover in a later chapter. But it's up to you, as the query will still run if the INNER keyword is not used.

Let's add in a new record into the customer_meeting table, without an employee, to confirm the behavior of an INNER JOIN.

```
INSERT INTO customer_meeting (id, employee_id, company, meeting_date)
VALUES (3, NULL, 'WXC Services', DATE'2018-08-23');
```

Once this query is run, the customer_meeting table will look like this:

ID	EMPLOYEE_ID	COMPANY	MEETING_DATE
1	5	ABC Construction	10/Aug/2018
2	2	BW Signage	21/Aug/2018
3	(null)	WXC Services	23/Aug/2018

The new record does not have an associated employee. Now, run your SELECT query with the join from earlier in the chapter.

```
SELECT
c.id,
c.employee_id,
c.company,
c.meeting_date,
```

```
e.last_name
FROM customer_meeting c
INNER JOIN employee e ON c.employee_id = e.id;
```

The results are:

```
ID   EMPLOYEE_ID    COMPANY             MEETING_DATE    LAST_NAME
1    5              ABC Construction    10/Aug/2018     ANDERSON
2    2              BW Signage          21/Aug/2018     SMITH
```

You can see that the `customer_meeting` record with an `id` of 3 is not shown. This is because there is no related record in the employee table, and because an `INNER JOIN` is used, the record is not shown. There are other join types that let you see this data, which we'll learn about in later chapters.

Summary

A join is a feature in SQL that allows you to relate two or more tables to each other inside a single query, allowing you to display data from these tables without using other programming languages. A join criterion is needed, which specifies how the two tables are related.

It's good practice to display your `SELECT` columns on separate lines, and to use table aliases, to make it easier to read and edit your queries.

The basic type of join we looked at is an `INNER JOIN`, which shows records that match in both tables. There are other join types, which we'll look at in the next few chapters.

CHAPTER 19

Outer Join

In the last chapter, we learned how to join tables together using the JOIN keyword. This was a type of join called an *inner join*, which displays records that exist in both tables being joined. The other type of join is an *outer join*.

What is an Outer Join?

An outer join is where two tables are joined together, but if there is no related record in one of the tables, the data from the other table is still shown.

Using our sample data and joining the employee table to the customer_meeting table, you saw customer_meeting and employee records. You didn't see any customer_meetings that had no employees, or any employees that had no customer_meetings. This is what an inner join does.

An outer join, on the other hand, will show all the data from one table and matching data from the other table, or a NULL value. It will show all customer_meeting records, and either the employee that is related or a NULL value if an employee is not related.

An outer join is helpful if you want to show all records from a table and not exclude those just because there are no records in another table.

There are three different types of outer joins:

- Left outer joins

- Right outer joins

- Full outer joins

We'll look at each of them in this chapter.

© Ben Brumm 2019
B. Brumm, *Beginning Oracle SQL for Oracle Database 18c*,
https://doi.org/10.1007/978-1-4842-4430-2_19

Writing a Left Outer Join

When you write a SELECT query that uses a JOIN, it's helpful to think of the two tables involved as one being on the left and the other being on the right. The table mentioned first is the table on the left.

We can represent a left outer join graphically as a Venn diagram, with each circle representing a table and the shaded area as the records that are found. Figure 19-1 shows this Venn diagram.

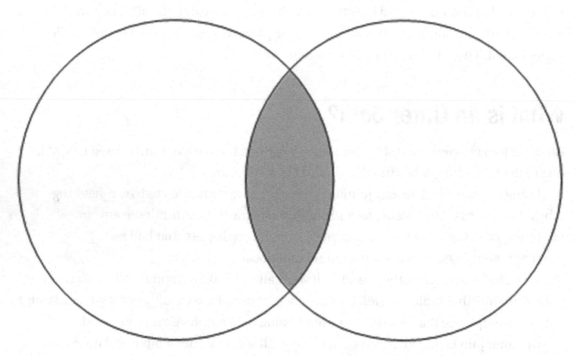

Figure 19-1. *An Inner Join, with table1 on the left and table2 on the right*

Our example query from the last chapter used an INNER JOIN:

```
SELECT
s.id,
s.employee_id,
s.company,
s.meeting_date,
e.last_name
FROM customer_meeting s
INNER JOIN employee e ON s.employee_id = e.id;
```

In this example the customer_meeting table is on the left and the employee table is on the right.

For a LEFT OUTER JOIN, all of the records in the left table are shown. If there is a match from the right table, it is shown; otherwise, a NULL value is shown.

In this example, if you use a LEFT OUTER JOIN, the query would show all of the customer_meeting records. It would show employee last_name values if a match was found, but otherwise show NULL.

You can write a LEFT OUTER JOIN in the same way as an INNER JOIN. You just need to change the keyword from JOIN or INNER JOIN to LEFT JOIN or LEFT OUTER JOIN. The keyword OUTER is optional, so it's up to you if you add it.

A query that uses a LEFT OUTER JOIN would look like this:

```
SELECT columns
FROM table1
LEFT [OUTER] JOIN table2 ON condition;
```

You can adjust the example query from earlier to see it as a LEFT JOIN:

```
SELECT
s.id,
s.employee_id,
s.company,
s.meeting_date,
e.last_name
FROM customer_meeting s
LEFT JOIN employee e ON s.employee_id = e.id;
```

The join criterion is still needed. You still need to specify how the data in the two tables is related, and in this case the customer_meeting's employee_id is related to the employee's id column.

Our LEFT JOIN query will display the following results:

ID	EMPLOYEE_ID	COMPANY	MEETING_DATE	LAST_NAME
1	5	ABC Construction	10/Aug/2018	ANDERSON
2	2	BW Signage	21/Aug/2018	SMITH
3	(null)	WXC Services	23/Aug/2018	(null)

These results show all of the records from the customer_meeting table. The results show both ANDERSON and SMITH for the first two employees, as the customer_meeting mentions employees 5 and 2 for their `employee_id` records. The third record has a `NULL` `employee_id`, and therefore a `NULL` last_name from the employee table. It is still shown, as we are using a `LEFT JOIN` and not an `INNER JOIN`.

A left join is represented graphically, as shown in Figure 19-2.

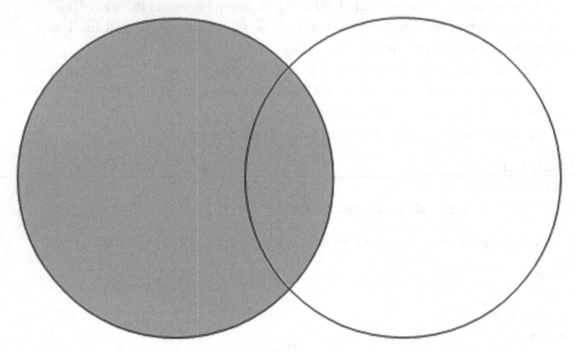

Figure 19-2. *A Left Outer Join, with table1 on the left and table2 on the right*

Showing All Employees with a Left Outer Join

Another example is this question: what if we wanted to see all employees, along with the `customer_meetings` they had, if any? We can do this using a `LEFT OUTER JOIN` as well.

Let's say we wanted to see the `id`, `last_name`, and `salary` of an employee, along with the `id`, `company`, and `meeting_date` of a `customer_meeting`. Our query could look like this:

```
SELECT
e.id,
e.last_name,
e.salary,
s.id,
s.company,
```

```
s.meeting_date
FROM employee e
INNER JOIN customer_meeting s ON e.id = s.employee_id;
```

This query uses an INNER JOIN, and would show us the following information:

ID	LAST_NAME	SALARY	ID	COMPANY	MEETING_DATE
2	SMITH	35000	2	BW Signage	21/Aug/2018
5	ANDERSON	31000	1	ABC Construction	10/Aug/2018

It only shows us employees that have a customer_meeting. We want to see all employees, regardless of if they have a customer meeting.

We can change our query to use a LEFT JOIN instead of an INNER JOIN, and include an ORDER BY:

```
SELECT
e.id,
e.last_name,
e.salary,
s.id,
s.company,
s.meeting_date
FROM employee e
LEFT JOIN customer_meeting s ON e.id = s.employee_id
ORDER BY e.id;
```

This will show the following results:

ID	LAST_NAME	SALARY	ID	COMPANY	MEETING_DATE
1	JONES	30000	(null)	(null)	(null)
2	SMITH	35000	2	BW Signage	21/Aug/2018
3	KING	45000	(null)	(null)	(null)
4	SIMPSON	52000	(null)	(null)	(null)
5	ANDERSON	31000	1	ABC Construction	10/Aug/2018
6	COOPER	(null)	(null)	(null)	(null)
7	(null)	(null)	(null)	(null)	(null)
8	SMITH	62000	(null)	(null)	(null)
9	PATRICK	40000	(null)	(null)	(null)

It shows all of the employee records, along with any `customer_meeting` values if they exist. `NULL` values are shown for employees that have no `customer_meeting` values.

Writing a Right Outer Join

Another type of outer join is a *right outer join*. A right outer join is where all of the records from the table on the right side of the join are shown, and if a record on the left side of the join exists it is shown, otherwise a `NULL` value is shown.

If you think this sounds like a left outer join, you're right. It's the opposite of a left outer join. In a left outer join, all the records from the left table are shown. In a right outer join, all of the records from the right table are shown.

A right outer can be shown as a Venn diagram as well, as seen in Figure 19-3.

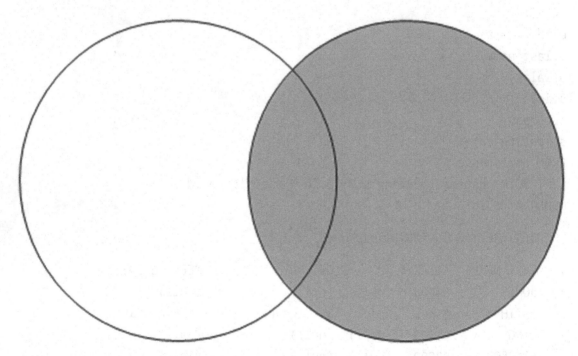

Figure 19-3. *A Right Outer Join, with table1 on the left and table2 on the right*

One of our examples from earlier displayed all of the employee records and any customer_meeting records they had. That example was written as a query with a LEFT JOIN:

```
SELECT
e.id,
e.last_name,
e.salary,
s.id,
s.company,
s.meeting_date
FROM employee e
LEFT JOIN customer_meeting s ON e.id = s.employee_id;
```

The same query can also be written as a RIGHT OUTER JOIN by simply swapping the order of the tables and changing LEFT JOIN to RIGHT JOIN. Here's an example:

```
SELECT
e.id,
e.last_name,
e.salary,
s.id,
s.company,
s.meeting_date
FROM customer_meeting s
RIGHT JOIN employee e ON e.id = s.employee_id;
```

The bolded part is the only part that has changed. The join criterion does not need to change. It doesn't matter which order the join conditions appear in.

The results from this query are the same as before:

ID	LAST_NAME	SALARY	ID	COMPANY	MEETING_DATE
1	JONES	30000	(null)	(null)	(null)
2	SMITH	35000	2	BW Signage	21/Aug/2018
3	KING	45000	(null)	(null)	(null)
4	SIMPSON	52000	(null)	(null)	(null)
5	ANDERSON	31000	1	ABC Construction	10/Aug/2018
6	COOPER	(null)	(null)	(null)	(null)

269

7	(null)	(null)	(null) (null)		(null)
8	SMITH	62000	(null) (null)		(null)
9	PATRICK	40000	(null) (null)		(null)

When Would You Use a Right Outer Join?

I haven't seen many queries at all that use a RIGHT OUTER JOIN or RIGHT JOIN, because such queries can always be written as a LEFT JOIN. I prefer writing the queries as a LEFT JOIN where possible, and so do most SQL developers whom I encounter.

The only scenario where I think a RIGHT JOIN may make more sense is if your output shows the columns with the NULL values first, and then the columns with the values.

For example, let's say you wanted an output like this:

ID	COMPANY	MEETING_DATE	ID	LAST_NAME	SALARY
(null)	(null)	(null)	1	JONES	20000
2	BW Signage	21/Aug/2018	2	SMITH	35000
(null)	(null)	(null)	3	KING	40000
(null)	(null)	(null)	4	SIMPSON	52000
1	ABC Construction	10/Aug/2018	5	ANDERSON	31000
(null)	(null)	(null)	6	COOPER	(null)
(null)	(null)	(null)	7	(null)	(null)
(null)	(null)	(null)	8	SMITH	62000
(null)	(null)	(null)	9	PATRICK	40000

These results show the customer_meeting columns on the left, if they exist, and then show all of the employee columns. In this example, it might make more sense to write the query as a RIGHT OUTER JOIN, because the output reflects the ordering of tables as they would occur when writing a RIGHT OUTER JOIN.

Writing a Full Outer Join

The final type of outer join is a *full outer join*. This behaves similar to both a left outer join and a right outer join. Joining two tables with a full outer join will show:

- All records from both tables that match

- All records from the first table that don't match the second table (which will show NULL values)

- All records from the second table that don't match the first table (which will show NULL values)

A full outer join can be displayed as a Venn diagram, as shown in Figure 19-4.

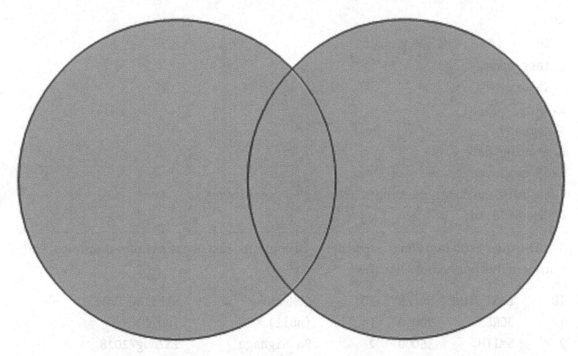

Figure 19-4. *A Full Outer Join, with table1 on the left and table2 on the right*

A full outer join is useful when you want to get all records from both tables and see which records match and don't match. A full outer join query looks like this:

```
SELECT columns
FROM table1
FULL [OUTER] JOIN table2 ON condition;
```

Just like the left join and right join, the word OUTER is optional when writing a FULL OUTER JOIN. Let's see an example.

Using a Full Outer Join on Our Tables

We can write a query that uses a full outer join on our employee and customer_meeting tables. Here's an example of such:

```
SELECT
e.id,
e.last_name,
e.salary,
s.id,
s.company,
s.meeting_date
FROM employee e
FULL JOIN customer_meeting s ON e.id = s.employee_id
ORDER BY e.id;
```

The query still joins on the employee_id columns, just like the earlier examples. The output of this query looks like this:

ID	LAST_NAME	SALARY	ID	COMPANY	MEETING_DATE
1	JONES	30000	(null)	(null)	(null)
2	SMITH	35000	2	BW Signage	21/Aug/2018
3	KING	45000	(null)	(null)	(null)
4	SIMPSON	52000	(null)	(null)	(null)
5	ANDERSON	31000	1	ABC Construction	10/Aug/2018
6	COOPER	(null)	(null)	(null)	(null)
7	(null)	(null)	(null)	(null)	(null)
8	SMITH	62000	(null)	(null)	(null)
9	PATRICK	40000	(null)	(null)	(null)
(null)	(null)	(null)	3	WXC Services	23/Aug/2018

You can see a few things in this output:

- Matching rows are shown, such as employee SMITH and their meeting with BW Signage, and employee ANDERSON and their meeting with ABC Construction.

- Employee rows with no meetings are shown, such as JONES and KIN.

- Customer_meeting rows with no employees are shown, such as the meeting with WXC Services.

This type of query shows more information than either a left join or right join.

Summary

An outer join is a type of join that shows all records in one table, along with records that match in another table if they exist. If no matches are found, a NULL value is shown. This allows you to see a full table as well as any matching records in another table.

A left outer join will show all records in the table mentioned on the left of the join keyword, and the right outer join will show all records in the table on the right of the join keyword. A full outer join does both.

CHAPTER 20

Other Join Types

There are several other types of join syntax offered in Oracle SQL. These join types aren't used as often, but it's worth knowing about them and why you should or should not use them.

The USING Keyword

In an earlier chapter you learned how to write a query that used an INNER JOIN to get data from two tables. As part of that you specified how the two tables were related, by indicating the two columns whose values needed to match. Here's the query you ran:

```
SELECT
s.id,
s.employee_id,
s.company,
s.meeting_date,
e.last_name
FROM customer_meeting s
INNER JOIN employee e ON s.employee_id = e.id;
```

There is another keyword in SQL that allows you to write an INNER JOIN or OUTER JOIN even easier: the USING keyword. This USING keyword allows you to specify a name for a column, and that column from both tables is used as the join criteria. The syntax looks like this:

```
SELECT columns
FROM table1
JOIN table2 USING (column_name);
```

With this syntax you replace the ON column=column with the USING(column). Let's demonstrate this with the office table.

© Ben Brumm 2019
B. Brumm, *Beginning Oracle SQL for Oracle Database 18c*,
https://doi.org/10.1007/978-1-4842-4430-2_20

Updating the Office Table

The office table isn't currently linking to anything, but the idea is that each employee will work from an office. To store this in our database, we need to add the id field from the office table to the employee table.

First, let's run an ALTER TABLE statement:

```
ALTER TABLE employee
ADD office_id NUMBER(5);
```

If you run this statement on your database in SQL Developer, a new column will be added to the employee table. I've called it office_id so it's clear what the value refers to. It's also a NUMBER data type with five digits, as that's the size of the id column in the office table.

When you run a SELECT query on the employee table, this column is blank:

```
SELECT id, last_name, salary, office_id
FROM employee;
```

ID	LAST_NAME	SALARY	OFFICE_ID
1	JONES	30000	(null)
2	SMITH	35000	(null)
3	KING	45000	(null)
4	SIMPSON	52000	(null)
5	ANDERSON	31000	(null)
6	COOPER	(null)	(null)
7	ADAMS	(null)	(null)
8	SMITH	62000	(null)
9	PATRICK	40000	(null)

You can run an UPDATE statement on this table to update these values. The update statements to run are shown as follows.

```
UPDATE employee SET office_id = 1 WHERE id IN (1, 4, 6, 9);
UPDATE employee SET office_id = 2 WHERE id IN (2, 3);
UPDATE employee SET office_id = 3 WHERE id IN (7, 8);
COMMIT;
```

These queries use the IN keyword to allow you to update multiple rows with one query and without specifying multiple OR statements.

After you run those UPDATE statements, you can run the same SELECT query on the employee table:

```
SELECT id, last_name, salary, office_id
FROM employee;
```

```
ID  LAST_NAME  SALARY   OFFICE_ID
1   JONES      30000    1
2   SMITH      35000    2
3   KING       45000    2
4   SIMPSON    52000    1
5   ANDERSON   31000    (null)
6   COOPER     (null)   1
7   ADAMS      (null)   3
8   SMITH      62000    3
9   PATRICK    40000    1
```

The employee records now have an associated office_id. Now let's write a SELECT query with the USING keyword.

Writing a Query with the USING Keyword

You can write a SELECT query with the USING keyword on the employee and office tables.

```
SELECT id,
last_name,
salary,
address
FROM employee
INNER JOIN office USING (office_id);
```

This query includes the USING keyword on the office_id column, which means it joins the two tables together based on the office_id column. Let's look at the results:

```
ORA-00904: "OFFICE"."OFFICE_ID": invalid identifier
```

This is unexpected. Why didn't you get a list of both employee and office records? The query includes both tables and several columns.

It's because the USING clause looks for the specified column in both tables, and the column names need to be the same. This query has joined the two tables on the employee.office_id column matching the office.office_id column. This has encountered an error, as the employee.office_id column identifies the office, but the office.office_id column does not exist.

The correct way to perform the join would be to match on employee.office_id = office.id. But this is not possible with the USING keyword. The USING keyword requires that both column names be the same.

You could rename the id column in the office table to be office_id but that's not always possible, especially if you're working on an existing system, as it may cause other queries to break. Renaming a column may also cause other queries that use the USING clause to break as well!

Note   The USING clause requires that both tables contain a column with the same name. If this column does not contain the same data, you will get unexpected results.

The requirement to make the column names the same is one of the reasons why I **don't recommend** the USING clause. Another reason is the restrictions on the column. We joined two tables together, and in our recent examples we've been using table aliases to make it clear which tables each column comes from. The previous query didn't have these aliases, so let's add them in.

```
SELECT e.id,
e.last_name,
e.salary,
o.address
FROM employee e
INNER JOIN office o USING (id);
```

If you run this query, you'll get this message:

```
ORA-25154: column part of USING clause cannot have qualifier
25154. 00000 -  "column part of USING clause cannot have qualifier"
*Cause:    Columns that are used for a named-join (either a NATURAL join
           or a join with a USING clause) cannot have an explicit qualifier.
*Action:   Remove the qualifier.
Error at Line: 9 Column: 8
```

This means that the id column inside the USING clause cannot have a table alias in the SELECT clause. This is because the value should be the same in both tables and therefore does not need a qualifier. Let's adjust the query to remove this:

```
SELECT id,
e.last_name,
e.salary,
o.address
FROM employee e
INNER JOIN office o USING (id);
```

This query will run and show the same results as earlier, even though they are incorrect in this example. Not being able to refer to this column with an alias is a small issue, but when the column in both tables is the same, it shouldn't matter.

A better way of writing this query is to use the ON keyword instead of the USING keyword:

```
SELECT e.id,
e.last_name,
e.salary,
e.office_id,
o.address
FROM employee e
INNER JOIN office o ON e.office_id = o.id;
```

You can add in the office_id here as well. The results from this query are:

ID	LAST_NAME	SALARY	OFFICE_ID	ADDRESS
1	JONES	30000	1	123 Smith Street
2	SMITH	35000	2	45 Main Street
3	KING	45000	2	45 Main Street
4	SIMPSON	52000	1	123 Smith Street
6	COOPER	(null)	1	123 Smith Street
7	ADAMS	(null)	3	10 Collins Road
8	SMITH	62000	3	10 Collins Road
9	PATRICK	40000	1	123 Smith Street

It's a little more typing to use the ON keyword, but it allows for more flexibility with your queries and prevents issues from arising with columns that don't match but have the same name.

What is a Natural Join?

A natural join is another Oracle feature that simplifies the process of joining tables. It's a variation of an inner join that allows you to join tables without specifying the column names.

The syntax for a natural join is:

```
SELECT columns
FROM table1
NATURAL JOIN table2;
```

How does Oracle know how to join the two tables together if you don't specify a column? With a natural join, the database will join based on the column or columns that have the same names.

It works in a similar way to the USING keyword. If the two tables have a column with the same name, the join is performed on that. If there are two columns with the same name, both columns are used.

Note   A natural join will perform an inner join on column names that have the same name. This is very restrictive and can give incorrect results.

Writing a Query with a Natural Join

Let's see an example of this using the employee and office tables again.

```
SELECT e.id,
e.last_name,
e.salary,
e.office_id,
o.address
FROM employee e
NATURAL JOIN office o;
```

If you run that query, you'll get this message:

```
ORA-25155: column used in NATURAL join cannot have qualifier
25155. 00000 -  "column used in NATURAL join cannot have qualifier"
*Cause:    Columns that are used for a named-join (either a NATURAL join
           or a join with a USING clause) cannot have an explicit qualifier.
*Action:   Remove the qualifier.
Error at Line: 49 Column: 8
```

This is the same error as the USING join. You'll have to remove the table alias from the id column. I'm guessing it's the id column, as I know that column is common between both tables.

```
SELECT id,
e.last_name,
e.salary,
e.office_id,
o.address
FROM employee e
NATURAL JOIN office o;
```

If you run this query, you'll get these results.

ID	LAST_NAME	SALARY	OFFICE_ID	ADDRESS
1	JONES	30000	1	123 Smith Street
2	SMITH	35000	2	45 Main Street
3	KING	45000	3	10 Collins Road

These are the same incorrect results we got with the USING keyword. This is because the join is performed on the id column in both tables, rather than employee.office_id = office.id. The worrying part of this is that an error is not shown. The results are shown but they are not correct.

Because the column names need to match, I don't recommend the NATURAL JOIN. There are a few other reasons why it's not a good idea to use a NATURAL JOIN:

- If there are multiple columns with the same name, they will also get included in the join criteria, giving you incorrect results without showing an error.

- You can't use table aliases with these columns, as we saw earlier.

- This can't be used with an outer join. It uses an inner join.

Just like the USING keyword, I don't recommend the natural join. I suggest using an inner join with the ON keyword instead.

What is a Cross Join?

A *cross join* is another type of join that is rarely used, but good to know about. Let's demonstrate this with an example.

Let's say you want to see all employees and their offices. You write a query like this:

```
SELECT e.id,
e.last_name,
e.salary,
e.office_id,
o.address
FROM employee e,
office o;
```

You run the query, and get results like this:

ID	LAST_NAME	SALARY	OFFICE_ID	ADDRESS
1	JONES	30000	1	123 Smith Street
2	SMITH	35000	1	123 Smith Street
3	KING	45000	1	123 Smith Street
4	SIMPSON	52000	1	123 Smith Street
5	ANDERSON	31000	1	123 Smith Street
6	COOPER	(null)	1	123 Smith Street
7	ADAMS	(null)	1	123 Smith Street
8	SMITH	62000	1	123 Smith Street
9	PATRICK	40000	1	123 Smith Street
1	JONES	30000	2	45 Main Street

2	SMITH	35000	2	45 Main Street
3	KING	45000	2	45 Main Street
4	SIMPSON	52000	2	45 Main Street
5	ANDERSON	31000	2	45 Main Street
6	COOPER	(null)	2	45 Main Street
7	ADAMS	(null)	2	45 Main Street
8	SMITH	62000	2	45 Main Street
9	PATRICK	40000	2	45 Main Street
1	JONES	30000	3	10 Collins Road
2	SMITH	35000	3	10 Collins Road
3	KING	45000	3	10 Collins Road
4	SIMPSON	52000	3	10 Collins Road
5	ANDERSON	31000	3	10 Collins Road
6	COOPER	(null)	3	10 Collins Road
7	ADAMS	(null)	3	10 Collins Road
8	SMITH	62000	3	10 Collins Road
9	PATRICK	40000	3	10 Collins Road

What has happened here? You were expecting eight or nine records but have found 27. This type of result is called a *Cartesian product*, and it is where every row in the first table is related to every row in the second table.

If you look closely at your results, you can see it lists all employees and shows the address for the first office, then lists all employees again and shows the address of the second office. It repeats this for the third office, and the 27 results come from nine employees multiplied by three offices. If we had more offices, we would get even more results.

Why did this happen? It's because we selected data from two tables without specifying a join condition. This was our query:

```
SELECT e.id,
e.last_name,
e.salary,
e.office_id,
o.address
FROM employee e,
office o;
```

There was no INNER JOIN or OUTER JOIN or mention of any columns that need to match. This results in a Cartesian product and is almost certainly not what you want. Running a query that shows 27 results instead of eight or nine is not so bad, but if you have hundreds or thousands of records, then you could end up with a very large result set.

It often happens accidentally, if you forget to add in the join condition like this. However, there is a way to specify that you do want this type of join.

Using a CROSS JOIN

A cross join is a type of join that will return a Cartesian product result. It will allow you to deliberately match all records in one table with all records in another table.

Why would you ever want to do this? It's an easy way to generate data for a table or a query, which may be something you need to do for the project you're working on.

The syntax of a cross join looks like this:

```
SELECT columns
FROM table1
CROSS JOIN table2;
```

You can apply this to your employee and office query like this:

```
SELECT e.id,
e.last_name,
e.salary,
e.office_id,
o.address
FROM employee e
CROSS JOIN office o;
```

This will show the same results as earlier: the same 27 records.

Why would you write a CROSS JOIN instead of the earlier method? In SQL, there are several ways of doing the same task, and sometimes you get a result that doesn't show an error but isn't quite what you wanted. The reason to use a CROSS JOIN is to specify that you intended to join every record in one table to every record in another table. From experience, it's very rare for a CROSS JOIN to be written on purpose. Most of the time if you see the kind of results shown previously, it is usually because of an error in your query. If you write the query using the first method, it isn't clear if you did this deliberately or accidentally.

Alternative Join Syntax

So far you have learned to join two tables together using variations of the JOIN keyword:

- JOIN, INNER JOIN

- LEFT JOIN, LEFT OUTER JOIN

- RIGHT JOIN, RIGHT OUTER JOIN

- CROSS JOIN

This set of keywords is called the ANSI join syntax, as it is part of the ANSI standard of SQL. There is an alternative syntax for joining tables together that's often called the Oracle syntax, as it's specific to Oracle SQL.

When you write a query that joins two tables together, you are essentially saying, "show me these columns where this table's column is equal to that table's column." This sounds a lot like the functionality of a WHERE clause.

The alternative join syntax does exactly that. It uses a WHERE clause to perform a join. There are some extra symbols for handling outer joins that are Oracle-specific.

Inner Join

What does this alternative join syntax look like? It's a WHERE clause:

```
SELECT e.id,
e.last_name,
e.salary,
e.office_id,
o.address
FROM employee e, office o
WHERE e.office_id = o.id;
```

Writing a query this way involves putting the table names into the FROM clause as a comma-separated list. By default, this is treated as a CROSS JOIN, where every record from both tables is joined together. You then use the WHERE clause to specify the columns that the two tables are joined on, so that you can reduce the results to something that makes sense.

285

The results of this query are:

```
ID   LAST_NAME   SALARY   OFFICE_ID   ADDRESS
1    JONES       30000    1           123 Smith Street
2    SMITH       35000    2           45 Main Street
3    KING        45000    2           45 Main Street
4    SIMPSON     52000    1           123 Smith Street
6    COOPER      (null)   1           123 Smith Street
7    ADAMS       (null)   3           10 Collins Road
8    SMITH       62000    3           10 Collins Road
9    PATRICK     40000    1           123 Smith Street
```

This shows all employees that have offices, and their office address. It's the same as performing an INNER JOIN, but the criteria for matching the tables is written in the WHERE clause instead of the ON keyword. The query we just wrote is equal to this one:

```
SELECT e.id,
e.last_name,
e.salary,
e.office_id,
o.address
FROM employee e
INNER JOIN office o ON e.office_id = o.id;
```

Outer Join

The example earlier showed how to write an inner join using the alternative syntax (in the WHERE clause). How can you write an outer join using this syntax?

Oracle has some symbols you can use in your queries to create an outer join with the WHERE clause. You can enter a + symbol inside brackets () next to the column in the WHERE clause that you expect could be NULL.

To write a LEFT OUTER JOIN, where the records from the left table are shown and the right table either shows matches or a NULL value, this query can be used:

```
SELECT e.id,
e.last_name,
e.salary,
```

```
e.office_id,
o.address
FROM employee e, office o
WHERE e.office_id = o.id(+);
```

Notice that the (+) symbol comes after the `o.id` column and before the semicolon. It's part of the SQL statement, and it's associated with the `office.id` column, which means that table's records may be blank.

The results are:

ID	LAST_NAME	SALARY	OFFICE_ID	ADDRESS
1	JONES	30000	1	123 Smith Street
2	SMITH	35000	2	45 Main Street
3	KING	45000	2	45 Main Street
4	SIMPSON	52000	1	123 Smith Street
6	COOPER	(null)	1	123 Smith Street
7	ADAMS	(null)	3	10 Collins Road
8	SMITH	62000	3	10 Collins Road
9	PATRICK	40000	1	123 Smith Street
5	ANDERSON	31000	(null)	(null)

This shows the same as a LEFT OUTER JOIN. All employee records are shown, and their office values are shown. A NULL value is shown for the `office_id` and `address` for employee 5, as they have no `office`.

A right outer join can be written by placing the (+) on the other column instead:

```
SELECT e.id,
e.last_name,
e.salary,
e.office_id,
o.address
FROM employee e, office o
WHERE e.office_id(+) = o.id;
```

ID	LAST_NAME	SALARY	OFFICE_ID	ADDRESS
1	JONES	30000	1	123 Smith Street
2	SMITH	35000	2	45 Main Street
3	KING	45000	2	45 Main Street

4	SIMPSON	52000	1	123 Smith Street
6	COOPER	(null)	1	123 Smith Street
7	ADAMS	(null)	3	10 Collins Road
8	SMITH	62000	3	10 Collins Road
9	PATRICK	40000	1	123 Smith Street

This query shows all office records and their associated employee records. Employee 5 is not shown as they do not have an office. This is the same as a RIGHT OUTER JOIN.

Why You Shouldn't Use the Alternative Join Syntax

Now you have seen there are two ways to perform joins in Oracle SQL. However, I recommend using the ANSI-style (with the JOIN keywords) rather than the alternative style (with the WHERE clause). There are several reasons for this.

Intention. The intention of the WHERE clause is to restrict data from your result set. Using the WHERE clause to join two tables together will work, but it's not the intention of the WHERE clause. This may seem simple to do when joining two tables together, but in the next chapter we'll learn how to join multiple tables. Once you start working with larger and more complex queries, they often have WHERE clauses with a lot of criteria, and it's easier to work with if the logic to filter the rows is separate to the logic to join tables.

Reduce Errors. With the JOIN keywords, there is a very low chance of getting errors or issues with your result set, because you're specifying how each table is joined as you're including it in your query. If you use the WHERE clause, you specify all of your tables in the FROM clause and then the criteria in the WHERE clause. As you join several tables together, there is a chance you will forget to add in the WHERE clause that joins the tables together. This can result in a Cartesian product, as we saw earlier, and will result in incorrect results. I've done this more times than I can count in my career.

Flexible. Using the JOIN keywords allows you to easily change the join types if needed and allows you to use other join types like a FULL OUTER JOIN. Using the joins in the WHERE clause, it's harder to do a FULL OUTER JOIN and takes a bit more work to change the symbol from one side to another.

So, whenever you need to join tables together, I recommend using the JOIN keywords rather than the WHERE clause. If you come across code that joins data in the WHERE clause, you'll be able to understand what it does and have the opportunity to change it.

Summary

The USING keyword allows you to join two tables together on a column name that is the same in both tables. It's easier to type but it relies on your column names matching, which won't always work.

The natural join is a type of inner join where the Oracle database joins the two tables based on all columns that have the same name. This is prone to issues, just like the USING keyword, as it relies on column names matching.

A cross join is a type of join that relates all records in one table with all records in another table. This results in a Cartesian product, which also happens if you don't specify a join type. This is often an accident, but there are some situations where you want a cross join, and Oracle provides the CROSS JOIN keyword to do this.

Finally, there is an alternative join syntax, or an Oracle join syntax, which allows you to perform inner and outer joins using the WHERE clause and some symbols. This is an older style syntax and is not recommended, as it's against the intention of the WHERE clause and prone to errors.

CHAPTER 21

Joining Many Tables

In this chapter, we'll learn how to use SQL to join many tables together in our query. So far, we've learned quite a bit about joins:

- What a join is (a way of relating two tables together in a query)

- What an inner and outer join is

- The different types of outer joins (left, right, full)

- Some other join types that are available if needed (cross join) or that are not recommended (natural join)

- The alternative join syntax (the WHERE clause)

All of the topics so far have only worked with two tables at a time: either the `employee` and `office` table, or the `employee` and `sales_meeting` table. What if we want to get data from three tables at once?

Joining Three Tables

In SQL, it's possible to join three or more tables together in a single query. In fact, it's where the strength of a database comes in. You're able to store data in different tables and relate it all together to view it in the way you need.

You have three tables in your database so far:

- employee

- office

- sales_meeting

What if you needed to display data from all three tables, such as the employee name, their office address, and the company and date of the meeting? You can do this using SQL by joining these three tables together.

291

© Ben Brumm 2019
B. Brumm, *Beginning Oracle SQL for Oracle Database 18c*,
https://doi.org/10.1007/978-1-4842-4430-2_21

Joining multiple tables works like the game of dominos. You know how in dominoes there was a set of small blocks with one symbol on each end, and the symbols were a dice number ranging from 1 to 6? I didn't play dominoes a lot, but I remember a rule that said you could only place a domino down next to a domino that had the same number. If a domino had a 4 at one end, you could only place a domino with a 4 on it next to the first domino, as shown in Figure 21-1.

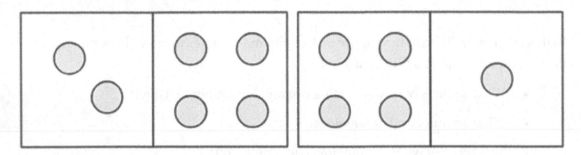

Figure 21-1. *Two dominoes are similar to a join with two tables*

Well, if you want to add a third domino, you need to find one that matches and add it to the end, as shown in Figure 21-2.

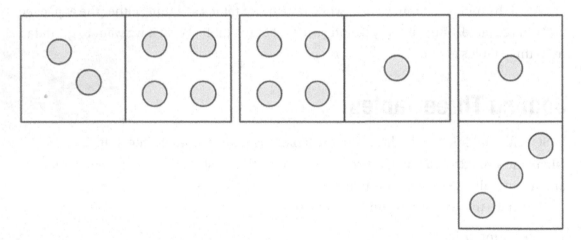

Figure 21-2. *Three dominoes are similar to a join with three tables*

You can keep doing this until you run out of pieces. This is like how joins work in SQL. The domino blocks are the tables and the numbers on them are columns. You can join many different tables together, as long as you can identify a common link between them.

You just add a new table to the end of your statement and specify the join criteria, and it's included.

A query that joins two tables may look like this:

```
SELECT columns
FROM table1
INNER JOIN table2 ON condition;
```

A query that joins three tables may look like this:

```
SELECT columns
FROM table1
INNER JOIN table2 ON condition
INNER JOIN table3 ON condition;
```

This query has joined three tables together and can display and work with data from all three tables.

Joining Our Tables Together

Let's see an example. You have your three tables (employee, office, and sales_meeting) and you want to see data from all three of them. Your query would look like this:

```
SELECT e.id,
e.last_name,
o.address,
s.company,
s.meeting_date
FROM employee e
INNER JOIN office o ON e.office_id = o.id
INNER JOIN sales_meeting s ON e.id = s.employee_id;
```

This query combines a few techniques you've learned so far and joins three tables. You are selecting from the employee table, which has been given an alias of "e". We have used the same inner join as previous chapters, joining this to the office table on the relevant IDs (employee.office_id and office.id).

You can then add an INNER JOIN to the sales_meeting table, with an alias of "s". You need to join this to your other tables on a certain condition. You can join it to any column that is in the tables specified above it, so anything in the office or employee table. In this example, you are joining it to the employee.id column, as that is how our data is set up.

Note   Table aliases are very helpful when you start adding more tables to your query.

If you run this query, you'll get this result.

ID	LAST_NAME	ADDRESS	COMPANY	MEETING_DATE
2	SMITH	45 Main Street	BW Signage	21/Aug/2018

This result is the only one shown, as it is the only employee that has an office record and a sales_meeting record:

- Employees 4, 6, 7, 8 and 9 are excluded because they have no office and no sales_meeting records.

- Employee 1 and 3 are excluded because they do not have a sales_meeting record

- Employee 5 is excluded as they do not have an office.

However, for the record that is showing, you can see the last_name from the employee table, the address from the office table, and the company and meeting_date from the sales_meeting table. This is because you have joined three different tables together.

Using Outer Join Types

In the earlier example, you joined three tables together but only saw one result, because that was the record that was common between all three tables. What if you want to see some records that match and NULL for those that don't match, like an outer join? You can do that with multiple tables.

Let's say you want to see the employee records and their `sales_meeting` and `office_` records if they exist, otherwise show NULL. You can do this by adjusting our earlier query to use LEFT JOIN instead of INNER JOIN.

```
SELECT e.id,
e.last_name,
o.address,
s.company,
s.meeting_date
FROM employee e
LEFT JOIN office o ON e.office_id = o.id
LEFT JOIN sales_meeting s ON e.id = s.employee_id;
```

Your results will display:

ID	LAST_NAME	ADDRESS	COMPANY	MEETING_DATE
1	JONES	123 Smith Street	(null)	(null)
2	SMITH	45 Main Street	BW Signage	21/Aug/2018
3	KING	45 Main Street	(null)	(null)
4	SIMPSON	123 Smith Street	(null)	(null)
6	COOPER	123 Smith Street	(null)	(null)
7	ADAMS	10 Collins Road	(null)	(null)
8	SMITH	10 Collins Road	(null)	(null)
9	PATRICK	123 Smith Street	(null)	(null)
5	ANDERSON	(null)	ABC Construction	10/Aug/2018

This result shows more records. You can see all of the `employee` records, their `offices` if they have any (otherwise NULL), and their `sales_meetings` if they have any (otherwise NULL).

The query is the same as the earlier example but uses LEFT JOIN instead of an INNER JOIN. This is a great way to see what data, if any, exists in other tables for your main record.

You can write a similar query for `sales_meetings`, where you can see all of the `sales_meeting` records, their `employees` (if they have any), and their `offices` (if they have any).

```
SELECT
s.id AS sales_meeting_id,
s.company,
```

```
s.meeting_date,
e.id AS employee_id,
e.last_name,
o.address
FROM sales_meeting s
LEFT JOIN employee e ON e.id = s.employee_id
LEFT JOIN office o ON e.office_id = o.id;
```

The results are:

SALES_MEETING_ID	COMPANY	MEETING_DATE	EMPLOYEE_ID	LAST_NAME	ADDRESS
1	ABC Construction	10/Aug/18	5	ANDERSON	(null)
2	BW Signage	21/Aug/18	2	SMITH	45 Main Street
3	WXC Services	23/Aug/18	(null)	(null)	(null)

This shows what we expect. The focus is on the sales_meeting, as the other tables are being "left joined" to it.

Mixing Join Types

The examples so far have demonstrated that you can show all matching records in many tables using INNER JOIN and matches or NULLs in all tables using a LEFT JOIN. Can you use a mix of both? The answer is yes, you can mix join types in a query.

What if you wanted to see all employees that had offices, and their sales_meetings if they had any sales_meetings? This could be done by selecting from the employee table, performing an INNER JOIN to the office table (to exclude employees that don't have offices and offices without employees), and then a LEFT JOIN to the sales_meeting table.

The query would look like this:

```
SELECT e.id,
e.last_name,
o.address,
s.company,
s.meeting_date
FROM employee e
INNER JOIN office o ON e.office_id = o.id
```

```
LEFT JOIN sales_meeting s ON e.id = s.employee_id;
```

The results from this query are:

ID	LAST_NAME	ADDRESS	COMPANY	MEETING_DATE
1	JONES	123 Smith Street	(null)	(null)
2	SMITH	45 Main Street	BW Signage	21/Aug/18
3	KING	45 Main Street	(null)	(null)
4	SIMPSON	123 Smith Street	(null)	(null)
6	COOPER	123 Smith Street	(null)	(null)
7	ADAMS	10 Collins Road	(null)	(null)
8	SMITH	10 Collins Road	(null)	(null)
9	PATRICK	123 Smith Street	(null)	(null)

You can see that this result is different to the earlier one. Employee id 5 is not shown (ANDERSON) because they do not have an office. Even though they have a sales_meeting, they are not shown because we were performing an INNER JOIN on employee and office, meaning the record had to exist in both tables.

This shows that you can use a mix of join types when working with multiple tables. The type of join you use should be dependent on the needs of your query and what result you want to see.

Joining Four or More Tables

You have seen some example queries that joined two and three tables together. You can use the same techniques to join four, five, and many more tables together. While we only have three tables at the moment, once you start working on real applications either in your job or on a side project, you'll start using many more than three tables.

The same techniques apply when joining more than three tables. For example, let's say you had a table called department that stored an id and a name of the department such as Accounting or Sales. Let's say there is also a column in the employee table called department_id that stores the id from the department table.

Our tables and fields would then be:

- employee: id, last_name, salary, job_title, office_id, department_id

- office: id, address

- sales_meeting: id, employee_id, company, meeting_date

- department: id, department_name

You could join all four of these tables together like this:

```
SELECT e.id,
e.last_name,
d.department_name,
o.address,
s.company,
s.meeting_date
FROM employee e
INNER JOIN office o ON e.office_id = o.id
INNER JOIN sales_meeting s ON e.id = s.employee_id
INNER JOIN department d ON e.department_id = d.id;
```

This would then show you the records that were related across all four tables. If you run this query at the moment using the sample data we have used so far, you'll get an error because the department table does not exist.

As you add more and more tables to our database, with related columns, you can join to them if you need to. You can also use the WHERE clause to filter data on any of these tables, the ORDER BY clause to order on any column, and other keywords you have learned so far.

You may end up with quite a long query, like the one shown here:

```
SELECT e.id AS employee_id
e.last_name,
e.salary,
e.job_title,
d.department_name,
o.address,
s.company,
s.meeting_date
FROM employee e
```

```
INNER JOIN office o ON e.office_id = o.id
INNER JOIN sales_meeting s ON e.id = s.employee_id
INNER JOIN department d ON e.department_id = d.id
WHERE o.address LIKE '%Main Street%'
AND e.salary > 30000;
```

This query would show all employee, department, office, and sales meeting information for employees that have an office on Main Street and a salary of greater than 30,000.

Once you set up your data, writing queries like this gets easier.

Summary

You can use the same method as joining two tables to join three, four, or more tables together. You can join all tables using an INNER JOIN, a type of OUTER JOIN, or a combination of joins. The exact joins needed will be determined by the data you want to view.

You can use other keywords and clauses with your joins, such as WHERE clauses to filter data and ORDER BY to sort data, to give you the exact data that you need.

PART V

Functions

CHAPTER 22

Using functions in SQL

There's more to SQL than reading the data that's stored in the table. You'll often need to manipulate it or perform calculations on it. That's where functions come in.

What is a Function?

A *function* is a piece of code stored in the database that allows you to perform a specific task that returns an output. There are three parts to a function:

- The input, which is the data you provide to the function

- The process, or what the function does

- The output, which is the result of the function's process

There are a lot of functions built into Oracle SQL to perform a lot of different calculations or processes. Why would you want to use a function? Functions are used to perform manipulation on data, such as:

- Count the number of records that meet a certain criteria

- Total a range of numbers

- Convert a date to another time zone

- Find a specific character in a string of characters

Whenever you need to see more than just the value that's stored in the database table, you'll probably need to use a function.

© Ben Brumm 2019
B. Brumm, *Beginning Oracle SQL for Oracle Database 18c*,
https://doi.org/10.1007/978-1-4842-4430-2_22

Where Can You Use Functions?

Functions can be used in many places in Oracle SQL, such as:

- The SELECT clause of a SELECT statement, viewing the result of a function

- The ON clause of the JOIN of a SELECT statement

- The WHERE clause of a SELECT statement, filtering data to the result of a function

- The ORDER BY clause

- The SET clause of an UPDATE statement

- The WHERE clause of a DELETE or UPDATE statement

- The VALUES clause of an INSERT statement

You've learned how to write a SELECT, INSERT, UPDATE, and DELETE statements. In this chapter, you'll see how functions can be used in these statements as well.

Simple Numeric Calculations

SQL lets you perform simple mathematical calculations using some standard mathematical symbols. These symbols are:

- \+ for addition

- \- for subtraction

- * for multiplication

- / for division

You may be able to get the result you need just using these symbols. Let's take a look at an example.

Let's say you need to see each employee's salary along with what their salary would be if you added 10000 to it. Your query would look like this:

```
SELECT id, last_name, salary, salary + 10000
FROM employee;
```

This query shows the employee id, last_name, and their current salary value. It also shows a new column that is the current salary value with 10000 added to it, which is what the "salary + 10000" does. This won't update any data in the table; it just shows what the current value is with 10000 added to it.

The results of this query are:

ID	LAST_NAME	SALARY	SALARY+10000
1	JONES	30000	40000
2	SMITH	35000	45000
3	KING	45000	55000
4	SIMPSON	52000	62000
5	ANDERSON	31000	41000
6	COOPER	(null)	(null)
7	ADAMS	(null)	(null)
8	SMITH	62000	72000
9	PATRICK	40000	50000

The new column is called "SALARY+10000." Oracle will label the column with the expression you have provided and remove the spaces. The values show what the salary is with 10000 added to it.

Any NULL values will continue to be displayed as NULL. This is because NULL is an unknown value, and adding anything to an unknown value will still make it an unknown value.

You can also subtract values by using the "-" symbol. For example, to see the salary value with 5000 less, your query would look like this:

```
SELECT id, last_name, salary, salary-5000
FROM employee;
```

The results would be:

ID	LAST_NAME	SALARY	SALARY-5000
1	JONES	30000	25000
2	SMITH	35000	30000
3	KING	45000	40000
4	SIMPSON	52000	47000
5	ANDERSON	31000	26000
6	COOPER	(null)	(null)
7	ADAMS	(null)	(null)
8	SMITH	62000	57000
9	PATRICK	40000	35000

Once again, the new column displays the result of this calculation. It shows a value that is 5000 less than the current salary value.

You can also use * for multiplication. You can multiply by whole numbers or decimal numbers. For example, you can see what the salary would look like if it had a 10% increase (by multiplying it by 1.1) or what it would look like if it was doubled (by multiplying it by 2).

```
SELECT id, last_name, salary, salary * 1.1, salary * 2
FROM employee;
```

ID	LAST_NAME	SALARY	SALARY*1.1	SALARY*2
1	JONES	30000	33000	60000
2	SMITH	35000	38500	70000
3	KING	45000	49500	90000
4	SIMPSON	52000	57200	104000
5	ANDERSON	31000	34100	62000
6	COOPER	(null)	(null)	(null)
7	ADAMS	(null)	(null)	(null)

ID	LAST_NAME	SALARY	SALARY*1.1	SALARY*2
8	SMITH	62000	68200	124000
9	PATRICK	40000	44000	80000

In an earlier chapter, you learned about column aliases, which are names you can give to your columns in the results. Using column aliases when performing these kinds of calculations is a great idea. This query makes the results much easier to read:

```
SELECT id,
last_name,
salary,
salary * 1.1 AS salary_inc_comm,
salary * 2 AS salary_double
FROM employee;
```

This shows the same data but indicates that the 1.1 multiplication is including commission and the multiplication by 2 is a doubling.

ID	LAST_NAME	SALARY	SALARY_INC_COMM	SALARY_DOUBLE
1	JONES	30000	33000	60000
2	SMITH	35000	38500	70000
3	KING	45000	49500	90000
4	SIMPSON	52000	57200	104000
5	ANDERSON	31000	34100	62000
6	COOPER	(null)	(null)	(null)
7	ADAMS	(null)	(null)	(null)
8	SMITH	62000	68200	124000
9	PATRICK	40000	44000	80000

Finally, you can perform division on numbers using the "/" symbol. To divide the employee salary by 2, you can write this query:

```
SELECT id,
last_name,
salary,
salary / 2
FROM employee;
```

ID	LAST_NAME	SALARY	SALARY/2
1	JONES	30000	15000
2	SMITH	35000	17500
3	KING	45000	22500
4	SIMPSON	52000	26000
5	ANDERSON	31000	15500
6	COOPER	(null)	(null)
7	ADAMS	(null)	(null)
8	SMITH	62000	31000
9	PATRICK	40000	20000

These operators or symbols can be very useful when performing these kinds of calculations. However, for more complex calculations, you can use Oracle's built-in functions.

The DUAL Table

Before we look into the functions available in Oracle, there's a concept that you should learn about first. When you write a SELECT statement in Oracle, both the SELECT and the FROM keyword are required. You can't write a SELECT statement without SELECT or without FROM.

This query will work:

```
SELECT id
FROM employee;
```

But this query will not:

```
SELECT id;
```

Sometimes you may not need to select from a table. For example, if you want to get the current date, you don't need to use a specific table for this, as the database should know the date (we'll learn the function for this later in this chapter). Or you may want to display a specific number to test out a function. For example, if you wanted to display the value 123, then you could write this query:

```
SELECT 123
FROM employee;
```

However, this would show a value of 123 for each row of the employee table:

123
123
123
123
123
123
123
123
123
123

This shows nine results plus the column heading. This isn't what you want to see. What if you removed the table from the query, as you don't want to get the employee records?

```
SELECT 123;
```

When you run this query, it will show an error:

```
ORA-00923: FROM keyword not found where expected
00923. 00000 -  "FROM keyword not found where expected"
*Cause:
*Action:
Error at Line: 1 Column: 10
```

This is because the FROM clause is required. So how can you see just the value of 123? You can use a special Oracle table called DUAL.

The DUAL table is a table built in to the Oracle database. It contains one row and one column. Its primary purpose is to allow you to run queries that use values or functions that don't need any table data.

You can see the DUAL table by running a query on it:

```
SELECT *
FROM dual;
```

DUMMY
X

The DUAL table has a single value of "X" in a single column called DUMMY. This means you can use the DUAL table for your earlier query to show the value of 123:

```
SELECT 123
FROM dual;
```

123
123

You can now see the value you have selected. This may not seem that useful now, but once we start using functions, you'll see the benefits of this DUAL table. This table is Oracle-specific: it doesn't exist in other SQL vendors such as Microsoft SQL Server or MySQL.

Number Functions

Oracle has a range of "number functions," or functions that perform calculations using numbers. Functions in Oracle can be referred to like this:

```
FUNCTIONNAME(parameters)
```

This includes:

- FUNCTIONNAME, or the name of the function

- Open brackets, which contain one or more parameters, or input values that you provide to the function

- Close brackets

The result of the function is used in the place where you specify the function. For example, if you use this function as one of the columns in the SELECT clause, the result of the function will be displayed in the column. Let's take a look at some examples.

One operation you may perform a lot is rounding numbers. Oracle allows you to store decimal numbers in the database, but sometimes you may want to display these in a whole number. There are a few functions that let you do this. One of those functions is called ROUND. I'll refer to Oracle functions in upper case, as that's what they are written as in the Oracle documentation, and it makes it easier to read in your SQL code.

The ROUND function takes two parameters, or inputs:

- The number you want to round

- The number of decimal places to round to

The result of the function is the number you specified rounded to the number of decimal places you specified. You can write this in an SQL query like this, using an example number:

```
SELECT ROUND(123.456, 0)
FROM dual;
```

We've used the DUAL table as mentioned earlier in the chapter. The ROUND function is also used, and it contains two parameters. The first is the number you want to round, which is 123.456. The second is the number of decimal places to round to, which is 0. This means the number 123.456 will be rounded to 0 decimal places.

If you run this query, you'll get this result:

ROUND(123.456,0)
123

The result of this ROUND function is 123. This is because 123.456 is rounded down, and not rounded up.

You can also use the ROUND function with a different number of decimal places. For example, to round to two decimal places, your query would look like this:

```
SELECT ROUND(123.456, 2)
FROM dual;
```

You simply change the second parameter to the number 2, to represent two decimal places. The results of this query are:

ROUND(123.456,2)
123.46

The result is 123.46 because 123.456 is rounded up to 123.46.

There are two other ways to round numbers in Oracle SQL, and they use the functions CEILING and FLOOR. The CEILING function will round a number up to the nearest whole number, and the FLOOR function rounds a number down to the nearest whole number.

The syntax for these functions is:

```
CEILING (input_number)
FLOOR (input_number)
```

Each of these functions takes a single parameter, which is the number to round. Unlike the ROUND function, these functions don't need the second parameter for the number of digits, as they always round to a whole number.

A query that uses these functions would be the one below. I've used column aliases to make the output neater.

```
SELECT
CEILING(123.456) AS num_ceilng,
FLOOR(123.456) AS num_floor
FROM dual;
```

NUM_CEILING	NUM_FLOOR
124	123

The CEILING function rounded the number up to 124, and the FLOOR function rounded the number down to 123. Other number functions in Oracle work in the same way, where you provide an input value and a result is calculated.

Let's see an example function that uses one of the columns in a table. Let's say that the salary stored in the employee table is an annual value, and we want to see what the monthly value would be. However, along with the monthly value, we want to see what the "left over" amount would be if we divide the salary by 12 and round it down. For example, the value of 30/12 would be 2 (2*12=24), with 6 left over (30-24=6). We can use functions for this in Oracle: the FLOOR function and the MOD function.

The MOD function performs a *modulo division*, which means it divides one number by another and returns the remainder.

Our query would look like this:

```
SELECT
Id,
last_name,
salary,
FLOOR(salary/12) AS monthly_salary,
MOD(salary, 12) AS monthly_remaining
FROM employee;
```

This query includes the FLOOR function to first divide the salary by 12, then round the result to the nearest whole number. The MOD function takes the salary value, divides it by 12, and displays the leftover value.

The result of this query would be:

ID	LAST_NAME	SALARY	MONTHLY_SALARY	MONTHLY_REMAINDER
1	JONES	30000	2500	0
2	SMITH	35000	2916	8
3	KING	45000	3750	0
4	SIMPSON	52000	4333	4
5	ANDERSON	31000	2583	4
6	COOPER	(null)	(null)	(null)
7	ADAMS	(null)	(null)	(null)
8	SMITH	62000	5166	8
9	PATRICK	40000	3333	4

This shows the salary, and the monthly salary rounded down. It also shows the remaining value after the salary was divided by 12. For example, the employee JONES has an annual salary of 30000, and can have a monthly salary of 2500 with 0 left over, because 2500*12 = 30000.

Concatenation of Strings

Earlier in this chapter you learned how to use symbols to perform mathematical operations, such as addition and subtraction. You can use another symbol to perform a different operation using string or text values: *concatenation*.

Concatenation is the process of joining two string values together. This is often done because values are stored in separate columns or in separate tables, but you want to display them both in one column. For example, if you had a column called first_name in our employee table, you may want to concatenate the first_name and last_name to make a full name.

How can you concatenate strings in Oracle? You use two pipe characters: "||". You place these two characters between two other strings, and the result will be a single value that combines them.

For example, you can combine the name "John" and the name "Smith" using concatenation:

```
SELECT 'John' || 'Smith'
FROM dual;
```

The result would be:

JOHN||SMITH
JohnSmith

This shows a single column with the combined value. However, there is no space between the values, as we didn't specify one with the concatenation. Concatenating does not automatically add spaces, so if you want one, you need to add it manually. Let's try this query:

```
SELECT 'John ' || 'Smith' AS full_name
FROM dual;
```

I've also added in a column alias to make the result easier to read. The result is:

FULL_NAME
John Smith

This now shows the value with a space between it. You can also concatenate values from a table. Let's say you needed to combine the last_name and salary values from the employee table:

```
SELECT id,
last_name || salary
FROM employee;
```

The results would be:

ID	LAST_NAME‖SALARY
1	JONES30000
2	SMITH35000
3	KING45000
4	SIMPSON52000
5	ANDERSON31000
6	COOPER
7	ADAMS
8	SMITH62000
9	PATRICK40000

The main issue with this result set is that it's hard to read the value from the concatenation, as the name leads straight into the number value.

How can you resolve the issue of the name leading right into the numbers? You can add in a space and a comma, for example. This can be done by adding in a third concatenated value into this. This means your value would show the last_name, then a comma and a space, then the salary. The query to do this is:

```
SELECT id,
last_name || ', ' || salary
FROM employee;
```

The results of this query are:

ID	LAST_NAME‖,‖SALARY
1	JONES, 30000
2	SMITH, 35000
3	KING, 45000
4	SIMPSON, 52000
5	ANDERSON, 31000
6	COOPER,

ID	LAST_NAME||||SALARY
7	ADAMS,
8	SMITH, 62000
9	PATRICK, 40000

These results are easier to read. You've added a space and a comma, and the results are now in a single column. If you ever need to combine string values, or strings with numbers or dates, you can use this concatenation technique.

String Functions

Oracle also offers some functions to work with strings, just like you learned when working with numbers earlier. There are a lot of these types of functions, and they let you do a wide range of things to string values such as:

- Change case (upper and lower case)

- Find strings within other strings and extract the position or the string

- Add or remove characters, such as spaces, from the ends of a string

- Translate ASCII codes

In this section, you'll see how to use a few of these functions.

Changing Case

There are two functions for changing the case of a string that you'll learn about in this section: one for changing to upper case, and one for changing to lower case. These functions are used to transform your string or character data into a consistent format.

Why do you want data in a consistent format? Perhaps you allow users to enter data in a form, in a mix of upper and lower case, and you want to store it the same way to make it easier to display and search at a later date.

To transform a string value to an uppercase value, you use the UPPER function. The syntax of the UPPER function looks like this:

```
UPPER (input_string)
```

It only takes one parameter, which is the input_string, or the string you want to convert to upper case. The function returns the same value in upper case.

You can see how this function works by querying the office table, as the address field has data that is in upper case and lower case:

```
SELECT id,
address,
UPPER(address)
FROM office;
```

The results of this query are:

ID	ADDRESS	UPPER(ADDRESS)
1	123 Smith Street	123 SMITH STREET
2	45 Main Street	45 MAIN STREET
3	10 Collins Road	10 COLLINS ROAD

You can see the id column, the original address, and the address as a result of the UPPER function. The value reads the same way but has just been converted to an uppercase value (123 SMITH STREET instead of 123 Smith Street). Any letters that are already uppercase letters are unchanged, lowercase letters are translated to uppercase letters, and numbers are unchanged.

You can use a similar query for converting data to lowercase. Oracle's LOWER function lets you do that, and the syntax is similar to the UPPER function:

```
LOWER (input_string)
```

The function converts all of the characters to lowercase characters. A query to do this for the office table would look like this:

```
SELECT id,
address,
LOWER(address)
FROM office;
```

The results are:

ID	ADDRESS	LOWER(ADDRESS)
1	123 Smith Street	123 smith street
2	45 Main Street	45 main street
3	10 Collins Road	10 collins road

These results show the address in lowercase. The numbers and existing lowercase characters are unchanged, and the uppercase characters were converted to lowercase.

Checking for Matches on the Same Case

A common way that I've seen the UPPER and LOWER functions work is when comparing data or looking for data in a table. This would be done inside the WHERE clause.

To demonstrate an example of this, you'll need to insert a new record into the employee table for the employee "Jones."

```
INSERT INTO employee (id, last_name, salary, office_id)
VALUES (10, 'Jones', 42000, 2);
```

When you run a SELECT statement on the table, it will look like this:

```
SELECT id,
last_name,
salary,
office_id
FROM employee;
```

ID	LAST_NAME	SALARY	OFFICE_ID
1	JONES	30000	1
2	SMITH	35000	2
3	KING	45000	2
4	SIMPSON	52000	1
5	ANDERSON	31000	(null)

ID	LAST_NAME	SALARY	OFFICE_ID
6	COOPER	(null)	1
7	ADAMS	(null)	3
8	SMITH	62000	3
9	PATRICK	40000	1
10	Jones	42000	2

Now let's say you wanted to find all employees with the name of JONES. You've seen a few of the records and understand that employee last_names are stored in uppercase, so your query looks like this:

```
SELECT id,
last_name,
salary,
office_id
FROM employee
WHERE last_name = 'JONES';
```

When you run this query, you get this result:

ID	LAST_NAME	SALARY	OFFICE_ID
1	JONES	30000	1

What about the new record you just inserted for Jones? Shouldn't that have shown up as well? In this case, the Oracle database has shown the correct result. This is because the WHERE clause in Oracle is case sensitive. This means that "JONES" does not equal "Jones" and it does not equal "jones."

Note   The WHERE clause in Oracle is case sensitive, which means that "JONES," "Jones," and "jones" are all different values.

How can you get this query to show both values? You use either the UPPER or LOWER function. Instead of looking for "all records with a last_name of JONES," you want to look for "all records where the uppercase version of the last_name is JONES." You can also look for "all records where the lowercase version of the last_name is jones." They would show the same result.

The query to do this would be:

```
SELECT id,
last_name,
salary,
office_id
FROM employee
WHERE UPPER(last_name) = 'JONES';
```

This will compare the uppercase version of the last_name value to the value of JONES. The following result will be displayed:

ID	LAST_NAME	SALARY	OFFICE_ID
1	JONES	20000	1
10	Jones	42000	2

Both "Jones" records are displayed: the one with the uppercase value and the one with the mixed case value.

You can get the same result by converting both sides to lowercase:

```
SELECT id,
last_name,
salary,
office_id
FROM employee
WHERE LOWER(last_name) = 'jones';
```

Which ones should you use? For me, it's a personal preference to use UPPER. It also makes more sense in this situation, as most of the values in the table are uppercase. But they will both show the same results.

Getting Part of a String

Another common operation to perform on a string value is to get a certain part of a string. This concept is called a *substring*, as the smaller part of a larger string is called a substring. The Oracle function SUBSTR will let you extract one string from another string. The syntax looks like this:

```
SUBSTR (string, start_position [, length])
```

There are three parameters in this function:

- string: the string that is being looked in

- start_position: the starting position of the substring to extract

- length: the length of the substring to return

In the preceding syntax, you'll notice some square brackets "[" and "]". These indicate that a parameter is optional. You don't have to specify the length parameter. This means you can run the function in two ways:

```
SUBSTR (string, start_position)
SUBSTR (string, start_position, length)
```

If you don't add the length parameter, the default behavior means the rest of the string will be returned.

Let's see an example on the office table. You may want to find the first two characters of the address field. You can do that using the SUBSTR function with a starting position of 1 and a length of 2.

```
SELECT id,
address,
SUBSTR(address, 1, 2)
FROM office;
```

This will show the following results:

ID	ADDRESS	SUBSTR(ADDRESS,1,2)
1	123 Smith Street	12
2	45 Main Street	45
3	10 Collins Road	10

It's taken the first two characters of the address field and displayed those in the new column here.

You can try the same function without the length parameter. Let's say you wanted to extract the rest of the address starting from the 5th character. Your query could look like this:

```
SELECT id,
address,
SUBSTR(address, 5)
FROM office;
```

The results would be:

ID	ADDRESS	SUBSTR(ADDRESS,5)
1	123 Smith Street	Smith Street
2	45 Main Street	ain Street
3	10 Collins Road	ollins Road

The function has taken the entire string starting with the character in position 5.

In Oracle, there are a lot more string functions that let you do a range of transformations on strings. These are just a few of them.

Calculations on Dates

You've learned in this chapter how to do basic operations on strings and numbers. You can also do basic operations on dates. Adding and subtracting days from a date is the most common operation I've seen, so you'll learn how to do that in this section.

The sales_meeting table has a meeting_date column that stores a date value.

ID	EMPLOYEE_ID	COMPANY	MEETING_DATE
1	5	ABC Construction	10/Aug/2018
2	2	BW Signage	21/Aug/2018
3	(null)	WXC Services	23/Aug/2018

You can add or subtract days from a date value by simply adding or subtracting a number to this date value. For example, to add 7 days to the meeting_date value, you would specify meeting_date + 7. The query to do this would be:

```
SELECT id,
meeting_date,
meeting_date + 7
FROM sales_meeting;
```

When you run this query, you'll get this result.

ID	MEETING_DATE	MEETING_DATE+7
1	10/Aug/2018	17/Aug/2018
2	21/Aug/2018	28/Aug/2018
3	23/Aug/2018	30/Aug/2018

Each of these dates has had 7 days added to it. You can add a longer period or subtract days if needed. Here's a query that shows the same dates with 14 days added and with 30 days subtracted.

```
SELECT id,
meeting_date,
meeting_date + 14,
meeting_date - 30
FROM sales_meeting;
```

The results are:

ID	MEETING_DATE	MEETING_DATE+14	MEETING_DATE-30
1	10/Aug/2018	24/Aug/2018	11/Jul/2018
2	21/Aug/2018	4/Sep/2018	22/Jul/2018
3	23/Aug/2018	6/Sep/2018	24/Jul/2018

This is a simple way to find a date in the future or the past. You can also use it to find hours in the future or the past as well. Remember that the DATE data type also includes time. We can use the same process as well as a function called TO_CHAR to show time.

The `meeting_date` column stores a date and time value, but only shows a date. One way to see the time value is to use the `TO_CHAR` function, which converts a date value to a string or character value. The `TO_CHAR` function syntax looks like this:

```
TO_CHAR (input_value [, format_mask [, nls_parameter] ] )
```

This includes several parameters:

- input_value: the value to convert to a character value

- format_mask: the format that the input_value should be displayed as. This is optional, and if it's omitted, a default format will be used.

- nls_parameter: This optional parameter allows you to specify any location-specific values.

First, let's display the `meeting_date` value as a date and time value:

```
SELECT id,
meeting_date,
TO_CHAR(meeting_date, 'DD/MON/YYYY HH:MI:SS AM') AS meeting_datetime
FROM sales_meeting;
```

The second parameter is the format mask. This is how the date value will be displayed. It includes:

- DD, which is a two-digit day (e.g., 27), followed by a forward slash "/"

- Then MON, which is a three-letter month (e.g., AUG), followed by a forward slash "/"

- Then a four-digit year (e.g., 2018), followed by a space

- Then a two-digit hour, followed by a colon ":"

- Then a two-digit minute, followed by a colon ":"

- Then a two-digit second, followed by a space

- Then an AM or PM indicator

The results of this query are:

ID	MEETING_DATE	MEETING_DATETIME
1	10/Aug/18	10/Aug/2018 12:00:00 AM
2	21/Aug/18	21/Aug/2018 12:00:00 AM
3	23/Aug/18	23/Aug/2018 12:00:00 AM

As you can see, the meeting_datetime column shows the meeting_date value including a time. The time is midnight, as this is the default value when a time is not specified.

Now, let's say you wanted to add 6 hours to these dates. Earlier you added whole numbers to the dates to add another day. You can add hours to dates by adding numbers and then dividing by 24. For example, adding 1/24 to a date will increase it by 1 hour.

To add 6 hours to each of the meeting_date values, your query will look like this:

```
SELECT id,
TO_CHAR(meeting_date, 'DD/MON/YYYY HH:MI:SS AM') AS meeting_datetime,
TO_CHAR(meeting_date + 6/24, 'DD/MON/YYYY HH:MI:SS AM') AS meeting_
datetime_future
FROM sales_meeting;
```

The results of this query are:

ID	MEETING_DATE	MEETING_DATETIME
1	10/Aug/18	10/Aug/2018 06:00:00 AM
2	21/Aug/18	21/Aug/2018 06:00:00 AM
3	23/Aug/18	23/Aug/2018 06:00:00 AM

This shows the current date and time and then the date and time after 6 hours have been added. All of the times are showing as 6AM, because you added the "+6/24" where the meeting_date column was mentioned. It's added inside the function because we want the addition of 6 hours to be done before the formatting is done by TO_CHAR.

These are just some examples of the kind of addition and subtraction you can do with dates and numbers. A lot more can be done with dates by using date functions.

Date Functions

In this section you'll learn how to use two of the most common date functions. The first one lets you find the current date and time.

Current Date and Time

There are many situations where you want to know what the current date and time is, such as:

- Recording when an event happened in an application

- Recording when errors occur

- Displaying the current date and time to the user

There are a few functions to display the current date and time, but the most commonly used one that I've seen is SYSDATE. This function will return the current date and time of the database server. It's a quick and easy way to get the current date and time. There are no parameters involved; just add the word SYSDATE into your query. To get the current date and time, use this query:

```
SELECT SYSDATE
FROM dual;
```

Your results will show the current date, such as:

SYSDATE
30/AUG/2018

The SYSDATE function actually includes a time component, but like the meeting_date column earlier, it doesn't show by default. You can show the date and time by using the TO_CHAR column on the SYSDATE column. Yes, you can use functions inside other functions, and this is a common way to get the data you need in many situations.

Your query may look like this:

```
SELECT
TO_CHAR(SYSDATE, 'DD/MON/YYYY HH:MI:SS AM') AS time_now
FROM dual;
```

The results of this query will show something like this:

SYSDATE
30/AUG/2018 12:30:14 PM

This shows the current date along with the time. Each time you run this query the time will change to reflect the current time.

If you need to insert the current date into a column, you can use this in an INSERT statement. For example, a query like this will insert a new record with a meeting on the current date and time:

```
INSERT INTO sales_meeting (id, employee_id, company, meeting_date)
VALUES (4, 7, 'McMahon', SYSDATE);
```

So, instead of specifying an actual date value, you use the SYSDATE function. You don't need to run this query on your database.

Adding Months

Earlier in this chapter you learned how to add days to a date by simply adding a number to a date:

```
SELECT meeting_date + 7
FROM sales_meeting;
```

However, what if you needed to add several months to a date? Three months, six months, 24 months? You could do this by adding the number of days. But what number would you choose: 30, or 31? Different months have different numbers of days, so adding a number of 30 won't work in all situations. If you need the date to be exactly a number of months in the future, this method won't work.

There's an Oracle function called ADD_MONTHS, which lets you add a specific number of months to a date:

```
ADD_MONTHS (input_date, number_of_months)
```

This includes two parameters. The input_date is the date you're adding to, and the number_of_months is a number that represents the number of months to add. This will add the specified number of months to a date and ensure the day remains the same, and only the month (or year) changes.

Let's say you needed to add six months to your meeting_dates. Your query would look like this:

```
SELECT
meeting_date,
ADD_MONTHS(meeting_date, 6) AS new_date
FROM sales_meeting;
```

The results of this query are:

ID	MEETING_DATE	NEW_DATE
1	10/Aug/2018	10/Feb/2019
2	21/Aug/2018	21/Feb/2019
3	23/Aug/2018	23/Feb/2019

The new_date column, with the ADD_MONTHS function, shows the meeting date 6 months into the future. It has kept the same day, but the month and year have been changed.

If you wanted to add a specific number of years to a date, you can add this in a number of months. This will work because a year always has 12 months. You can do this by adding the representation of years in months (e.g., 24 for 2 years) or by multiplying the number of years by 12 (e.g., 2 * 12). This query includes both examples:

```
SELECT
meeting_date,
ADD_MONTHS(meeting_date, 24) AS new_date,
ADD_MONTHS(meeting_date, 2*12) AS new_date_ex2
FROM sales_meeting;
```

The results are:

ID	MEETING_DATE	NEW_DATE	NEW_DATE_EX2
1	10/Aug/2018	10/Aug/2020	10/Aug/2020
2	21/Aug/2018	21/Aug/2020	21/Aug/2020
3	23/Aug/2018	23/Aug/2020	23/Aug/2020

Both the new_date and new_date_ex2 columns show the meeting_date value 2 years into the future. This is an easy way of adding months or years to an existing date value.

Summary

Functions in Oracle will let you perform calculations on columns and values in your queries. You can do some basic operations using mathematical symbols such as +, -, * and /. You can also concatenate string values using ||. If you want to perform operations more than that, you can use one of Oracle's many functions.

The Oracle functions are grouped into three groups based on the type of data they work with: number, string, and date. These functions take parameters, perform a process, and return a value. They can be used in many different areas of queries, such as WHERE clauses in SELECT queries and INSERT and UPDATE queries.

CHAPTER 23

Writing Conditional Logic

Many programming languages include the ability to perform conditional logic, or "if this is true, then do something, otherwise do something else." SQL is different to other programming languages and doesn't include a lot of features such as variables and loops. However, SQL does have the ability to use conditional logic.

This is often called an IF statement in other languages, which looks like this:

```
if (some condition) {
  do_something;
}
else {
  do_something_else;
}
```

In SQL, you can do the same kind of thing, but it's done a little differently. You can use a type of statement called the *CASE statement*.

The CASE Statement

In SQL, the CASE statement allows you to perform this "if-then-else" logic or conditional logic in your query. It's similar to an IF statement in other languages. It's called a statement rather than a function because it's a combination of keywords and not a keyword with several parameters inside brackets.

The CASE statement can be used in many of the same places that a function can, such as:

- The SELECT, WHERE, and ORDER BY clause of a SELECT statement

- The UPDATE, SET, and WHERE clause of an UPDATE statement

- The WHERE clause of a DELETE statement

331

© Ben Brumm 2019
B. Brumm, *Beginning Oracle SQL for Oracle Database 18c*,
https://doi.org/10.1007/978-1-4842-4430-2_23

It's good for displaying a particular value depending on another value in the same row. Because values in each row can be different, adding in a CASE statement to look at them and display a value in different situations is sometimes useful.

What does a CASE statement look like?

```
CASE [expression] WHEN condition_1 THEN result_1
WHEN condition_2 THEN result_2
...
WHEN condition_n THEN result_n
ELSE result
END case_name
```

The parameters for this statement are:

- expression: This is the expression or the condition that the CASE statement will look for. If you compare this to an IF statement, this is the first part of the condition that comes after the IF. This is an optional parameter.

- condition_1/2/n: This is the possible result of the expression just mentioned. You can have as many of these conditions as you like in your CASE statement, depending on how many different possible values you want to handle.

- result_1/2/n: This is the value that should be displayed or shown if the condition mentioned is met. This comes after the THEN keyword and is equivalent to the THEN part of an IF-THEN-ELSE statement in other programming languages.

- ELSE result: This is the value to show if none of the conditions in the CASE statement are met. It's equivalent to the ELSE part of an IF-THEN-ELSE statement.

- case_name: This is an optional parameter and indicates what the column should be called when it's used in the query. It's similar to a column alias that you've used in earlier chapters.

It's quite a long statement, but it's very useful if you need to perform this kind of logic in your query. In Oracle SQL, you can use a CASE statement in two ways: a *simple case statement*, and a *searched case statement*.

Simple Case Statement

A *simple case statement* is where the expression parameter is used. The same expression is checked for each of the WHEN condition lines.

For example, your statement may look like this:

```
CASE last_name
WHEN 'JONES' THEN 'The name is Jones'
WHEN 'SMITH' THEN 'The name is Smith'
WHEN 'KING' THEN 'The name is King'
ELSE 'The name is something else'
END namecheck
```

This statement looks at the last_name column and displays different values if it is equal to JONES, SMITH, or KING. If it doesn't match any of those, another value is displayed. You don't need to specify WHEN last_name = 'JONES' or WHEN last_name = 'SMITH' because, using this method, the WHEN automatically applies to the last_name mentioned at the start of the statement.

There is also no mention of a table name or a FROM clause here, as it's assumed this statement is part of another statement (such as a SELECT) that includes a FROM clause. For example, this CASE statement can be added to a SELECT query:

```
SELECT
last_name,
CASE last_name
WHEN 'JONES' THEN 'The name is Jones'
WHEN 'SMITH' THEN 'The name is Smith'
WHEN 'KING' THEN 'The name is King'
ELSE 'The name is something else'
END namecheck
FROM employee;
```

LAST_NAME	NAMECHECK
JONES	The name is Jones
SMITH	The name is Smith
KING	The name is King
SIMPSON	The name is something else
ANDERSON	The name is something else
COOPER	The name is something else
ADAMS	The name is something else
SMITH	The name is Smith
PATRICK	The name is something else
Jones	The name is something else

You can see that a few of these results show a sentence that describes the name correctly, and others show "something else." The last row shows "Jones", but this CASE statement shows it as "something else". This is because the CASE statement and the WHEN clause are case sensitive, just like the WHERE clause you learned about in an earlier chapter. This means that "Jones" does not equal "JONES."

The good news is that you can use functions inside a CASE statement. You can convert the last_name to an uppercase value for checking inside the CASE statement:

```
SELECT
last_name,
CASE UPPER(last_name)
WHEN 'JONES' THEN 'The name is Jones'
WHEN 'SMITH' THEN 'The name is Smith'
WHEN 'KING' THEN 'The name is King'
ELSE 'The name is something else'
END namecheck
FROM employee;
```

LAST_NAME	NAMECHECK
JONES	The name is Jones
SMITH	The name is Smith
KING	The name is King
SIMPSON	The name is something else
ANDERSON	The name is something else
COOPER	The name is something else
ADAMS	The name is something else
SMITH	The name is Smith
PATRICK	The name is something else
Jones	The name is Jones

Using this UPPER function has converted "Jones" to "JONES" and it has met the criteria inside the CASE statement that said WHEN 'JONES'.

Let's look at another example, where you need to determine if a `salary` is equal to 20000 or 40000, then it's eligible for a pay rise. Your query would look like this:

```
SELECT id,
last_name,
salary,
CASE salary
WHEN 20000 THEN 'Eligible'
WHEN 40000 THEN 'Eligible'
ELSE 'Not Eligible'
END salary_check
FROM employee;
```

This query looks at the `salary` column. If it's equal to 20000 it shows a value of Eligible. It shows the same value if it's equal to 40000. If it doesn't match either of those values, it shows as Not Eligible. If you run the query, you'll get this result:

ID	LAST_NAME	SALARY	SALARY_CHECK
1	JONES	30000	Not Eligible
2	SMITH	35000	Not Eligible
3	KING	45000	Not Eligible
4	SIMPSON	52000	Not Eligible
5	ANDERSON	31000	Not Eligible
6	COOPER	(null)	Not Eligible
7	ADAMS	(null)	Not Eligible
8	SMITH	62000	Not Eligible
9	PATRICK	40000	Eligible
10	Jones	42000	Not Eligible

This shows the word Eligible for employees with a salary of 20000 or 40000, and Not Eligible for the other records. However, both of the WHEN clauses inside the CASE statement look very similar:

```
WHEN 20000 THEN 'Eligible'
WHEN 40000 THEN 'Eligible'
```

We can try to improve this by using the OR keyword to combine them into one, just like we would if this was a WHERE clause. This makes it easier to read and write, as there is less code.

```
WHEN 20000 OR 40000 THEN 'Eligible'
```

Let's add this to the overall query and run it.

```
SELECT id,
last_name,
salary,
CASE salary
WHEN 20000 OR 40000 THEN 'Eligible'
ELSE 'Not Eligible'
END salary_check
FROM employee;
```

We get this error:

```
ORA-00905: missing keyword
00905. 00000 -  "missing keyword"
*Cause:
*Action:
Error at Line: 28 Column: 12
```

Does this mean we can't have the OR keyword inside a CASE statement? We can, but not inside a simple case statement. For anything more than these simple checks, we need to use the other type of case statement.

Searched Case Statement

The other type of CASE statement in Oracle is the *searched case statement*. The difference between the searched case statement and the simple case statement is where you specify the expression. In the simple case statement, the expression goes right after the CASE keyword. In the searched case statement, the expression goes in each WHEN clause.

The searched case statement allows for more complex criteria to be used, such as multiple conditions, wildcard checks, greater than and less than checks, and checks on several fields. You can see an example of this using the same logic as the simple case statement you saw earlier, but in the format of a searched case statement:

```
CASE
WHEN last_name = 'JONES' THEN 'The name is Jones'
WHEN last_name = 'SMITH' THEN 'The name is Smith'
WHEN last_name = 'KING' THEN 'The name is King'
ELSE 'The name is something else'
END namecheck
```

This method involves a little more typing, but it's more flexible. Let's add this into a SELECT query and add in the UPPER function as you did earlier.

```
SELECT
last_name,
CASE
WHEN UPPER(last_name) = 'JONES' THEN 'The name is Jones'
```

```
WHEN UPPER(last_name) = 'SMITH' THEN 'The name is Smith'
WHEN UPPER(last_name) = 'KING' THEN 'The name is King'
ELSE 'The name is something else'
END namecheck
FROM employee;
```

LAST_NAME	NAMECHECK
JONES	The name is Jones
SMITH	The name is Smith
KING	The name is King
SIMPSON	The name is something else
ANDERSON	The name is something else
COOPER	The name is something else
ADAMS	The name is something else
SMITH	The name is Smith
PATRICK	The name is something else
Jones	The name is Jones

The results show the same as the earlier example. The namecheck column shows a short description, based on how we wrote the CASE statement. This method might seem like a bit too much effort for a simple check, so in this situation, perhaps the simple case statement is preferred. However, there are times where a searched case statement is better.

Let's take a look at another example. Let's say you've been asked to find out the eligibility of a pay raise for several employees based on their current salary. If an employee is paid less than 40000, then show it as a low salary. If they are paid between 40000 and 50000, then show it as a medium salary, and anything 50000 or more should be shown as a high salary.

Your query would look like this:

```
SELECT id,
last_name,
salary,
CASE
```

```
WHEN salary < 40000 THEN 'Low salary'
WHEN salary > 40000 AND salary < 50000 THEN 'Medium salary'
WHEN salary > 50000 THEN 'High salary'
END salary_check
FROM employee;
```

We haven't added in an ELSE here. It's an optional clause. Let's see what happens when you run this query.

ID	LAST_NAME	SALARY	SALARY_CHECK
1	JONES	30000	Low salary
2	SMITH	35000	Low salary
3	KING	45000	Medium Salary
4	SIMPSON	52000	High salary
5	ANDERSON	31000	Low salary
6	COOPER	(null)	(null)
7	ADAMS	(null)	(null)
8	SMITH	62000	High salary
9	PATRICK	40000	(null)
10	Jones	42000	Medium salary

You can see that some records have a value of either Low salary, Medium salary, or High salary. The other records are showing as NULL. This is because they didn't meet the criteria mentioned in the CASE statement.

What about the record that has a salary of 40000? Why didn't it show a value? It's because the criteria you used was this:

```
CASE
WHEN salary < 40000 THEN 'Low salary'
WHEN salary > 40000 AND salary < 50000 THEN 'Medium salary'
WHEN salary > 50000 THEN 'High salary'
END salary_check
```

The first WHEN clause looks for salary values less than 40000. The second WHEN clause looks for salary values greater than 40000. There's no mention of a salary being equal to 40000. There are two ways to fix this:

- Change the signs to include "equal to"

- Change the WHEN clause to overlap

The first way to solve it is to change the signs to include an equal to. The description we used earlier was: "If an employee is paid less than 40000, then show it as a low salary. If they are paid between 40000 and 50000, then show it as a medium salary." This shows that the salary values of 40000 should be marked as 'Medium salary'. You can change your query to put an "equal to":

```
SELECT id,
last_name,
salary,
CASE
WHEN salary < 40000 THEN 'Low salary'
WHEN salary >= 40000 AND salary < 50000 THEN 'Medium salary'
WHEN salary >= 50000 THEN 'High salary'
END salary_check
FROM employee;
```

ID	LAST_NAME	SALARY	SALARY_CHECK
1	JONES	30000	Low salary
2	SMITH	35000	Low salary
3	KING	45000	Medium salary
4	SIMPSON	52000	High salary
5	ANDERSON	31000	Low salary
6	COOPER	(null)	(null)
7	ADAMS	(null)	(null)
8	SMITH	62000	High salary
9	PATRICK	40000	Medium salary
10	Jones	42000	Medium salary

The right values are now shown. The final two NULL values are displaying because the salary value is NULL.

The other way of resolving this problem is taking advantage of the way that Oracle processes CASE statements. Oracle will find the first condition that is true, and use that for your CASE statement. This means if both the first and second WHEN clauses are true, then the first WHEN clause result will be used. You can update your query to use this:

```
SELECT id,
last_name,
salary,
CASE
WHEN salary < 40000 THEN 'Low salary'
WHEN salary < 50000 THEN 'Medium salary'
WHEN salary >= 50000 THEN 'High salary'
END salary_check
FROM employee;
```

ID	LAST_NAME	SALARY	SALARY_CHECK
1	JONES	30000	Low salary
2	SMITH	35000	Low salary
3	KING	45000	Medium salary
4	SIMPSON	52000	High salary
5	ANDERSON	31000	Low salary
6	COOPER	(null)	(null)
7	ADAMS	(null)	(null)
8	SMITH	62000	High salary
9	PATRICK	40000	Medium salary
10	Jones	42000	Medium salary

The same values are shown as the earlier example. The CASE statement, as you can see, is quite a powerful statement

There is another way to handle conditional logic in SQL, and that's the DECODE function.

The DECODE Function

DECODE is a function available in Oracle that lets you perform conditional logic. It's similar to the CASE statement. The function syntax looks like this:

```
DECODE (expression, search, result [, search, result]... [,default] )
```

The parameters of this Oracle DECODE function are:

- expression (mandatory): This is the value to compare to in the function.

- search (mandatory): This is the value to compare against the expression.

- result (mandatory): This is what is returned if the search value matches the expression value. There can be many pairs of search and result values, and the result value is related to the previous search value.

- default (optional): If none of the search values match the expression, then this value is returned. If the default value is not provided then NULL is used.

If you compare this to an IF-THEN-ELSE statement, it would look like this:

```
IF (expression = search) THEN result
[ELSE IF (expression = search) THEN result]
ELSE default
END IF
```

You can write the earlier CASE statement as a DECODE function as well. It would look like this:

```
SELECT
last_name,
DECODE(UPPER(last_name), 'JONES', 'The name is Jones', 'SMITH', 'The name
is Smith', 'KING', 'The name is King', 'The name is something else') AS
namecheck
FROM employee;
```

This function is all on a single line, so can be formatted a little better:

```
SELECT
last_name,
DECODE(UPPER(last_name),
  'JONES', 'The name is Jones',
  'SMITH', 'The name is Smith',
  'KING', 'The name is King',
  'The name is something else') AS namecheck
FROM employee;
```

You can run this query and get the following result.

LAST_NAME	NAMECHECK
JONES	The name is Jones
SMITH	The name is Smith
KING	The name is King
SIMPSON	The name is something else
ANDERSON	The name is something else
COOPER	The name is something else
ADAMS	The name is something else
SMITH	The name is Smith
PATRICK	The name is something else
Jones	The name is Jones

The DECODE function in this example looks similar to a CASE statement and shows the same results. However, there are situations where the DECODE function can be a bit messy, such as using the LIKE keyword for partial matches or using greater than or less than symbols.

DECODE can only be checked for exact matches. You can use some operators and a SIGN function to check for greater than or less than other values. Earlier we had a CASE statement that grouped salaries:

```
CASE
WHEN salary < 40000 THEN 'Low salary'
WHEN salary < 50000 THEN 'Medium salary'
WHEN salary >= 50000 THEN 'High salary'
END salary_check
```

To write the same logic in a DECODE statement, our function would look like this:

```
DECODE(SIGN(40000-salary),1,'Low salary', -1, 'Medium or high salary', 'Unsure')
```

This function first subtracts the salary from 40000 and encloses it in a SIGN function. This function will return a 1 if the result is positive, and -1 if the result is negative. So, if the salary is less than 40000 then the value will be positive, and SIGN returns 1.

You'll then need to substitute the 'Medium or high salary' for another DECODE function to check for the value of 50000:

```
DECODE(SIGN(40000-salary),1,'Low salary', -1, DECODE(SIGN(50000-
salary),1,'Medium salary', -1, 'High salary', 'Unsure'),'Unsure')
```

As you can see, this is getting quite messy, with functions inside other functions. It's also hard for you or others to understand what it means.

So, in this situation, it might work, but a CASE statement would be better.

CASE or DECODE?

If the CASE statement and the DECODE function do the same thing, which one should you use? I recommend using the CASE statement in every situation, for a few reasons:

- CASE was introduced in Oracle 8 (quite a while ago) to replace DECODE, which is an older function.

- CASE is more flexible than DECODE.

- CASE is more readable for simple and complicated logic than DECODE.

- Performance is the same between both CASE and DECODE.

If you use CASE in all situations, then you're being consistent. Sometimes it might seem easier to use a DECODE for simple logic, but if you use DECODE in some places and CASE in others, it makes your SQL code a little harder to understand.

Summary

Oracle SQL includes the ability to use conditional logic, which is equivalent to "if then else" statements. This can be done in two ways: CASE and DECODE.

The CASE statement lets you perform conditional logic, either as a simple case statement or a searched case statement. These statements are almost the same and only differ in where the expression is used, but the searched case statement allows for more flexibility in logic.

The DECODE function can also be used for conditional logic in a similar way. However, it is more restrictive, older, and harder to read. I recommend using CASE statements rather than DECODE functions.

CHAPTER 24

Understanding Aggregate Functions

In the last chapter, you learned what a function was. You looked at a few examples of functions, such as LOWER, that performed a specific operation on a particular column's value for every record. The LOWER function was used to convert every record's last_name value into a lowercase version of the last_name.

```
SELECT id,
last_name,
LOWER(last_name)
FROM employee;
```

The results of this query show the last_name records in lowercase.

ID	LAST_NAME	LOWER(LAST_NAME)
1	JONES	jones
2	SMITH	smith
3	KING	king
4	SIMPSON	simpson
5	ANDERSON	anderson
6	COOPER	cooper
7	ADAMS	adams
8	SMITH	smith
9	PATRICK	patrick
10	Jones	jones

© Ben Brumm 2019
B. Brumm, *Beginning Oracle SQL for Oracle Database 18c*,
https://doi.org/10.1007/978-1-4842-4430-2_24

This function, and others we looked at, are performed on each record individually. There are some functions in SQL that allow you to perform an operation on multiple records

Aggregate Functions

An *aggregate function* is a type of function in SQL that can use data form more than one row. They are called aggregate functions because they aggregate data. While the functions you learned about earlier, such as ADD_MONTHS and LOWER, are operating on each row that is returned, aggregate functions look at data in multiple rows and return a single result.

Why would this be useful? There are five commonly used aggregate functions in SQL, and they allow you to perform the following tasks:

- Find the number of records in a column or a table

- Find the total of a set of numbers

- Find the maximum or highest value

- Find the minimum or highest value

- Find the average from a list of values

You'll learn about these functions and how to use them in this chapter.

The SUM Function

The first of the aggregate functions you'll learn about is called SUM. The SUM function is used to total or add up numbers. It looks like this:

SUM ([DISTINCT] expression)

The SUM function takes two parameters:

- expression: This is the expression to be added up, which could be a column in a table or some other representation of number values.

- DISTINCT: This is an optional parameter that specifies the SUM function should only sum the distinct or unique values in the expression. I haven't used this very often, but it's good to know that it's available.

A Simple SUM Example

Let's see some examples of the SUM function, using the salary value in the employee table. The table looks like this:

```
SELECT id,
last_name,
salary
FROM employee;
```

ID	LAST_NAME	SALARY
1	JONES	30000
2	SMITH	35000
3	KING	45000
4	SIMPSON	52000
5	ANDERSON	31000
6	COOPER	(null)
7	ADAMS	(null)
8	SMITH	62000
9	PATRICK	40000
10	Jones	42000

To find the SUM of the salary values, you can write a query like this:

```
SELECT SUM(salary)
FROM employee;
```

This will show the total of all of the salary values.

SUM(SALARY)
337000

The NULL values are ignored in the SUM calculation, and the total of the salary values is 337,000. Notice how there is only one row returned, even though there are ten rows in the employee table. This is because the SUM function is an aggregate function. It returns a single row regardless of how many rows are in the underlying table.

SUM with WHERE

The SUM function can work if you use it with a WHERE clause. The database will perform the WHERE clause first, and then perform the SUM on those values that match the WHERE clause.

Let's say you want to find the total of all salary values for employees excluding SIMPSON. The query for that would be:

```
SELECT SUM(salary)
FROM employee
WHERE last_name <> 'SIMPSON';
```

The result from this query is:

SUM(SALARY)
285000

This is the same salary total as before, minus the 52000 salary for SIMPSON.

SUM with Expression

You can use the SUM function with values that have had other functions or calculations performed on them. Let's say you wanted to find the total of salary values if they had all been given a 20% pay increase. This means the salary value would be multiplied by 1.2 and then added together.

```
SELECT SUM(salary * 1.2)
FROM employee;
```

The results are:

SUM(SALARY)
404400

Anything that can be turned into a number can be used as a parameter in the SUM function.

SUM with DISTINCT

Let's see what the DISTINCT keyword does when used inside the SUM function. This will find the unique or distinct values in the column, and sum those together.

```
SELECT SUM(DISTINCT salary)
FROM employee;
```

The results are:

SUM(SALARY)
337000

It shows 337,000 because it has calculated the sum of all of the unique salary values.

The COUNT Function

Another function available in Oracle SQL is the COUNT function. This function is used to count the number of records in a table or in your result set. It works in a similar way to the SUM function:

```
COUNT( [DISTINCT] expression)
```

The two parameters to this function are the same as the SUM function:

- expression: This is the expression to be counted, which could be a column in a table or some other representation of number values.

- DISTINCT: This is an optional parameter that specifies the COUNT function should only count the distinct or unique values in the expression.

Let's take a look at some examples.

Counting All Records

A common use of the COUNT function is to count all records in a table. This can be done using a * for the parameter:

```
SELECT COUNT(*)
FROM employee;
```

This will count all records in the table and show a single number.

COUNT(*)
10

Just like the SUM function, the COUNT function is an aggregate function, so it aggregates multiple rows into one row. This is an easy way to see how many records are in a table. You can run it on any table:

```
SELECT COUNT(*)
FROM office;
```

COUNT(*)
3

There are three records in the office table, so this COUNT shows a value of 3.

Count a Specific Column

Another way to use the COUNT function is to count the number of values in a specific column. This is slightly different to COUNT(*), because counting a specific column will ignore any NULL values, but COUNT(*) will include rows with NULL values.

If you perform a COUNT on the id column, it will count the values that are not NULL and show the result. In this situation, all of the values are populated. You can confirm this by selecting some of the columns from the employee table.

```
SELECT id, last_name, salary
FROM employee;
```

ID	LAST_NAME	SALARY
1	JONES	30000
2	SMITH	35000
3	KING	45000
4	SIMPSON	52000
5	ANDERSON	31000
6	COOPER	(null)
7	ADAMS	(null)
8	SMITH	62000
9	PATRICK	40000
10	Jones	42000

You can use the COUNT function on the id column:

```
SELECT COUNT(id)
FROM employee;
```

COUNT(ID)
10

However, if you count the last_name column, the value will be different because there is a NULL value:

```
SELECT COUNT(last_name)
FROM employee;
```

COUNT(LAST_NAME)
9

You can also count the salary column, which will show a different value again:

```
SELECT COUNT(salary)
FROM employee;
```

COUNT(SALARY)
8

As you can see, performing a COUNT on different columns will show different results if there are NULL values in that column.

Count with DISTINCT

Sometimes you'll need to find out the number of distinct or unique values in a column, such as a "status" column or employee last_name values. You can use the SELECT DISTINCT to see what the values are, but if you just want to see how many there are, you can use COUNT with DISTINCT.

The query to do this would look like this:

```
SELECT COUNT(DISTINCT last_name)
FROM employee;
```

Notice that the DISTINCT is inside the brackets, as we are counting the distinct last_name values. The results of this query are:

COUNT(DISTINCTLAST_NAME)
9

This result shows 9, because there are 10 rows in the table including the value of SMITH mentioned twice, which is excluded from the count. It shows there are 9 distinct last_name values. We can see what the actual values are by running a SELECT query:

```
SELECT DISTINCT last_name
FROM employee;
```

LAST_NAME
JONES
SMITH
KING
SIMPSON
ANDERSON
ADAMS
COOPER
PATRICK
Jones

Both "JONES" and "Jones" are treated as different values, as the DISTINCT keyword is case sensitive.

What happens if we put the DISTINCT outside the COUNT function? This is something I've done before and I've seen others do. In order to count the number of distinct records, a query could look like this:

```
SELECT DISTINCT COUNT(last_name)
FROM employee;
```

If you run this query, you'll get this result:

COUNT(LAST_NAME)
10

The value of 10 is shown. This is because this query is not counting the distinct last_name values; it's counting all of the last_name values and then performing a DISTINCT on the COUNT function. These steps are performed:

1. Look at the last_name values in the employee table

2. Count the number of last_name values that are not NULL and return a single value (the value of 10)

3. Show the unique results. There is only one row, so no duplicates are found.

This process performs the COUNT before the DISTINCT, so while the query will return a result, it doesn't show you the distinct number of last_name values.

Note   To count the number of distinct values, the DISTINCT must go inside the COUNT function, not outside.

Count with WHERE

Another way you can use the COUNT function is with a WHERE clause in the SELECT query. The previous examples have involved counting all records in a table, but sometimes you may want to count records that meet certain criteria. This is as simple as adding a WHERE clause to the SELECT query as you've previously done.

Let's say you needed to find the number of employees with a salary of less than or equal to 40000. A query to do this would be:

```
SELECT COUNT(*)
FROM employee
WHERE salary <= 40000;
```

This uses the COUNT(*) function along with a WHERE clause for just the employees we want to count. The results are:

COUNT(*)
4

This query has determined there are 4 employees that meet that criterion.

The AVG Function

Oracle includes a function called AVG, which is short for "average." This function is used to find the average of a set of number values. An average value is calculated by adding together all of the non-NULL values and dividing by the number of non-NULL values. The function looks similar to the SUM and COUNT functions:

```
AVG ( [DISTINCT] expression)
```

The parameters to this function are the same as the COUNT function:

- expression: This is the expression to calculate the average of, which could be a column in a table or some other representation of number values.

- DISTINCT: This is an optional parameter that specifies the AVG function should only average the distinct or unique values in the expression.

Let's take a look at some examples.

Average of All Values

One way to use the AVG function is to find the average of all values in a column. This only works with number values, so for this example you'll need to find the average salary for all employees:

```
SELECT AVG(salary)
FROM employee;
```

Like the COUNT and SUM functions earlier, you specify the column name inside the brackets. The database will look at all values in this column that are not NULL, find the average of them, and display the value to you. The result of this query is:

AVG(SALARY)
42125

This shows the average salary is 42,125. You can check what `salary` values are in the table by selecting those values:

```
SELECT id, salary
FROM employee;
```

ID	SALARY
1	30000
2	35000
3	45000
4	52000
5	31000
6	(null)
7	(null)
8	62000
9	40000
10	42000

Average with DISTINCT

You can also use the AVG function to average the number of unique or distinct values. It works the same way as the COUNT function, where it eliminates the duplicate values in the column and averages the remaining values. The query could look like this:

```
SELECT AVG(DISTINCT salary)
FROM employee;
```

AVG(DISTINCTSALARY)
42125

This query has found the average of the distinct values.

Average with WHERE

Finally, just like the SUM and COUNT function, you can use AVG with a query that has a WHERE clause. You can add the WHERE clause to the query separately from the AVG function.

Let's say you needed to find the average salary of employees who were in office number 2. To do this, your query could be:

```
SELECT AVG(salary)
FROM employee
WHERE office_id = 2;
```

The results are:

AVG(SALARY)
40666.66666

This query will find all employees with an office_id of 2, and then find the average salary of those employees. You can run a SELECT query to see which records it is using:

```
SELECT id, last_name, salary
FROM employee
WHERE office_id = 2;
```

ID	LAST_NAME	SALARY
2	SMITH	35000
3	KING	45000
10	Jones	42000

These three records were used in the AVG function, and the average of the salary values is 40,666.

The MIN Function

MIN is another aggregate function, and it's used to find the minimum or lowest value in a list of values. It's used with number values, just like AVG and SUM, and it ignores any NULL values.

To use the MIN function, follow this syntax:

```
MIN (expression)
```

The expression here refers to the values to use to calculate the minimum. Most often this will be a column in a table. Let's see some examples of the MIN function.

Minimum of All Records

You can write a simple query that uses MIN to find the minimum value of all records. For example, to find the minimum salary, your query could look like this:

```
SELECT MIN(salary)
FROM employee;
```

The results of this query are:

MIN(SALARY)
30000

This shows that the minimum or smallest salary is 20000. You can see how this is the case by looking at all salary values in the table.

```
SELECT id, salary
FROM employee;
```

ID	SALARY
1	30000
2	35000
3	45000
4	52000

ID	SALARY
5	31000
6	(null)
7	(null)
8	62000
9	40000
10	42000

You could order this query by the salary column to make it easier to look for the lowest value.

```
SELECT id, salary
FROM employee
ORDER BY salary ASC;
```

ID	SALARY
1	25000
5	31000
2	35000
9	40000
10	42000
3	45000
4	52000
8	62000
6	(null)
7	(null)

Now you can see that the lowest salary is 30000. NULL values are ignored, as they represent unknown values, which is different to zero.

Minimum with WHERE

Just like the previous functions, you can use the MIN function in a query with a WHERE clause. Let's say you wanted to find the minimum salary of all employees that are in office_id 3. To do this, your query would look like this:

```
SELECT MIN(salary)
FROM employee
WHERE office_id = 3;
```

The results are:

MIN(SALARY)
62000

This is the minimum value because there are only two employees with an office_id of 3, and one of them has a salary value of NULL.

The MAX Function

The final aggregate function you'll learn about is the MAX function. This function will find the maximum or highest value in a set of values. It's the opposite of the MIN function. To use this function, follow this syntax:

```
MAX (expression)
```

The expression here refers to the values to use to calculate the maximum. Most often this will be a column in a table. Let's see some examples of the MAX function.

Maximum of All Records

You can use the MAX function to find the highest value for a column in a table, just like you used the MIN function to find the smallest. A query to do this would look like this:

```
SELECT MAX(salary)
FROM employee;
```

This will show the following result:

MAX(SALARY)
62000

This shows the highest salary in the table, which is 62,000. You can confirm this by selecting all salary values from the table and ordering by salary in descending order:

```
SELECT id, salary
FROM employee
ORDER BY salary DESC NULLS LAST;
```

ID	SALARY
8	62000
4	52000
10	42000
3	40000
9	40000
2	35000
5	31000
1	20000
6	(null)
7	(null)

Just like with all other functions in this chapter, the NULL values are ignored.

Maximum with WHERE

You can also use the MAX function when using a WHERE clause in your query. The MAX function will be used on all values in rows that match the WHERE clause.

For example, to find the maximum `salary` for all `employees` in office 1 or 2, the following query can be used:

```
SELECT MAX(salary)
FROM employee
WHERE office_id IN (1, 2);
```

The results are:

MIN(SALARY)
52000

This is the highest `salary` for employees in either office 1 or 2.

Summary

Aggregate functions are functions that look at one or many rows and aggregate that data into a single result. The five most common functions are SUM (which adds up values), COUNT (which counts the number of values), AVG (which finds an average value), MAX (which finds the maximum value), and MIN (which finds the lowest value). All of them ignore NULL values and can be used with a WHERE clause.

CHAPTER 25

Grouping Your Results

In the last chapter, you learned about aggregate functions. These functions calculated a value, such as a sum or a count, over the values in a column and showed you a single row of results. In this chapter, you'll learn how to write a query that groups your results. What does that mean?

Grouping Your Data

To understand the concept of grouping data, let's take a look at the employee table.

```
SELECT id, last_name, salary, office_id
FROM employee;
```

ID	LAST_NAME	SALARY	OFFICE_ID
1	JONES	30000	1
2	SMITH	35000	2
3	KING	45000	2
4	SIMPSON	52000	1
5	ANDERSON	31000	(null)
6	COOPER	(null)	1
7	ADAMS	(null)	3
8	SMITH	62000	3
9	PATRICK	40000	1
10	Jones	42000	2

© Ben Brumm 2019
B. Brumm, *Beginning Oracle SQL for Oracle Database 18c*,
https://doi.org/10.1007/978-1-4842-4430-2_25

In the last chapter, you learned how to find the total of all of the salary values using SUM and how to count the number of records using COUNT. These functions look at all of the values in the table and show you a value. They let you find the answer to questions like:

- Find the sum of all salary values

- Find the sum of all salary values for employees in office_id 1

- Find the number of employees

- Find the number of employees in office_id 2

What if you wanted to find the number of employees in each office? You could write a query like this:

```
SELECT COUNT(*)
FROM employee
WHERE office_id = 1;
```

This would show the number of employees with an office_id value of 1. You would then have to run another query for the next office_id:

```
SELECT COUNT(*)
FROM employee
WHERE office_id = 2;
```

You would then run these queries until you got the COUNT results for all of your office_id values. There are a few disadvantages to doing it this way:

- You have to write queries for each different office_id value, which takes time.

- You need to know what each of the office_id values are before writing the query.

- You'll have to combine the results of all of these separate queries.

There is a better way to do this though: grouping. Oracle SQL allows you to create groups of data when using aggregate functions. This will let you find the answer to questions such as "find the number of employees in each office_id" without having to run separate queries. For this example, this is the kind of result we are looking for.

OFFICE_ID	COUNT(*)
1	4
2	3
3	2
(null)	1

How can you do this with SQL? There's a keyword called GROUP BY that can be used with a SELECT statement.

The GROUP BY Keyword

In SQL, the GROUP BY keyword lets you group data when running a SELECT query. To use GROUP BY, you need:

- An aggregate function, such as SUM or COUNT

- Columns to group this data by

In our example, you want to find the number of employees in each office_id. This means the column you want to group this data by is the office_id, as the description says "in each office_id." You also want to see the number of employees, which is done using COUNT.

To start the SELECT query, you specify the column to display and then COUNT:

```
SELECT office_id, COUNT(*)
```

This will display the office_id column, and then a COUNT column. You then add in the table name:

```
SELECT office_id, COUNT(*)
FROM employee
```

Now you add in a GROUP BY keyword. This defines how you want to group your data, or how the COUNT function should be calculated. You want to calculate the COUNT for each different value of office_id, so your GROUP BY clause will look like this:

```
SELECT office_id, COUNT(*)
FROM employee
GROUP BY office_id;
```

367

One easy way to remember this is that any column in the SELECT clause that is not an aggregate function should be in the GROUP BY clause. In this query, the office_id is in the SELECT clause and is also in the GROUP BY clause. The COUNT(*) function is not in the GROUP BY clause because it is an aggregate function. Let's run this query now.

OFFICE_ID	COUNT(*)
1	4
2	3
3	2
(null)	1

This shows you the exact result that you want. This simple query lets you find the number of employees in each office, without having to know what the office_id values are and without having to write separate queries.

What if you didn't use the GROUP BY clause?

```
SELECT office_id, COUNT(*)
FROM employee;
```

If you run this query, you might expect to see the same results. However, this is what you see:

```
ORA-00937: not a single-group group function
00937. 00000 -  "not a single-group group function"
*Cause:
*Action:
Error at Line: 1 Column: 8
```

This error means that you have a column with an aggregate function, but no GROUP BY clause. This SQL is invalid, as the GROUP BY clause is needed. This is a common error that you'll get when writing SQL, but fortunately it's an easy fix.

SQL Developer will also show a colored underline under your SELECT columns if you forget to add a GROUP BY:

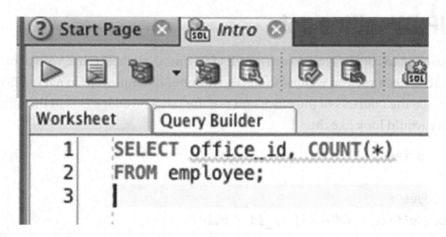

Figure 25-1. *Colored underline*

If you hover over this, it will display a warning message.

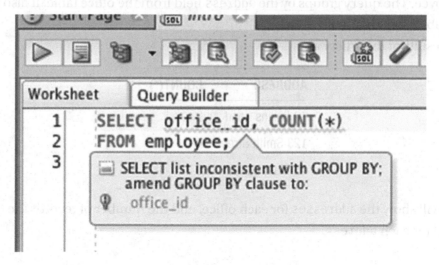

Figure 25-2. *Warning message for missing GROUP BY*

This way you can see that you have an issue before you run the query.

GROUP BY with a Join

You can use the GROUP BY clause with any SELECT query, such as those with a join to another table. Let's say you wanted to see the number of employees in each office, but wanted to see the address of the office and not the ID. The address is in the office table. Your query would look like this:

```
SELECT o.address,
COUNT(*)
FROM employee e
INNER JOIN office o ON e.office_id = o.id
GROUP BY o.address
ORDER BY o.address;
```

This query includes a few things. It has table aliases, which are "o" for office and "e" for employee. The query groups by the address field from the office table. It also joins the two tables together.

The results of this query are:

ADDRESS	COUNT(*)
10 Collins Road	2
123 Smith Street	4
45 Main Street	3

This will show the addresses for each office, and the number of records the query has found for each address.

GROUP BY and SUM

You can use the GROUP BY clause with any aggregate function. The earlier examples used COUNT, but you can use SUM instead if needed. To find the sum of salary values for each office, your query could look like this:

```
SELECT office_id,
SUM(salary)
FROM employee
GROUP BY office_id;
```

It's very similar to the query with COUNT, but instead you are using SUM on the salary column. Your results will look like this:

OFFICE_ID	SUM(SALARY)
1	122000
2	122000
3	62000
(null)	31000

This shows each office_id value and the sum of the salary values for employees with that office_id. You could add this up manually but using this function, and a GROUP BY clause will calculate it automatically.

GROUP BY with WHERE

Just like with any other SELECT query, you can filter your results using the WHERE clause if you're using a GROUP BY clause. The WHERE clause will filter any results that don't match your criteria, and then the GROUP BY and aggregate functions will be performed on the records that are left.

Let's say you wanted to find the total salary for each office, excluding the employee SIMPSON. Your query would look like this:

```
SELECT office_id,
SUM(salary)
FROM employee
WHERE last_name <> 'SIMPSON'
GROUP BY office_id;
```

The WHERE clause comes before the GROUP BY clause. If it's around the other way, you'll get an error.

The results from this query are:

OFFICE_ID	SUM(SALARY)
1	70000
2	122000
3	62000
(null)	31000

The results are almost the same as the earlier query, except office_id 1 has a lower salary. It's 52,000 lower because SIMPSON was excluded, and they have an office_id of 1. In this situation, the query has:

1. Looked at all employee records

2. Excluded those that have a last_name of SIMPSON

3. Displayed each of the unique office_id values from these results

4. Calculated a SUM for each of these office_id values from these results

Using a combination of WHERE, aggregate functions, and GROUP BY makes it easy in SQL to get the kind of aggregate results you're looking for.

Restricting Results After Grouping

The WHERE clause in a query allows you to restrict the results that you perform your aggregate function and grouping on. In the preceding example, you excluded employee SIMPSON from the SUM of salary by office.

Let's try a different example to see another feature of SQL. Let's say you wanted to find the number of employees in each office where there are more than two employees in that office.

You can start by listing the office_id values and the count of employees:

```
SELECT office_id, COUNT(*)
FROM employee
GROUP BY office_id;
```

The results will look like this:

OFFICE_ID	COUNT(*)
1	4
2	3
3	2
(null)	1

This shows the number of employees in each office. Now, the next step is to only show the offices that have more than two employees. To do this, you could exclude office_id 3, but it's better to exclude the records based on your criteria. Excluding the data based on the id values you find will require you to know these id values. So, let's exclude records with 2 or fewer employees:

```
SELECT office_id, COUNT(*)
FROM employee
WHERE COUNT(*) > 2
GROUP BY office_id;
```

This should only show records where the COUNT function has returned a value greater than 2. Let's run this query and see what happens:

```
ORA-00934: group function is not allowed here
00934. 00000 -  "group function is not allowed here"
*Cause:
*Action:
Error at Line: 3 Column: 7
```

You've gotten an error. Why is this? This error has happened because of the way the SQL statements are processed and the rules behind it. One rule in SQL is that you can't use a WHERE clause on any value that is a result of a GROUP BY clause. This is because the clauses in an SQL statement are processed in the following order, which is different to the order they are written:

1. FROM

2. WHERE

3.   GROUP BY

4.   SELECT

5.   ORDER BY

This means that when the WHERE clause is processed, all it knows is the columns and tables you are selecting from. It has no knowledge of the result of the COUNT function for each group, as that is done by the GROUP BY clause.

How can you get the result you need? You can use a clause called HAVING.

The HAVING Clause

In SQL, there is a clause called the HAVING clause. The HAVING clause will restrict rows in your result after the GROUP BY has been applied. The HAVING clause looks like this:

```
HAVING criteria
```

It works in a similar way to the WHERE clause, as you need to specify criteria. However, the criteria here are meant to be the aggregate functions used in your SELECT query.

In the earlier example, you tried to find the offices and the number of employees in each office where there are more than two employees. To do this, you need to only show records where the COUNT(*) is greater than 2. Because this is an aggregate function, you'll need to use the HAVING clause for this:

```
SELECT office_id,
COUNT(*)
FROM employee
GROUP BY office_id
HAVING COUNT(*) > 2;
```

The HAVING clause looks the same as a WHERE clause would, except the keyword is different. Also, the HAVING clause goes after the GROUP BY clause, rather than after the FROM clause.

If you run this query, you'll get this result:

OFFICE_ID	COUNT(*)
1	4
2	3

Both of the first two office_ids are displayed, as they have 4 and 3 employees in them. The record with an office_id of 3 is not shown, as it had two employees in it. You can see the underlying data by querying the employee table, and ordering by the office_id to make it easier to see:

```
SELECT id,
last_name,
office_id
FROM employee
ORDER BY office_id ASC;
```

ID	LAST_NAME	OFFICE_ID
1	JONES	1
4	SIMPSON	1
6	COOPER	1
9	PATRICK	1
2	SMITH	2
3	KING	2
10	Jones	2
7	ADAMS	3
8	SMITH	3
5	ANDERSON	(null)

You can see the number of employees by looking at this result.

GROUP BY, HAVING, and SUM

You can use the HAVING clause with any aggregate function. The earlier example used the COUNT function, but it can also be used with other functions such as SUM, MAX, MIN, or AVG.

Let's say you needed to find the number of employees and total salary for each office where the total salary is greater than 100,000. This can be done by expanding the query from the earlier example:

```
SELECT office_id,
COUNT(*),
SUM(salary)
FROM employee
GROUP BY office_id
HAVING SUM(salary) > 100000;
```

This query has a few differences. It has two aggregate functions: COUNT and SUM. This is acceptable to do in SQL. It also has a HAVING clause that only shows records where the SUM of salary is greater than 100,000. The results of this query are:

OFFICE_ID	COUNT(*)	SUM(SALARY)
1	4	122000
2	3	122000

It shows both offices 1 and 2, as their total salary is greater than 10000. The record with an office_id of 3 is excluded as the total salary is less than 100000.

This example shows that you can include two aggregate functions in your query and use the HAVING clause on only one of them.

Finding Duplicate Records

The final example you'll learn in this chapter is how to find duplicate records. In your tables, it's easy to store data that is the same as existing records. There are features you can use in both your database and application code to prevent this; however, they are not always used.

Let's take a look at the employee table again:

```
SELECT id,
last_name,
salary,
office_id
FROM employee;
```

The results are:

ID	LAST_NAME	SALARY	OFFICE_ID
1	JONES	30000	1
2	SMITH	35000	2
3	KING	45000	2
4	SIMPSON	52000	1
5	ANDERSON	31000	(null)
6	COOPER	(null)	1
7	ADAMS	(null)	3
8	SMITH	62000	3
9	PATRICK	40000	1
10	Jones	42000	2

You can see that there are ten employees. Some of the last_name values are the same, even though the salary is different. If you wanted to find duplicate records in this table, you may want to start with the last_names that were repeated. Just because the records have the same last_name doesn't mean they are duplicates, but it's a good place to start. You may also just want to know which last_names are used more than once.

The query you want to write will show you the last_name and the number of employees with each last_name where there is more than one employee for that last name. This query will look like this:

```
SELECT UPPER(last_name),
COUNT(*) AS empcount
FROM employee
GROUP BY UPPER(last_name)
```

```
HAVING COUNT(*) > 1
ORDER BY empcount DESC;
```

There are a few things in this query. We're selecting the uppercase version of the `last_name` and the `COUNT` of each `last_name` and have given an alias to the `COUNT` column called "empcount." We're grouping by the `last_name` column and using the `HAVING` clause to eliminate `last_name` records where there is 1 employee or less. Finally, we're ordering by the empcount column.

Why are we using the `COUNT(*)` function in the `HAVING` clause but using the empcount alias in the `ORDER BY`? This is due to the way the query is processed in Oracle and it means that the `ORDER BY` clause can refer to column aliases, but the `GROUP BY` and `HAVING` can't. The same result could be achieved with `ORDER BY COUNT(*) DESC`, but for this example, I've used the column alias.

Let's see the results:

LAST_NAME	EMPCOUNT
JONES	2
SMITH	2

The results show JONES and SMITH with two employees each. The `last_name` of JONES shows two because we have converted the `last_name` to uppercase, so it includes the record of "Jones." All other `last_names` are not shown here because they only have one matching `employee`.

So, by using a combination of aggregate functions, grouping, and ordering, you can find out which records may be duplicates and can investigate your data further.

Summary

Grouping your data means performing aggregate functions for each different value in a particular column. If you use aggregate functions and columns that are not aggregate functions, you'll need to group by all nonaggregate columns in your query in order to avoid an error. You can use the `WHERE` clause to filter records before the grouping. You can also use the `HAVING` clause to filter records after the grouping has been applied, which is done on the aggregate functions used.

Using a combination of `GROUP BY` and `HAVING` can make it easy to get the results you need.

CHAPTER 26

What Are Indexes?

Indexes are a feature that's worth knowing about in SQL. They are useful for making your queries perform better, and as you gain more experience in SQL, you'll need to know how to create them and why they are needed.

What Is an Index?

An *index* is an object in the database that improves the performance, or reduces the run time, of your SQL query. I like to think of it like an index in the back of a textbook.

Have you ever tried to look at a textbook for a specific topic? For example, you're looking at a textbook on the history of human civilization and want to know more about Julius Caesar. You know this was part of the Roman times, so you might guess that it was somewhere in the middle of the book. You would flip to somewhere in the middle of the book and scan the pages to look for something about Julius Caesar. Or, you could start ate page 1 and look through each page for information on Julius Caesar until you get to the current year.

Either of those methods would take a while and wouldn't be very efficient. When you read every page from start to finish until you find the information you need is how Oracle looks up data in your table. When you look for the `employee` record where the `last_name` is SIMPSON, Oracle will look at every row to find the record you need. This can also take some time if the table is large.

There is a better way. Textbooks often have an index at the back of the book. This index will list all of the key topics in the book and the pages they are referenced on. To find information about Julius Caesar, you can simply look that up in the index and it will show you all of the pages in the book where it's mentioned:

Julius Caesar... pg 43, 210, 548-570

You can then flip to those pages to find the information you need.

© Ben Brumm 2019
B. Brumm, *Beginning Oracle SQL for Oracle Database 18c*,
https://doi.org/10.1007/978-1-4842-4430-2_26

An index in Oracle works the same way. You can create an index, which includes information on where to find records in a table. When you run an SQL statement that looks for data using that information, Oracle will use the index to find the records you need. This is usually much faster than looking through the entire table without the index.

So why do you need to know about indexes? Indexes are good to know because they can make a big difference in the performance of your queries. It's also very common in databases in the "real world" to have indexes on their tables. Knowing what they are, what they do, and how to create them is a skill that will be useful for you in your career.

How to Create an Index

An index is an object on the database, just like a table. To create an index, we use the CREATE statement. The syntax for this statement is:

```
CREATE INDEX index_name
ON table_name (columns);
```

You start with CREATE INDEX. You then need to provide a name for the index. The index name must be unique on the database. Next, you have the keyword ON and then a table name, followed by the column (or columns) you want the index to be created on.

An index is created on a single table and on one or more columns. The index will store the information about the columns you specify, making it easier for the database to look up records based on those columns. Let's see some examples.

Example of Creating an Index

Let's say you wanted to create an index on the last_name column in the employee table, so that any queries that looked up the last_name column would run faster. To do this, your statement would look like this:

```
CREATE INDEX idx_emp_lname
ON employee (last_name);
```

It's a short statement but there are a few things to notice. First, the index name is idx_emp_lname. You can make up almost any name you like, as long as it's within Oracle's naming rules (must start with a letter, can't be more than 30 characters long, for example). Why have I called this index idx_emp_lname?

If you've done any programming before, then you may be aware of certain coding standards or guidelines. These aren't rules enforced by the programming language, but are standards set by the team or the community. These standards can relate to spacing, line breaks, characters, and object naming. You might have noticed I've used a few already in the SQL code in this book:

- SQL keywords all in upper case, such as SELECT and FROM

- Column and table names in lower case, such as employee and salary

- Each of the keywords in a SELECT statement is on a new line.

The reason the index is named `idx_emp_lname` is because it's a standard that I like to encourage. It's broken down into three parts:

- The idx is short for index, which means this object is an index.

- The emp is short for employee, which is the table that the index applies to

- The lname is short for last_name, which is the column that the index applies to.

Why is this name helpful? It's so you can quickly tell what it is by looking at the name. There are two places that you'll often see the name of an index or other objects in the database. The first is error messages, as error messages often include the names of objects, and being able to see that an error is related to `idx_emp_lname` gives you a good idea what it's about. The second is using a database feature called an *execution plan*, which includes the planned steps that Oracle will take to execute a query. When you see the name `idx_emp_lname`, you know it's an index on the `employee` table on the `last_name` column, without having to look it up.

Let's look at that statement again:

```
CREATE INDEX idx_emp_lname
ON employee (last_name);
```

The index is called `idx_emp_lname`. Then we have the word `ON`, and then specify the `employee` table. Inside brackets, we have the `last_name` column. This means an index will be created on the database, which contains all of the different `last_name` values and information about where they are stored in the `employee` table. This means that when you run certain queries on this table, they will run faster, as the database knows where these last_name values are stored.

Run the query on the database using the same process as running a SELECT query. This will work in either SQL Developer or Live SQL (the web-based SQL tool) if you're using that. The output should show:

```
Index IDX_EMP_LNAME created.
```

Unlike a table, you can't run queries on an index. You can't run a query like SELECT * FROM idx_emp_lname. This is because the index stores all of its information behind the scenes in the database. All you need to do is create it.

Now, let's see some examples of using the index. Remember the earlier example of looking up a value in an index in the back of a book? The index in Oracle works the same way. However, you need to write a query that will actually look up the value in the table for the index to be used. One of the easiest ways to do this is to use the WHERE clause. Let's say you had this query:

```
SELECT id,
last_name,
salary
FROM employee;
```

This query will display the last_name for all employees, but it won't use the index. It's the equivalent of "show me every page in the book" if we use that textbook example from earlier. Using an index in the back of the book won't help if you want to show everything.

ID	LAST_NAME	SALARY
1	JONES	30000
2	SMITH	35000
3	KING	45000
4	SIMPSON	52000
5	ANDERSON	31000
6	COOPER	(null)
7	ADAMS	(null)

ID	LAST_NAME	SALARY
8	SMITH	62000
9	PATRICK	40000
10	Jones	42000

Let's say you wanted to find a specific employee called COOPER. Your query would look like this:

```
SELECT id,
last_name,
salary
FROM employee
WHERE last_name = 'COOPER';
```

Before you created the index, Oracle would have to:

1. Look at every row in the table

2. Check if the row matched the last_name of COOPER

3. If it did, show the row to you

This might not seem like a lot of work for ten rows, but once you start getting into the thousands and hundreds of thousands of rows, then this makes a big difference.

Now that you have an index on this table and on this column, Oracle will:

1. Look up the entry for COOPER in the index, which shows the rows that have that value

2. Show those rows to you

This will be much faster in larger tables.

If you run the query now, you'll get this result:

ID	LAST_NAME	SALARY
6	COOPER	(null)

The index doesn't change what is shown. It just changes how fast it is shown.

Why Is Performance Important?

Performance of an SQL query is important because a fast query gives a much better user experience than slower queries. There are a few situations where this may apply.

Web Application

One example is when you are developing an application for people to use. This application would access a database to add new data, update existing data, and view existing data. Usually when a user loads a page, a query is run on the database to display data to the user. While the query is running, the user has to wait, either looking at a blank screen or a loading screen, for the data to be displayed. If this data is displayed instantly or in a few seconds, it's likely going to be a good experience for the user. It's something they would expect. However, if the page doesn't display for 20 to 30 seconds or longer because of a SELECT query that takes this long to run, the users are not going to be happy.

In most situations, they would expect a faster load time in an application that displays data. A query that displays data in a couple of seconds could only be slightly different to one that takes 30 seconds to run, but it's a big difference in performance and experience for the user.

Overnight Batch Jobs

Another example of where the performance of a query is important is overnight batch jobs. In many organizations, there are applications that users operate that store data. These users also have a need to run reports on this data, to find out how many sales they made per month or how many customers have signed up. The reporting of this data is often done in a separate system to where it is captured, because the reporting could impact the performance of the live application.

In order for the reporting and the live application to work efficiently, the data from the application is transferred to a reporting system. This reporting system is optimized for viewing data, using a process called extract, transform, load (ETL). This process has a lot of different SQL queries in it, such as populating tables to show the total sales amounts per day and per month.

This process, and these queries, are often performed overnight so that the users of the application are unaffected and the reporting system is ready for the next day. There's roughly a 12-hour window for these steps to run. Seems like a long time, right? Well, these queries can be very complicated and can take quite a long time to run. The goal is for these queries to be completed sometime in the middle of the night, so the data is ready for the next day. However, if the queries do not perform well, then they could still be running at 9 in the morning, meaning the reporting system is not ready for use and the server that it's running on is still under load.

It's common for these kinds of queries to take 20 minutes or more for a particular step in the process. If the query takes 3 hours instead of 20 minutes, that can cause the rest of the process to be delayed. The performance of the SQL queries in this case is important.

Reporting System

The last example where query performance is important is in a reporting system. As mentioned earlier, the system that does the reporting is usually different to the system that captures the data. The reporting system will be used by people all across the company to see different information based on the data captured in different systems.

Every time a report is generated, a query is run to SELECT the data from the database. These reports may take a little time to generate. If the report generates in 30 seconds for example, then the users may be satisfied with that. However, if the report starts taking several minutes to generate, then the users will be frustrated and have a poor experience with the system.

So those are a few examples of how the performance and running time of a query can impact the user experience.

Index Using a Join

A common situation where an index is useful is on columns that are used as part of joins. Take a look at this query for example:

```
SELECT
e.id,
e.last_name,
e.salary,
o.address
FROM employee e
INNER JOIN office o ON e.office_id = o.id;
```

This query will show the following results.

ID	LAST_NAME	SALARY	ADDRESS
1	JONES	30000	123 Smith Street
2	SMITH	35000	45 Main Street
3	KING	45000	45 Main Street
4	SIMPSON	52000	123 Smith Street
6	COOPER	(null)	123 Smith Street
7	ADAMS	(null)	10 Collins Road
8	SMITH	62000	10 Collins Road
9	PATRICK	40000	123 Smith Street
10	Jones	42000	45 Main Street

This query gets data from two tables (the employee and office tables) and joins them on the office's id value. When the Oracle database processes this query, it will do something like this:

1. Look up all data in the employee table

2. Look at each employee's office_id value

3. Using that office_id value, look at all values in the office table for the matching id value

4. Get the address from the matching row and use that for the employee

5. Repeat steps 2-4 for each employee record

In the preceding list, step 3 is where the link between the two tables is used. Without an index, each row in the office table is scanned for the office id for that employee. For example, the employee with an id of 1 (JONES) has an office_id of 1. The database will then look through the office table for the row with and id of 1 and use the address from that row. This is repeated for the employee with and id of 2 (SMITH), and so on.

This may be OK when there are three rows in the office table. But when there are hundreds or thousands, it can really impact the performance.

Creating an Index

The query in the example we just saw was using a join between the primary key from the office table and a foreign key from the employee table:

```
SELECT
e.id,
e.last_name,
e.salary,
o.address
FROM employee e
INNER JOIN office o ON e.office_id = o.id;
```

The primary key on the office table is id, and the foreign key on the employee table is office_id. In an Oracle database, whenever you define a primary key on a table, an index is automatically created on that column. An index will exist on the office.id column. However, an index is not automatically created when a foreign key is created.

Creating an index on a foreign key column is a great way to improve the performance of a query. A foreign key column (such as the employee.office_id) is often used to look up values in another table.

Note   In Oracle, an index is automatically created on a primary key. An index is **not** automatically created on a foreign key.

To create an index on the employee.office_id column, you can run this statement:

```
CREATE INDEX idx_emp_officeid
ON employee (office_id);
```

Once again, I've used a naming convention with the name of the index. It's called idx_emp_officeid, which means it is an index on the employee table on the office_id column. Once you run this statement, an index is created on the database.

```
Index IDX_EMP_OFFICEID created.
```

Now the index is created, the way the Oracle database runs the query will mean the index can be used and the query will run faster.

The Disadvantages of Indexes

Creating indexes is a good way to improve the performance of a query. However, they're not a "silver bullet" to good-performing SQL. They're not a single magical solution. There are some disadvantages.

First, each index requires some space on the database. Depending on the number of records in the related table, this could be a large amount of space. The more indexes you create, the more space is taken up. You might have a maximum size for your database, set by your IT department, so this may be something to be conscious of.

Another disadvantage is keeping the index updated. Indexes on a table improve the performance of SELECT queries, but they reduce the performance of INSERT, UPDATE, and DELETE queries. This is because each time an INSERT, UPDATE, or DELETE query is run, the index needs to be updated along with the table. This can slow down the query. If there are multiple indexes on a table (which is possible), then these INSERT/UPDATE/DELETE queries can take much longer. This might not seem like much for a simple query, but with more complicated queries, the run time can easily expand.

So, there is a tradeoff between creating too many indexes and not enough indexes. How do you know what indexes to create?

Best Practices for Creating Indexes

There are a few best practices that I can recommend for knowing when and how to create indexes:

- Consider creating indexes on columns used in WHERE clauses of queries (e.g., WHERE last_name = 'SMITH'). This will help the lookup on this column.

- Consider creating indexes on columns used in JOINs, which will also help the lookup on this column.

- Don't create indexes on every column in the table, as this can slow down the INSERT, UPDATE, and DELETE queries on this table.

- Consider creating indexes on columns that have a lot of different unique values.

There are several different types of indexes that are not covered in this book. If you are doing performance tuning on your database and are considering indexes, it would be useful to learn about the other types of indexes so you can determine what's best for your query.

A large part of knowing when to create indexes is knowing the types of queries that your database runs, and what data is stored in the tables. This often comes from speaking with other team members and even database administrators, who are responsible for the administration of the database server and often are quite knowledgeable in database performance.

Summary

An index in a database is an object that improves the performance of queries. They are created on a table and include one or more columns. Queries that perform well are important as they improve the user experience, whether it is in an application, an overnight batch job, or a reporting system.

Indexes are useful to create on columns that are used in WHERE clauses of queries, or on fields in a JOIN clause. However, indexes can slow down INSERT, UPDATE, and DELETE queries, so it's not advisable to create indexes on every column in a table.

PART VI

Command Line

CHAPTER 27

Using the Command Line

So far, we've used an application called SQL Developer to run our SQL queries. At the start of the book, you downloaded this software from the Oracle website and used it to run queries.

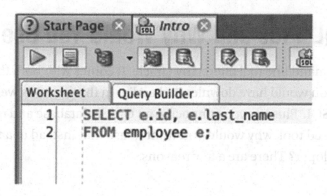

Figure 27-1. *Oracle SQL Developer*

Another way you can run these queries is using LiveSQL, which is Oracle's web-based SQL editor. You can create tables and run queries using an account you create on Oracle's website for this tool. However, this will only work on tables you create within LiveSQL. You can't use it to connect to your databases on your own computer.

There's a third way you can run SQL, and that's using the command line. The command line is a name for a tool on every operating system that lets you run commands using text only.

© Ben Brumm 2019
B. Brumm, *Beginning Oracle SQL for Oracle Database 18c,*
https://doi.org/10.1007/978-1-4842-4430-2_27

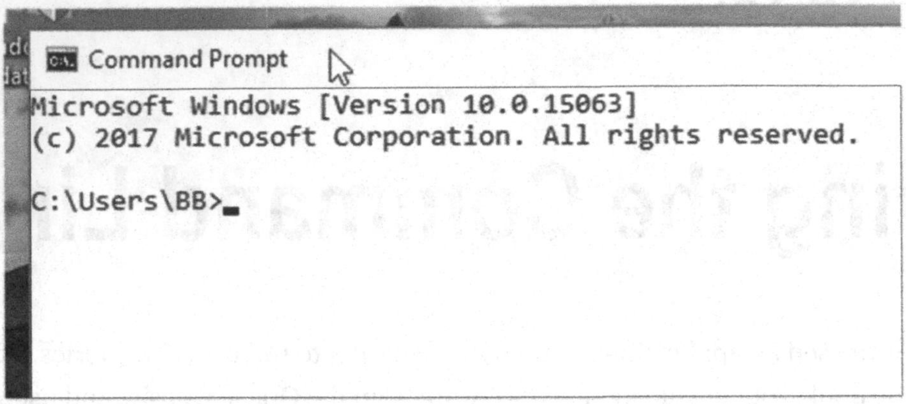

Figure 27-2. *The command line on Windows*

What is SQL*Plus and Why Would You Use It?

SQL*Plus is a command line tool offered by Oracle. It comes with both the Express Edition of Oracle (which you would have downloaded earlier in this book) as well as the full edition of Oracle. SQL*Plus lets you connect to an Oracle database and run queries on it.

If it's a text-based tool, why would you want to use that instead of a full user interface such as SQL Developer? There are a few reasons.

It's Fast

The SQL*Plus tool is pretty fast. It's a small tool that does a lot. It's faster to load and run than IDEs such as SQL Developer. Sure, it has fewer features and you can't click buttons, but it starts up very quickly and it's great for running queries.

Like many software tools, the more you use it, the more efficient you'll become at it. After a while, you'll start getting better at using SQL*Plus. Many software developers prefer using text-based editors such as vim and emacs for their development work for this reason: it's fast.

It's Easy to Run Scripts

A script is a file that contains a set of SQL statements. Running one of these in SQL*Plus is quite easy. In SQL Developer, you'll have to open the file by browsing through the directories on your computer. In SQL*Plus, you can copy and paste or enter the path to the file and run it.

It's Available on Every Oracle Database

Another advantage of SQL*Plus is that it comes with every Oracle database. Whether you're running Oracle Express or the full version of Oracle, you'll have access to SQL*Plus and are able to run SQL commands with it.

You Don't Always Have Access to SQL Developer

While SQL Developer is a free application and doesn't require an installation process, you may not be able to use it in your workplace. At my first role in the industry, we used a tool called "PL/SQL Developer," which is a paid application similar to SQL Developer. This means we didn't use SQL Developer for our queries, so any habits or techniques with SQL Developer that I or my team learned were not able to be used.

Another situation where you may not have access to SQL Developer is on client sites. Some people have jobs where they visit different clients quite regularly and are not able to install software at the client's site. This means they will have to use SQL*Plus, rather than use SQL Developer.

How to Start SQL*Plus

To start SQL*Plus, you need to open a command window. These steps will assume you're running Oracle on Windows, but the steps are similar for other operating systems as well. SQL*Plus was included with Oracle Express that you installed at the beginning of this book.

1. Open the Command Prompt by clicking Start and typing "cmd".

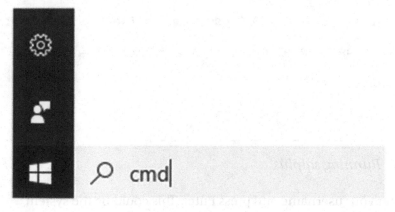

Figure 27-3. *Running the cmd command*

If you're on an older version of Windows, you may need to click Start then click Run, then type "cmd".

2. Press Enter. The command window is now open.

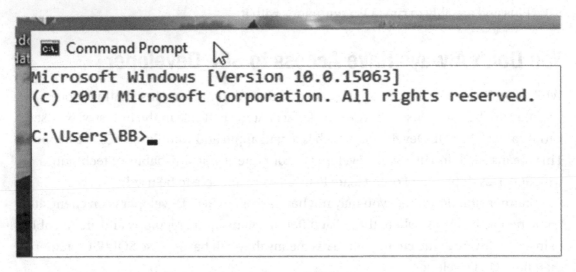

Figure 27-4. *The Windows command window*

3. Enter the command sqlplus and press Enter.

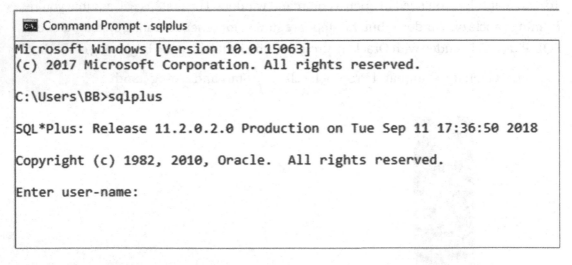

Figure 27-5. *Running sqlplus*

4. Enter your username and press Enter. This could be the system username, or the username you set up earlier in the book.

5. Enter your password and press Enter. If you're using the system account, this is the same password you entered when you installed Oracle Express and when you set up the connection in SQL Developer earlier in this book. If you're using the user you created, then enter their password here.

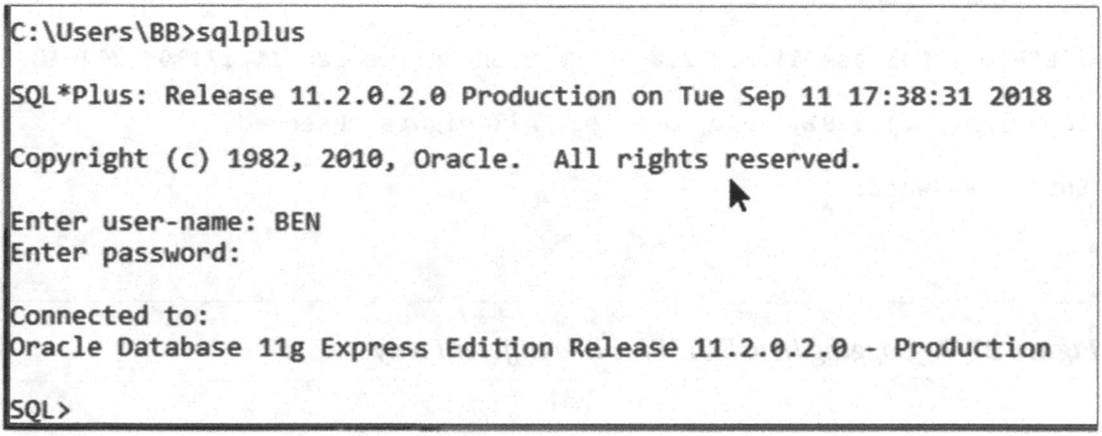

```
C:\Users\BB>sqlplus

SQL*Plus: Release 11.2.0.2.0 Production on Tue Sep 11 17:38:31 2018

Copyright (c) 1982, 2010, Oracle.  All rights reserved.

Enter user-name: BEN
Enter password:

Connected to:
Oracle Database 11g Express Edition Release 11.2.0.2.0 - Production

SQL>
```

Figure 27-6. *Logging in to SQL*Plus*

You are now logged in to SQL*Plus and your database.

Note   Your output will include Oracle version 18c (unlike the screenshot here, which mentions version 11).

Alternative Login Syntax

There are other ways you can enter your username and password when logging in to SQL*Plus. These are used as a personal preference or as a quicker way of logging in. To use these other methods:

Login with Two Steps

You can log in to your database with two steps: specifying the username as a parameter when launching sqlplus and entering the password separately.

1. Open the command window as explained in the earlier steps.

2. Enter sqlplus username, where username is the name of the user you want to enter, and press Enter.

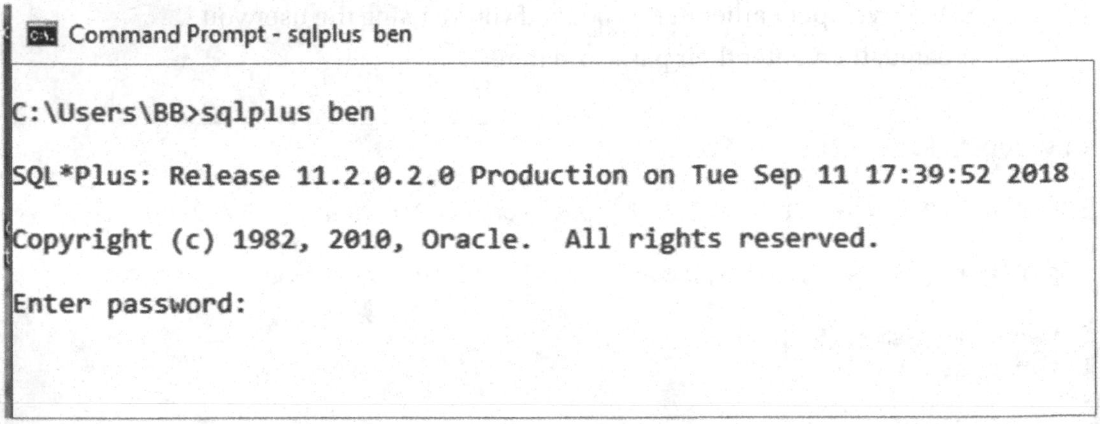

```
■ Command Prompt - sqlplus ben

C:\Users\BB>sqlplus ben

SQL*Plus: Release 11.2.0.2.0 Production on Tue Sep 11 17:39:52 2018

Copyright (c) 1982, 2010, Oracle.  All rights reserved.

Enter password:
```

Figure 27-7. *Logging in to SQL*Plus in a different way*

3. Enter the password for this user, and press Enter.

You are now logged in to your database.

Log in with One Step

You can also log in to your database in one step, where you specify the username and password as parameters to the sqlplus command.

1. Open the command window as explained in the earlier steps.

2. Enter sqlplus username password, where username is the name of the user you want to enter and the password is that account's password, and press Enter.

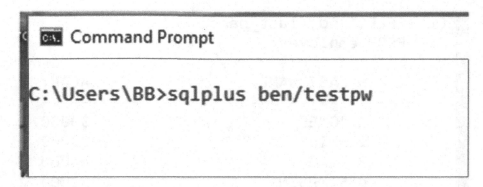

Figure 27-8. *Logging in to SQL*Plus in a different way*

You are now logged in to your database.

Running a Query in SQL*Plus

To run a query in SQL*Plus, simply type the query at the prompt after logging in. For example, to select all records from the employee table, enter this query:

```
SELECT id, last_name, salary
FROM employee;
```

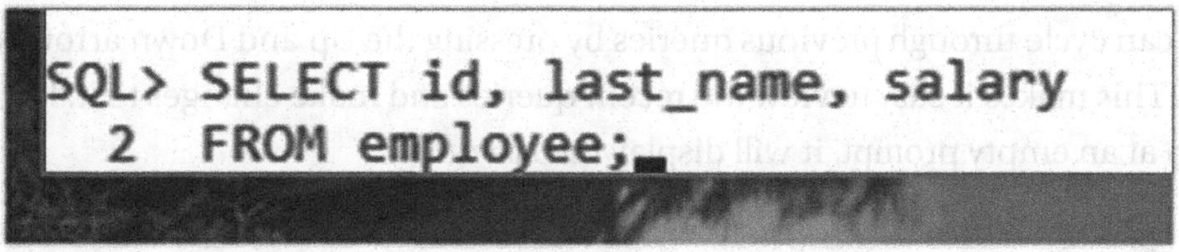

Figure 27-9. *A SELECT query in SQL*Plus*

You can press Enter while writing a query to go to a new line. The query is not run until you enter a semicolon and press Enter. This means you can add new lines whenever you like, such as for each SQL keyword or for each column.

Once you have entered the semicolon after this query, press Enter. The results of the query are shown.

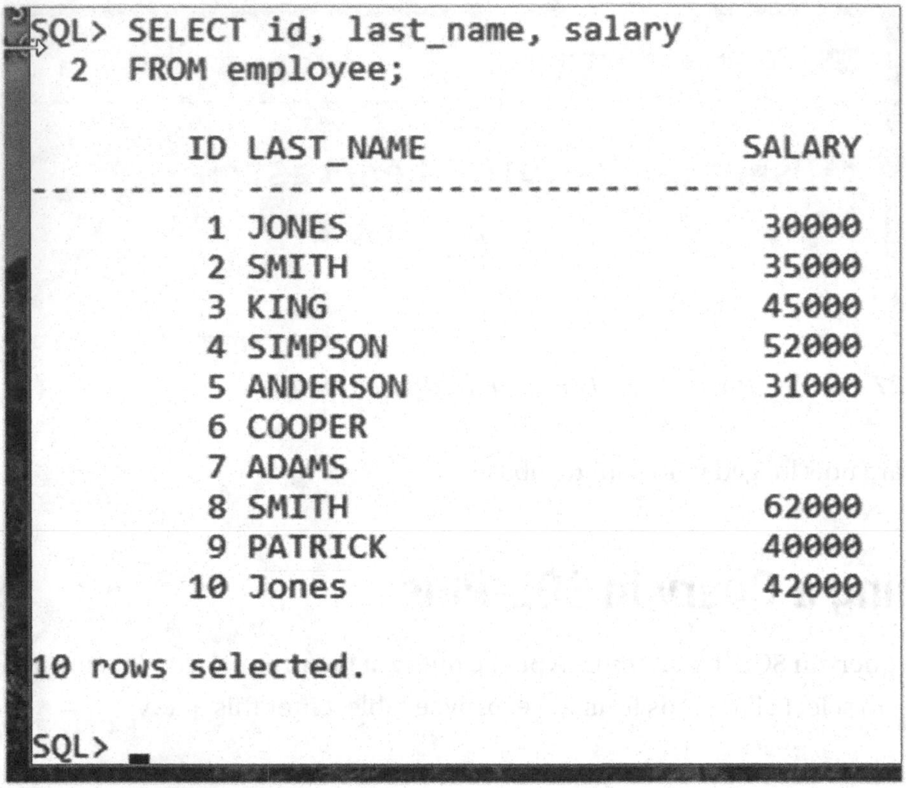

```
SQL> SELECT id, last_name, salary
  2  FROM employee;

        ID LAST_NAME                    SALARY
---------- --------------------- ----------
         1 JONES                         30000
         2 SMITH                         35000
         3 KING                          45000
         4 SIMPSON                       52000
         5 ANDERSON                      31000
         6 COOPER
         7 ADAMS
         8 SMITH                         62000
         9 PATRICK                       40000
        10 Jones                         42000

10 rows selected.

SQL>
```

Figure 27-10. *Running a SELECT query*

You can cycle through previous queries by pressing the Up and Down arrows at the prompt. This makes it easy to view the recent queries and make changes to it. If you press Up at an empty prompt, it will display the last query.

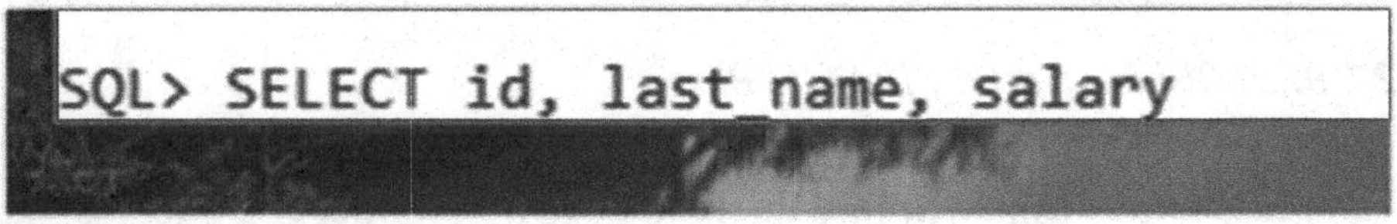

```
SQL> SELECT id, last_name, salary
```

Figure 27-11. *Recent SQL statements*

SQL*Plus also gives you a cursor in your query. You can move the cursor using the arrow keys, and make edits to the query before running it. For example, you can add an ORDER BY to this query by moving the cursor to the end of the query and typing ORDER BY last_name ASC;

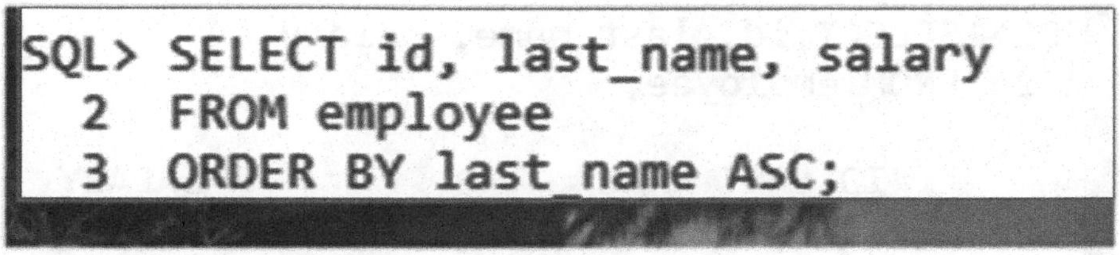

```
SQL> SELECT id, last_name, salary
  2  FROM employee
  3  ORDER BY last_name ASC;
```

Figure 27-12. *Making changes to an SQL query*

Press Enter to run the query, and the results are shown.

Formatting Output in SQL*Plus

You've probably noticed when running these queries in SQL*Plus that the output doesn't look very neat. This is because each column's width is sized according to the potential number of characters in the column, not the actual number of characters, unlike SQL Developer. This means you'll get a lot of blank spaces in columns and rows spread over multiple lines.

For example, running our SELECT query on the employee table looks like this:

```
SELECT id, last_name, salary
FROM employee;
```

```
SQL> SELECT id, last_name, salary
  2  FROM employee;

        ID LAST_NAME                          SALARY
---------- -------------------------- ----------
         1 JONES                               30000
         2 SMITH                               35000
         3 KING                                45000
         4 SIMPSON                             52000
         5 ANDERSON                            31000
         6 COOPER
         7 ADAMS
         8 SMITH                               62000
         9 PATRICK                             40000
        10 Jones                               42000

10 rows selected.

SQL>
```

Figure 27-13. *The output of a SELECT query*

However, it's possible to clean this up to make it more readable. We can run commands to format the columns in SQL*Plus. The syntax for this command looks like this:

```
column column_name format value;
```

An example of this command would be:

```
column last_name format a10;
```

This specifies that the last_name column should be formatted as an alphanumeric field with a width of 10 characters. We run this command before our SQL query.

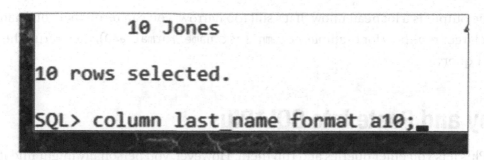

```
        10 Jones

10 rows selected.

SQL> column last_name format a10;
```

Figure 27-14. *Formatting columns*

Then, you can run the SQL query again. Press Up a few times to load the query again and press Enter.

```
SQL> column last_name format a10;
SQL> SELECT id, last_name, salary
  2   FROM employee;

        ID LAST_NAME       SALARY
---------- ---------- ----------
         1 JONES            30000
         2 SMITH            35000
         3 KING             45000
         4 SIMPSON          52000
         5 ANDERSON         31000
         6 COOPER
         7 ADAMS
         8 SMITH            62000
         9 PATRICK          40000
        10 Jones            42000

10 rows selected.

SQL>
```

Figure 27-15. *Formatted output from a SELECT statement*

The output is a lot neater now. If it's still too narrow, you can rerun that command with a larger number (for example, `column last_name format a40`), then rerun the `SELECT` query.

Copy and Paste into SQL*Plus

SQL*Plus lets you enter queries and run them. However, you personally might find it easier to write queries in a text editor and copy and paste them into the command line. This is something you can do in SQL*Plus. To do this:

1. Enter your query into a text editor, such as Notepad++ or Sublime Text.

2. Copy your query from the text editor.

3. Open SQL*Plus, right click at your prompt, and select Paste. The query will now be shown in SQL*Plus.

4. Run the query by pressing Enter.

The query results will then be displayed.

The Forward Slash Character

Sometimes when looking at SQL code you might see the forward slash character "/" at the end of a statement:

```
SELECT id, last_name, salary, office_id
FROM employee
/
```

You'll see these kinds of examples on websites, or in scripts that your current or future employers would use. What does this mean, and why do you need it if you have a semicolon?

In SQL*Plus, the semicolon character will ensure the most recent statement is run. The slash character will run whatever is in the buffer, which can include more than one statement. If you enter the preceding query into SQL*Plus, which has a slash at the end rather than a semicolon, and run the query, you'll get the same results.

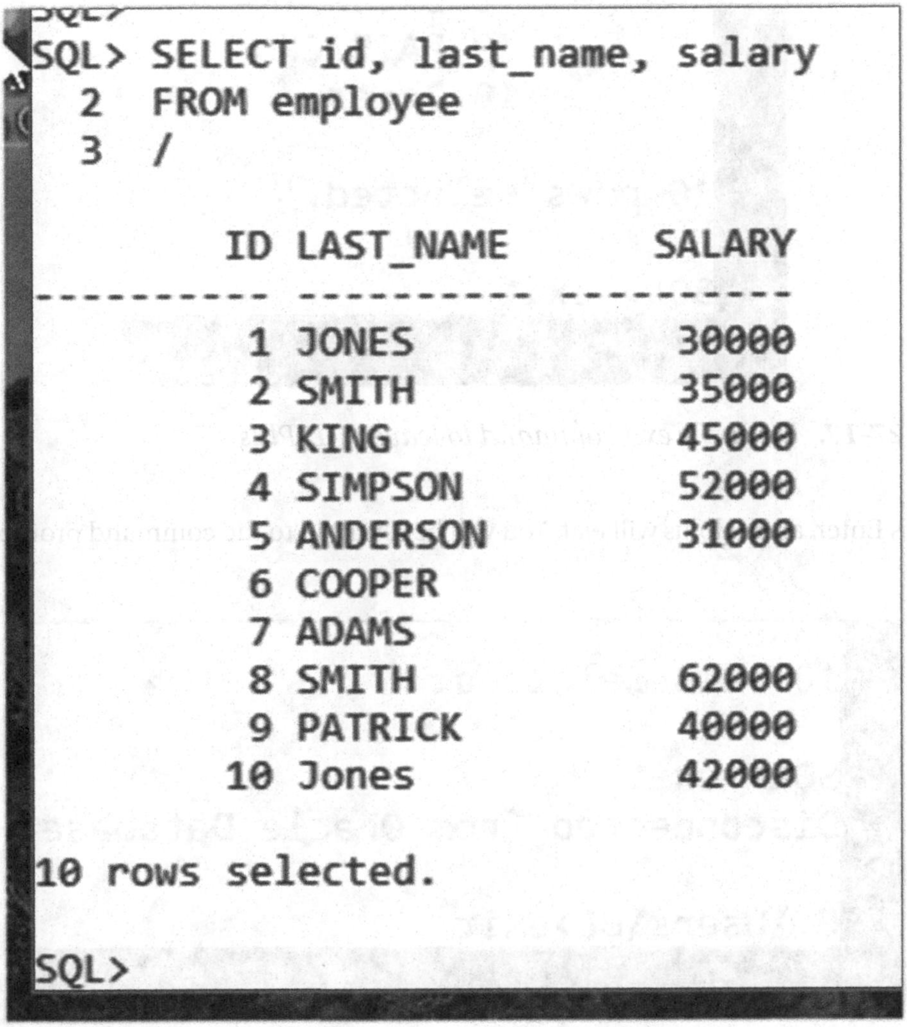

Figure 27-16. *The query results*

You'll often see the slash character in scripts that have more than one statement in them. This means all statements are run at the same time, rather than stopping between statements.

Exiting SQL*Plus

If you want to exit SQL*Plus at any time, you can type the command exit at the sqlplus prompt.

9 PATRICK
10 Jones
10 rows selected.
SQL> exit

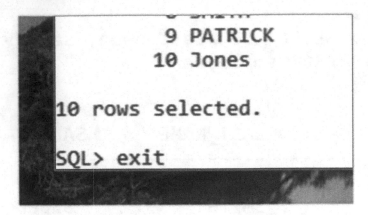

Figure 27-17. *Using the exit command to leave SQL*Plus*

Press Enter, and sqlplus will exit. You will be returned to the command prompt.

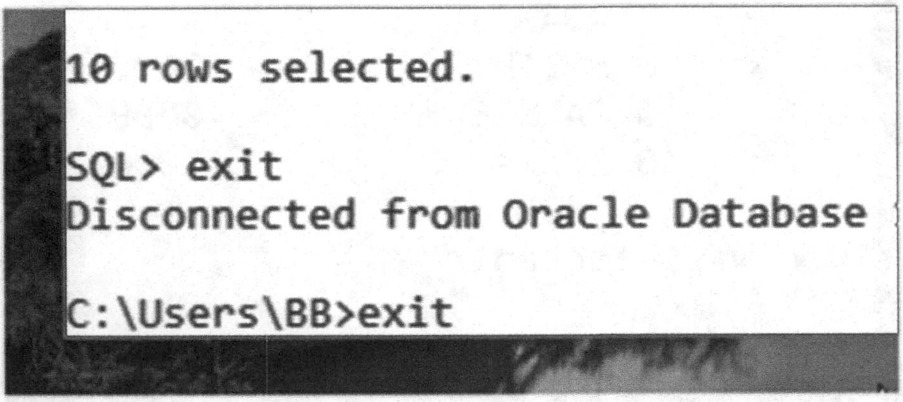

10 rows selected.
SQL> exit
Disconnected from Oracle Database
C:\Users\BB>exit

Figure 27-18. *Using the exit command to leave the command prompt*

You can then type exit again and press Enter, and the command prompt will exit.

What About SQLcl?

SQL*Plus has been around since the mid-1980s, which is a long time in the world of software. The features have remained pretty standard for most of this time. Recently, Oracle has released a new free command line tool, called "SQLcl," which is short for SQL

Command Line. This is a command line tool, similar in operation to SQL*Plus, but with a lot more features. SQLcl allows you to:

- Interact with the database (run SQL queries)

- Run batch scripts

- Edit SQL code

- Statement completion

- .. and much more

However, unlike SQL*Plus, SQLcl does not come with Oracle databases automatically. You can easily download it from the Oracle website though.

How to Download and Run SQLcl

You can download SQLcl from the Oracle website. To do this:

1. Visit Oracle's website and navigate to Developer Tools ➤ SQLcl. You can do this from www.oracle.com or navigating to the page directly: www.oracle.com/technetwork/developer-tools/sqlcl/ downloads/index.html.

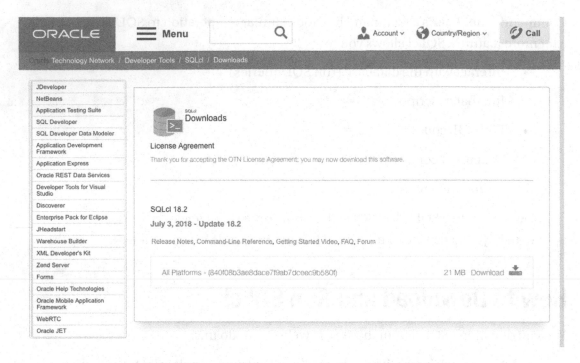

Figure 27-19. *The SQLcl download page*

2. Accept the license agreement.

3. Click the Download button. There is a single download file that works across all operating systems.

4. Once the ZIP file is downloaded, extract it to a location on your computer.

5. Open the command window (Start ➤ cmd).

6. Browse to the location where you extracted the files. For example, this could be done using the command cd c:\oraclexe\sqlcl\

Command Prompt

```
c:\>cd c:\Users\BB\Downloads\sqlcl-18.2.0_
```

Figure 27-20. *Changing to the new directory*

7.   Browse to the bin folder: cd bin

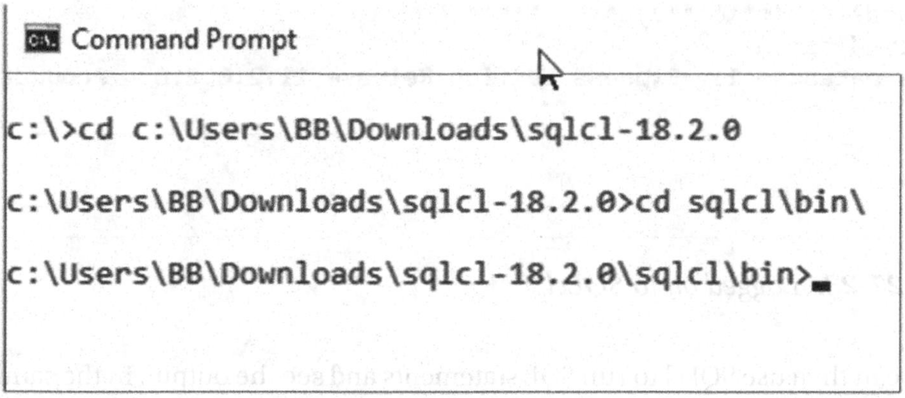

Command Prompt

```
c:\>cd c:\Users\BB\Downloads\sqlcl-18.2.0

c:\Users\BB\Downloads\sqlcl-18.2.0>cd sqlcl\bin\

c:\Users\BB\Downloads\sqlcl-18.2.0\sqlcl\bin>_
```

Figure 27-21. *Changing to the bin directory*

8.   Run the sql command. SQLcl will then start.

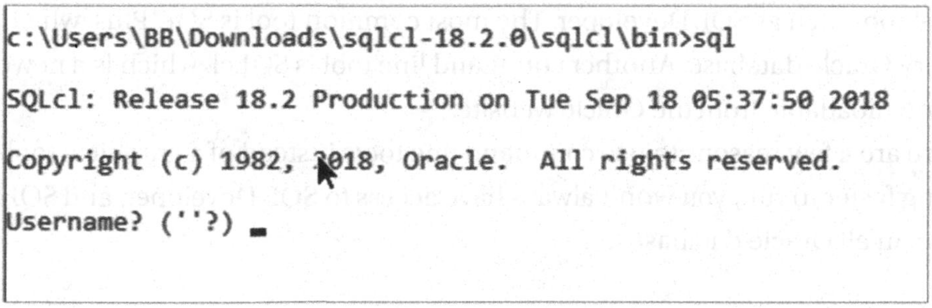

```
c:\Users\BB\Downloads\sqlcl-18.2.0\sqlcl\bin>sql

SQLcl: Release 18.2 Production on Tue Sep 18 05:37:50 2018

Copyright (c) 1982, 2018, Oracle.  All rights reserved.

Username? (''?) _
```

Figure 27-22. *Running SQLcl*

9. Now that SQLcl is running, you'll need to connect to your database. You can do this at the prompt that appears after entering sqlcl. Enter your username and password.

10. Press Enter, and your database connection will be made. Your screen should look like this:

```
c:\Users\BB\Downloads\sqlcl-18.2.0\sqlcl\bin>sql

SQLcl: Release 18.2 Production on Tue Sep 18 05:37:50 2018

Copyright (c) 1982, 2018, Oracle.  All rights reserved.

Username? (''?) intro_user
Password? (**********?) **********
Connected to:
Oracle Database 11g Express Edition Release 11.2.0.2.0 - Production


SQL> _
```

Figure 27-23. Logged on to SQLcl

You can then use SQLcl to run SQL statements and see the output, in the same way as you would for SQL*Plus.

Summary

Oracle offers command line tools, which can be used to access the database without a graphical tool such as SQL Developer. The most common tool is SQL*Plus, which comes with every Oracle database. Another command line tool is SQLcl, which is a newer tool and is downloadable from the Oracle website.

There are a few reasons to use command line tools instead of a graphical tool, such as it being faster to run, you won't always have access to SQL Developer, and SQL*Plus is available on all Oracle databases.

PART VII

Appendixes

APPENDIX

How to Find and Navigate the Oracle SQL Reference

There is a lot to learn and remember about Oracle SQL. We've learned a lot of different keywords in this book, such as:

- SELECT
- INSERT
- UPDATE
- DELETE
- CREATE TABLE

We've also learned a few different SQL functions, such as SUM and UPPER. Each of these commands and functions has a specific syntax, which is the way it needs to be run and the parameters that it accepts. This is easy to forget.

Fortunately, Oracle provides an online reference or documentation for their database. This contains detailed information about all of their commands and functions and is a great way to look up something specific if you've forgotten how it works or what to do.

Finding the Oracle SQL Reference

To find the Oracle reference:

1. Visit `https://docs.oracle.com`.

2. Click on Database, then Oracle Database on the left.

© Ben Brumm 2019
B. Brumm, *Beginning Oracle SQL for Oracle Database 18c*,
https://doi.org/10.1007/978-1-4842-4430-2_28

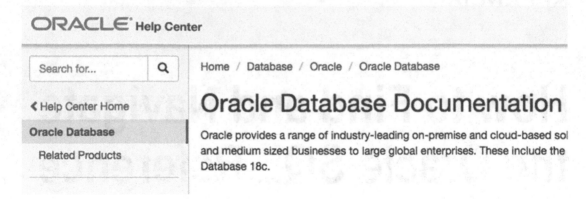

Figure A1-1. *The link to Oracle Database documentation*

3. Click on Development, which is under Topics.

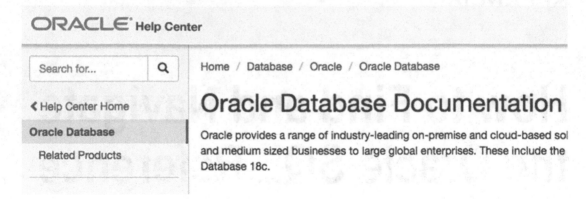

Figure A1-2. *The Development link*

4. Scroll down to the "SQL and PL/SQL" section and click on the HTML link under "SQL Language Reference." You can click the PDF link instead to download a PDF file for viewing offline.

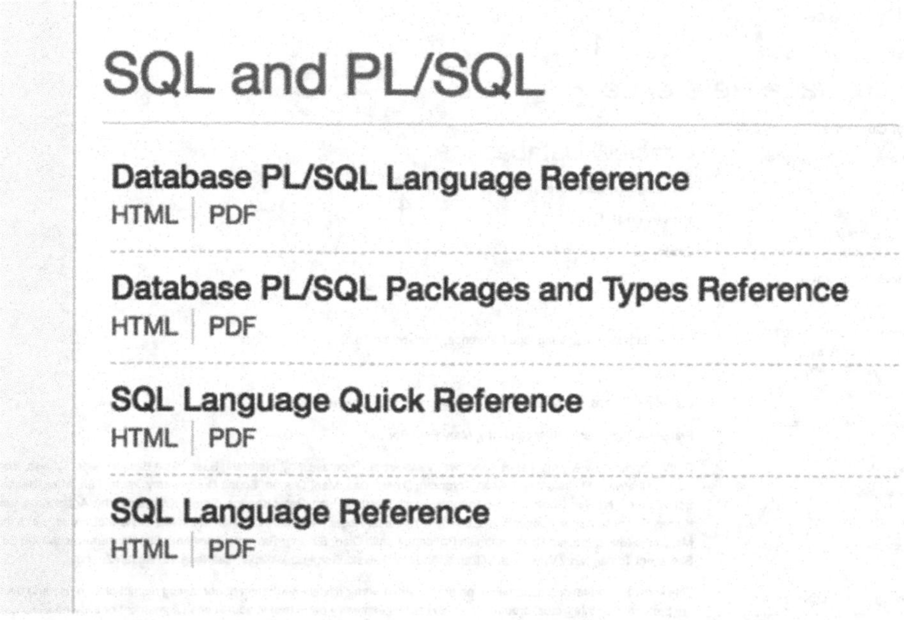

SQL and PL/SQL

Database PL/SQL Language Reference
HTML | PDF

Database PL/SQL Packages and Types Reference
HTML | PDF

SQL Language Quick Reference
HTML | PDF

SQL Language Reference
HTML | PDF

Figure A1-3. *The link to the SQL Language Reference*

The Oracle SQL Reference

The Oracle SQL Reference looks like this.

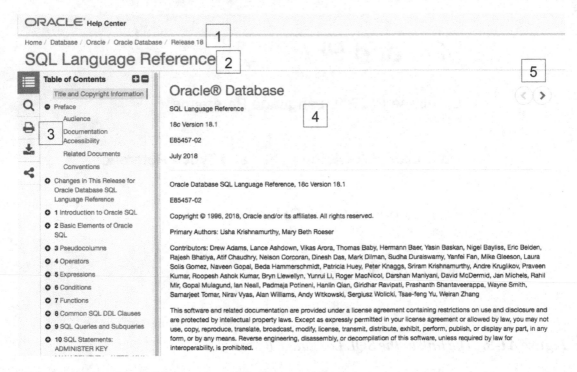

Figure A1-4. *The SQL Language Reference*

This page contains a few different areas:

1. **Breadcrumb navigation**. This can be used to navigate up and down in the page hierarchy. It also lets you know where in the documentation you currently are, as it changes depending on what page you are on.

2. **Page title**. This is the name of the page you are currently viewing.

3. **Sidebar**. This contains the Table of Contents, which is everything that the guide contains. You can click on the heading names to be taken to each section or click the + icons to expand a section where it applies. There are also buttons for Search, Print, Download, and Share.

4. **Main content**. This shows the content of the page you are currently viewing.

5. **Navigation arrows**. Clicking the left and right arrows will take you to the previous and next pages in the reference guide.

Find What You Need Using Table of Contents

One way to find what you need is to browse and expand the Table of Contents to the right section. For example, let's say you're looking for information on how to use the SUM function. To do this:

1. Click on the Functions link on the Table of Contents.

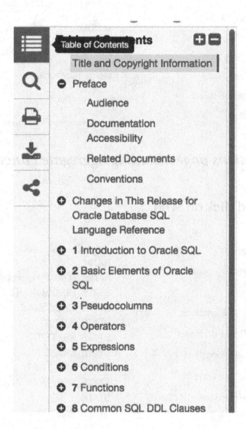

Figure A1-5. *The Table of Contents panel*

2. The SUM function is an aggregate function, so click on Aggregate functions on this page or on the Table of Contents.

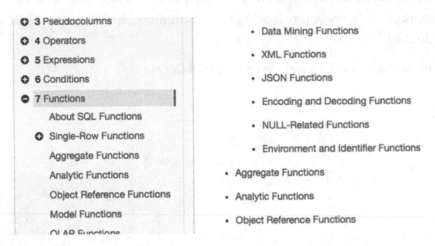

Figure A1-6. *The Functions page including Aggregate Functions*

3. Scroll down and click on SUM.

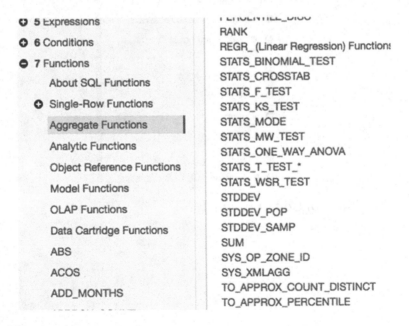

Figure A1-7. *The Aggregate Functions list*

4.   The SUM reference page is shown in Figure A1-8.

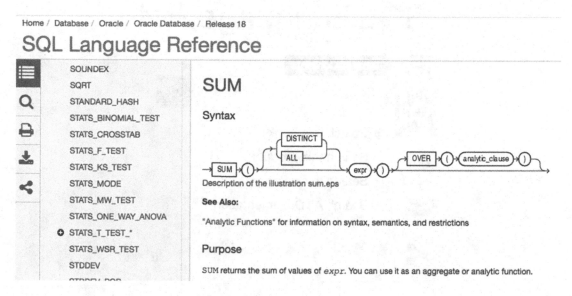

Figure A1-8. *The SUM reference page*

Find What You Need Using Search

The other way to find what you need is to use the Search function. To do this:

1.   Click on the Search icon on the left of the sidebar (the magnifying glass icon).

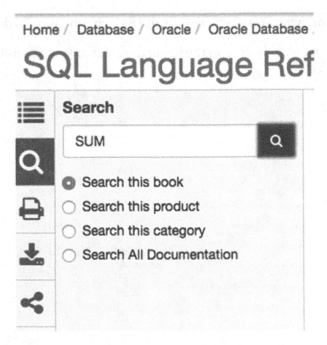

Figure A1-9. *The Search box on the left sidebar*

2.   Enter in a search term, such as SUM, and press Enter.

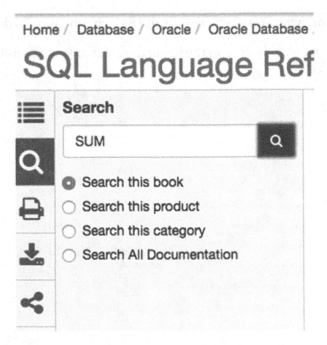

Figure A1-10. *Searching for SUM*

3. The search results are shown on a new tab, with your search term
    bolded in each result.

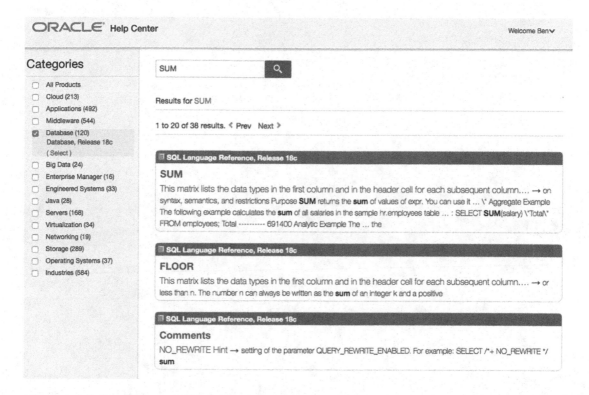

Figure A1-11. *The search results*

4. Click on the result that matches the one you are looking for. In this
    case, it may be the first result: the SUM page.

Index

A

ADD_MONTHS function, 329
Aggregate functions, 347
  AVG (*see* Average (AVG) function)
  COUNT function
    column, 352
    DISTINCT, 354
    parameters, 351
    SUM function, 351
    WHERE clause, 356
  definition, 348
  LOWER function, 347
  MAX function
    records, 362
    syntax, 362
    WHERE, 363
  MIN function
    records, 360
    syntax, 360
    WHERE clause, 362
  SUM (*see* SUM function)
  tasks, 348
ALTER TABLE statement
  CASCADE CONSTRAINTS, 248
  column, 241
  constraint, 243
  data type, 242
  DROP TABLE, 249
  foreign key, 245
  primary key, 243
  remove column, 247
  rename column, 246
  structure of, 240
  table rename, 248
AND keyword, 100–101
Average (AVG) function
  all values, 357
  COUNT function, 357
  DISTINCT, 358
  SUM and COUNT functions, 357
  WHERE clause, 359

B

BETWEEN operator
  don't match, values, 147
  greater than or equal to and less than
    or equal to, 149
  inclusive and exclusive check, 148
  syntax, 145
  text values, 147
  two values, 146
BINARY_FLOAT data type, 191
Binary large object (BLOB), 194

C

CASE statement
  case_name, 332
  conditions, 332
  vs. DECODE function, 344

© Ben Brumm 2019
B. Brumm, *Beginning Oracle SQL for Oracle Database 18c*,
https://doi.org/10.1007/978-1-4842-4430-2

D